LOCOMOTIVE PORTFOLIOS

British Atlantic Express Tender Locomotives

Front cover photo:
Great Northern C1 Atlantic 3286, built as 286 in 1904, superheated in 1924 and withdrawn as 2815 in 1947, at Hitchin, 1937. (Colour Rail)

Back cover photos:
Great Central 'Jersey Lily' C4 Atlantic 5262 at Leicester, c1930. (Manchester Locomotive Society – MLS)

LB&SCR Marsh Atlantic 32422 *North Foreland* in BR mixed traffic lined black livery at Brighton, 13 March 1952. (Colour Rail)

LOCOMOTIVE PORTFOLIOS

British Atlantic Express Tender Locomotives

DAVID MAIDMENT

PEN & SWORD TRANSPORT
AN IMPRINT OF PEN & SWORD BOOKS LTD.
YORKSHIRE – PHILADELPHIA

First published in Great Britain in 2025 by
Pen and Sword Transport
An imprint of
Pen & Sword Books Ltd.
Yorkshire – Philadelphia

ISBN 978 1 39908 075 0

A CIP catalogue record for this book is available from the British Library.

Typeset in Palatino by SJmagic DESIGN SERVICES, India.
Printed and bound in India by Replika Press Pvt. Ltd.

The Publisher's authorised representative in the EU for product safety is Authorised Rep Compliance Ltd., Ground Floor, 71 Lower Baggot Street, Dublin D02 P593, Ireland.
www.arccompliance.com

For a complete list of Pen & Sword titles please contact

PEN & SWORD BOOKS LIMITED
George House, Beevor Street, Off Pontefract Road, Hoyle Mill, Barnsley, South Yorkshire, England, S71 1HN.
E-mail: enquiries@pen-and-sword.co.uk
Website: www.pen-and-sword.co.uk

or

PEN AND SWORD BOOKS
1950 Lawrence Rd, Havertown, PA 19083, USA
E-mail: uspen-and-sword@casematepublishers.com
website: www.penandswordbooks.com

MIX
Paper | Supporting responsible forestry
FSC™ C016779

All David Maidment's royalties from this book will be donated to the Railway Children charity [reg. no. 1058991] [www.railwaychildren.org.uk]

Other books by David Maidment:

Novels (Religious historical fiction)
The Child Madonna, Melrose Books, 2009
The Missing Madonna, PublishNation, 2012
The Madonna and her Sons, PublishNation, 2015
The Reluctant Traitor, PublishNation, 2021

Novels (Railway fiction)
Lives on the Line, Max Books, 2013
Steamy Stories, PublishNation, 2021

Non-fiction (Railways)
The Toss of a Coin, PublishNation, 2014
A Privileged Journey, Pen & Sword, 2015
An Indian Summer of Steam, Pen & Sword, 2015
Great Western Eight-Coupled Heavy Freight Locomotives, Pen & Sword, 2015
Great Western Moguls and Prairies, Pen & Sword, 2016
Southern Urie and Maunsell 2-cylinder 4-6-0s, Pen & Sword, 2016
Great Western Small-Wheeled Double-Framed 4-4-0s, Pen & Sword, 2017
The Development of the German Pacific Locomotive, Pen & Sword, 2017
Great Western Large-Wheeled Double-Framed 4-4-0s, Pen & Sword, 2017
Great Western Counties, 4-4-0s, 4-4-2Ts *&* 4-6-0s, Pen & Sword, 2018
Southern Maunsell Moguls and Tank Engines, Pen & Sword, 2018
Southern Maunsell 4-4-0s, Pen & Sword, 2019
Great Western Granges, Pen & Sword, 2019
Cambrian Railways Gallery, Pen & Sword, 2019
Great Western Panniers, Pen & Sword, 2019
Great Western Kings, Pen & Sword, 2020
Great Western & Absorbed Railway 0-6-2Ts, Pen & Sword, 2020
Drummond's L&SWR Passenger & Mixed Traffic Locomotives, Pen & Sword, 2020
Southern 0-6-0 *Tender Locomotives,* Pen & Sword, 2021
LNER 4-6-0 *Locomotives*, Pen & Sword, 2021
Midland & LMS 4-4-0s, Pen & Sword, 2021
Great Western Castle 4-6-0 *Locomotives, 1923-1959,* Pen & Sword, 2022
Great Western Castle 4-6-0 *Locomotives, The Final Years 1960-1965, Pen & Sword,* 2022
Great Western Castle 4-6-0 *Locomotives, In the Preservation Era,* Pen & Sword, 2023
Four-coupled Tank Locomotives, Built by the Great Western Railway, Pen & Sword, 2023
Four-coupled Tank Locomotives, Absorbed by the Great Western Railway, Pen & Sword, 2023
The Princess Coronation Pacific Locomotives, 1937-1956, Pen & Sword, 2023
The Princess Coronation Pacific Locomotives, The Final Years & Preservation, Pen & Sword, 2023
Great Western 0-6-0 *tender locomotives*, Pen & Sword, 2024
LNER 4-4-0s *of Great Northern, Great Central, Great Eastern and Midland & Great Northern Design,* Pen & Sword, 2024
LNER 4-4-0s *of North Eastern, North British, Great North of Scotland & LNER Design,* Pen & Sword, 2024

Non-fiction (Street Children)
The Other Railway Children, PublishNation, 2012
Nobody ever listened to me, PublishNation, 2012

CONTENTS

ACKNOWLEDGEMENTS

Once again I have first and foremost to thank officers and members of the Manchester Locomotive Society for their friendship and assistance, and particularly Paul Shackcloth, club photograph archivist, for giving me access to and use of the Society's vast photographic collection and letting me publish them free of cost as I am donating my royalties as usual to the Railway Children charity (www.railwaychildren.org.uk) that I founded in 1995, a charity supported by both professionals and enthusiasts associated with the railway industry. Most of the photographs have been donated by past members of the Society but some do not identify the photographer. If I have therefore failed to credit the correct photographer in the caption, please contact the publisher. I also wish to acknowledge the help given by my editor, Carol Trow, Pen & Sword's Commissioning Editor, John Scott-Morgan, the Transport Production Manager, Janet Brookes and the Pen & Sword design and marketing team, whose work produces the quality of book production that I have come to rely on. I commend the book to all interested in the brief flowering of the Atlantic locomotive in the history of Britain's railways, whether from an engineering, historical, enthusiast or modelling perspective.

David Maidment
April 2024

INTRODUCTION

The first British Atlantic, the name derived from a locomotive of the 4-4-2 wheel arrangement delivered by the Baldwin Locomotive Company to the Atlantic City Railroad in 1894, was the Great Northern 'Klondyke' (later LNER C2) of 1898. This was swiftly followed by the inside cylinder 4-4-2 'Highflyer' of the Lancashire and Yorkshire Railway (L&YR) and then in 1902 by probably the most famous and numerous of British Atlantics, the Great Northern 251 and its successors (LNER C1) with its outside cylinders and wide firebox over the trailing axle. The Great Central and North Eastern railways both produced their first Atlantics in 1903 and the Great Western, intrigued by the performance of the de Glehn Atlantics of the Chemin de Fer du Nord in France, purchased 102 *La France* in the same year and followed it up with the purchase of two more based on the Paris-Orleans Railway design. Churchward then produced the most powerful of all British Atlantics, the 4-cylinder No.40, later converted to a 4-6-0 as 4000 *North Star,* and built a number of his powerful 2-cylinder engines as 4-4-2s to compare with the French engines and his own 4-6-0s. The London, Brighton and South Coast Railway (LB&SCR) entered the fray in 1906 with Douglas Earle Marsh's 'H1', remarkably similar to the GN C1. The Great Central and North Eastern built further developments of the wheel arrangement and then the North British constructed their Reid Atlantics also in that year. The final flowering of the wheel arrangement in Britain came in 1911 with the North Eastern 'Z' class (LNER C7), an unsuperheated version of the Reid North British Atlantic (the LNER C10) and the LB&SCR 'H2'.

All of these locomotives will be described in the following chapters – their basic design and dimensions, their construction, history, their operation and performance. It is interesting that of the 310 British Atlantics built over the decade between 1898 and 1911, the vast majority belonged to the East Coast railways that later formed the LNER. Ten of the sixteen British Atlantic classes became LNER assets. Only the L&YR's forty 'Highflyers' were built in reasonable numbers apart from the East Coast classes, the Great Western Atlantics being short-lived, converted to very successful 4-6-0s not because of any performance weakness, but because the 4-6-0s gave better adhesion on the formidable banks of the GW system especially in Devon and Cornwall. The Southern just had the handful of Brighton Atlantics for the London-Brighton route and the Newhaven Boat Trains. By the end of the first decade of the twentieth century, the 4-6-0 was the chosen preference to take over from the front line 4-4-0s which still excelled particularly on the London & South Western, the South Eastern & Chatham, the LNWR, the Midland, the Caledonian, the Great Central and the Great Eastern railways. Most of the Atlantics were withdrawn before the outbreak of the Second World War with a few of the Great Central, Great Northern and North Eastern Atlantics just making it to around nationalisation on humdrum duties. The last to go were a few of the 1911 Marsh Atlantics, the last of all, 32424 *Beachy Head*, going out in a flourish in 1958. Only the two Ivatt classes, the LNER C1 and C2, had examples preserved, though the Reid North British *Midlothian* was a near miss. The failure to preserve a Brighton Atlantic has been remedied by the construction of a full-size operational replica *Beachy Head.*

The book will conclude with a chapter on some of the most notable Atlantics overseas, to compare them briefly with the British examples, from the most numerous examples in the USA, to the famous French de Glehn compounds and their final swansong with the four USA 'Hiawathas' of 1935 and the six Belgian streamlined Atlantics of 1939. In total, 3,544 Atlantics were built in the world, the vast majority, 2,127, being in the Americas. Germany had the most in Europe – most of the State railways prior to 1920 having significant examples, especially the Prussian Railway in the flat north of the country, although they were forced to surrender many of these to France as reparations after the First World War. With their lower adhesion than that of 4-6-0s, 4-6-2s or 2-8-2s, they blossomed briefly on the fastest lightweight expresses over the flatter main lines of the world.

THE ENGINEERS

Sir John Aspinall, Chief Mechanical Engineer, L&YR, 1886–99

John Audley Frederick Aspinall was born on 25 August 1851 in Liverpool, the son of a Roman Catholic judge. He was educated at Beaumont Roman Catholic College in Berkshire and then apprenticed to John Ramsbottom and Francis Webb at Crewe. Webb sent him to observe locomotive practice in the USA in 1872 and he was appointed Works Manager at Inchicore, Dublin, on the Great Southern & Western Railway of Ireland in 1875. A major advance was his introduction of the vacuum brake system there, which he adopted in the UK later.

In 1883 he became the GS&WR's Locomotive Superintendent in which post he was succeeded by Henry Ivatt when he moved to become the Chief Mechanical Engineer of the Lancashire & Yorkshire Railway in 1886, a post he held until 1899 when he became the railway's General Manager. He completed the construction and equipping of Horwich Works and within three years of its building the town had grown from 4,000 to 14,000. His main locomotive design and construction activity took place between 1891 and 1900, which included the well-known numerous 2-4-2 tank engines. At the peak around 1894/5 Horwich Works was turning out seven new locomotives a month. He also introduced electrification of some suburban lines.

He was keen on providing activities for his staff outside their daily duties and provided comprehensive facilities at Horwich for staff education, similar to those provided at Swindon and Crewe. Sporting activities were not neglected, and land was purchased for a bowling green, tennis courts and a cricket pitch. A gymnasium was added in 1895. In the 1890s nearly half of the 5,000 men employed in the Works took part in the educational and sporting activities of the company.

In 1914 he was in Germany at the outbreak of war and was interned initially until negotiations secured his release. Had the Germans foreseen his later contribution to the war effort for which he was knighted in 1917, his release might have been thwarted. He was President of the Institute of Mechanical Engineers in 1909/10 and President of the Institute of Civil Engineers in 1918/19. He wrote seven academic papers and was the holder of fourteen patents. His son, John, was a barrister and first class cricketer. Sir John died on 19 January 1937, aged 85.

Henry A. Ivatt, Locomotive Engineer, GNR, 1895–1911

Henry Ivatt was born on 16 September 1851 at Wentworth in Cambridgeshire and was educated at Liverpool College. At the age of seventeen he was apprenticed to John Ramsbottom at Crewe Works. He then acted as a locomotive fireman for six months, and held various other posts including work in the Traffic Department, culminating in an appointment as Assistant Foreman at Stafford depot. He was appointed as Head of Holyhead Locomotive Depot in 1874 and in 1876 was made Head of the Chester Motive Power District. In 1877 he moved to Cork in Ireland as District Locomotive Superintendent of the Southern Division of the Great Southern & Western Railway. In 1882 he moved to Inchicore as Assistant Locomotive Engineer & Works Manager and in 1886 became Locomotive Engineer of the company.

In 1895 he returned to the mainland, following Patrick Stirling as Locomotive Engineer of the Great Northern Railway (GNR), based at Doncaster. He was a popular manager with his staff and had a strong family life, fathering six children, although the eldest died in 1898. One of his sons, Henry George, followed in his father's footsteps, becoming Chief Mechanical Engineer of the LMS in 1946.

He became a member of the Institute of Mechanical Engineers in 1887, and a member of its Council between 1900 and 1922. He was elected Vice-President of the I.Mech.E in 1922-3, a role he held until his death, aged 72, at Haywards Heath in Sussex, on 25 October 1923.

George Jackson Churchward, Chief Mechanical Engineer, GWR, 1902–22

Churchward, Dean's successor and virtual co-manager during the latter's final five years, was born in 1857 in Stoke Gabriel on the River Dart between Kingswear and Totnes and joined the South Devon Railway at Newton Abbot in 1873. After absorption of that railway by the Great Western in 1876, he transferred, aged just 19, to the Swindon Drawing Office, and after a few rapid promotions, was appointed as Carriage and Wagon Works Manager in 1885. Ten years later he became Swindon Works Manager and identified as Dean's successor when he became his Chief Assistant in 1897, at a salary of £900 a year. Although he was not appointed as Locomotive Superintendent until 1 June 1902 – with his salary increased to £2,500 – he had been developing his ideas within the ample scope given him by Dean, and had already written a paper on a scheme for a limited number of 'standard' locomotive designs by January 1901, although in the interim he maintained a steady production of Dean designed engines, albeit showing an increasing influence of his own ideas, especially boiler design.

The 1901 paper outlined a scheme for six standard locomotive classes, a 2-8-0, two 4-6-0s, a 4-4-0, a 2-6-2 tank, and a 4-4-2 tank. The first 4-6-0, No. 100 (later 2900), was built within a month of Churchward's formal appointment and the 2-8-0, No.97 (later 2800), was the second standard locomotive to emerge from Swindon Works in June 1903. By 1905 he had amassed sufficient experience of these prototypes to proceed with confidence and the standard 4-6-0s, 2-8-0s and 2-6-2 tanks began to be built in quantity. Only then did the building of double-framed passenger 4-4-0s cease. Churchward finalised his plans for the full range of standard locomotives to meet all the Great Western Railway's needs, which, as well as the passenger locomotives, included the 2-6-0 mixed traffic 4300, which would cover the traffic needs that the small-wheeled 4-4-0s were still meeting. Its introduction in 1911 eliminated the need to build further 'Bulldog' 4-4-0s.

Churchward interested himself in locomotive, carriage and wagon matters, leaving the rest to his Chief Assistant, F.G. Wright. Churchward selected bright young engineers, involved them in frequent discussions, talked regularly to the draughtsmen and was active in seeking the views of practical men in the Works and running sheds, as well as maintaining his interest in developments overseas. The 1950s Western Region Chairman, Reggie Hanks, an apprentice himself at Swindon Works in 1912, recounted a couple of anecdotes about Churchward's hands-on involvement. On one occasion on Frome station, he observed the fireman leaning far out over the cabside to see the injector overflow. He promptly had the overflow pipe moved from behind to the leading edge of the cab steps, so that the fireman did not have to lean out so far. On another occasion he was discussing some detail of design with his Chief Draughtsman and one of the younger office staff who had prepared the detailed work. The Chief Draughtsman began to answer Churchward's questions but was told brusquely to 'Shut up – let the young man speak for himself. He did the work!' In such ways, Swindon design developed step by step and it put the Great Western a decade or more ahead of any other railway in the country as far as locomotives were concerned.

Churchward had an even temperament and a dignified bearing suggesting a 'country squire', strengthened by his interest in country pursuits, especially fishing. But he was also a good administrator and leader of men. He drew out the best from his staff and created a culture of good teamwork, a tradition and practice he inherited from Dean and his predecessors. In 1916 his title was changed to that of Chief Mechanical Engineer, he was awarded the CBE at the end of the war and in October 1920 he was the first Honorary Freeman of Swindon, of which he'd been the first Mayor as far back as 1900.

It is well known that his life ended run down by one of his

successor's engines whilst crossing the line from his home to the Works, nearly twelve years after his retirement. He'd retained his interest to the end and kept himself abreast of developments without obviously interfering with the policies and decisions of his successor. When he'd retired in 1922, the *Railway Magazine* had published a tribute, which included the words, 'It would be invidious to suggest that Mr G.J. Churchward CBE, who retired from the position of Chief Mechanical Engineer of the Great Western Railway, is the greatest locomotive engineer in modern British practice.'

Behind this reputation were a number of significant facts – he'd established a fleet of 888 new locomotives, his passenger and freight locomotives had been compared against those of other railways and had been shown to shine in both performance and economy, influencing design on the other major companies. Locomotives to his basic designs were still being built more than a generation later and were at the forefront of Western Region power at nationalisation in 1948, although by then Dean's double-framed 4-4-0s and Churchward's developments of them were almost extinct. His early designs developed from the Dean double-framed engines had been completely eclipsed and although good and successful in their day, performing widespread secondary duties efficiently enough, most were withdrawn from service by the mid-1930s, superseded by Collett's mixed traffic developments of Churchward's basic standard 4-6-0 designs.

John G. Robinson, Chief Mechanical Engineer, GCR, 1900–22

John George Robinson was born in Newcastle-upon-Tyne on 30 July 1856. He was the second son of the locomotive engineer Matthew Robinson and his wife, Jane. He was educated at Chester Grammar School and in 1872 was a Great Western Railway apprentice at Swindon, a pupil of Joseph Armstrong. In 1878 he was appointed as Assistant Engineer to his father at Bristol.

In 1884 he moved to Ireland as Assistant Carriage & Wagon Superintendent of the Waterford and Limerick Railway and the following year was appointed as Locomotive, Carriage and Wagon Superintendent. In 1900, following the sudden resignation of Harry Pollitt, he moved back to the mainland as Locomotive and Marine Superintendent of the Great Central Railway, his post retitled as Chief Mechanical Engineer in 1902. He held that post until the Grouping at the end of 1922 and was offered the similar post in the new LNER organisation, but being already 66 felt the post should go to a younger man and recommended Nigel Gresley. He was persuaded to remain for a while as an engineering consultant to the new company.

His design of the 2-8-0 freight locomotive had played a key role in military activities on the Continent in the First World War and he was awarded the CBE in the 1920 Honours List. He died aged 87 on 7 December 1943.

Wilson Worsdell, Chief Mechanical Engineer, NER, 1890–1910

Wilson Worsdell was from a Quaker family, the tenth child, fourth son, of Nathaniel and Mary Worsdell and younger brother of William Worsdell, who would precede him as Locomotive Superintendent of the North Eastern Railway. He was born on 7 September 1850 at Monks Coppenhall in Crewe and was a pupil at the Friends' School at Ackworth in 1860. He left in 1867 and spent the first six months of that year in the Crewe Works Drawing Office. In July he went to America and became an engineering pupil working for Edward Williams, Superintendent of Motive Power and Machinery at the Pennsylvania Railroad's Altoona Works. He returned to Crewe in 1871 in the Works under Francis Webb. He got experience in both the erecting shop and drawing office and was appointed assistant foreman at Stafford locomotive shed in 1874. He moved to Bushbury as foreman in 1876 and was in charge of the Chester depot in 1877.

He married Mary Elizabeth Bradford in 1882 and his son, Geoffrey, was born the following year, who broke the Quaker tradition by being educated at Charterhouse public school. He left Chester in March 1883 with a glowing testimonial from his depot staff and went as Assistant Mechanical Engineer of the North Eastern Railway at Gateshead. The Chief, Alexander McDonnell, was a controversial character and resigned at short notice in 1884 and his brother William became

Locomotive Superintendent. Wilson was re-designated Assistant Locomotive Superintendent of the Northern Division in 1885 and his salary was increased by £100 to £600 a year. William retired on health grounds in 1890 and Wilson took over on 1 October at a salary of £1,100. He remained in charge until May 1910. He bought a home, Greenesfield House, adjacent to the Works, working closely with an outstanding General Manager, George Gibbs. Wilson's assistant was Vincent Raven and Walter Smith was his Chief Draughtsman.

He designed the M1 4-4-0 in 1895, an engine involved in the 1895 East/West Coast 'Race to Aberdeen' and went on a study tour to the USA in 1901. Influenced by what he saw, he designed larger 20 ton wagons and the outstanding Q6 0-8-0s and J27 0-6-0s which remained as last survivors of steam in the North East. He designed the enlarged 4-4-0 of class R (LNER D20) in 1899 and his five 4-6-0s were the first passenger 4-6-0s in the country.

He retired in May 1910 as Chief Mechanical Engineer, his duties including the design and maintenance of locomotives, carriage and wagons, tugboats and hydraulic machinery, having been responsible for the management of 18,500 staff, 2,142 locomotives, 4,000 passenger coaches and 98,000 goods wagons. He was involved in the electrification of North Tyneside in 1904 and the goods branch to Newcastle Docks and electric locomotive 26500, now preserved. He was well liked by his staff, ran a boys' club and became a JP in 1907. He was a keen fisherman, possessing a second house in Voss in Norway, and was President of the Association of Railway Engineers and Carriage & Wagon Superintendents of Great Britain and Ireland. He was much appreciated and remained as a consultant to the North Eastern Railway to the end of 1910. He moved home to South Ascot and died in 1920 aged 69 and was buried at All Souls, Ascot. He was honoured by the naming of a new Peppercorn A1 pacific, 60127 *Wilson Worsdell*, on 30 October 1950.

Sir Vincent Raven, CME, NER, 1910–22

Vincent Raven was born on 3 December 1859 at Great Fransham in Norfolk, the son of a clergyman and educated at Aldenham School in Hertfordshire. In 1877 he became a pupil of Edward Fletcher, Locomotive Superintendent of the North Eastern Railway, and after various posts in that railway, was appointed in 1893 as Assistant Mechanical Engineer to Wilson Worsdell. As well as the development of the Atlantic locomotives described on this book, he designed a pacific locomotive and was heavily involved in the promotion and design of electrification. As early as 1904 the North Tyneside suburban network was electrified (3rd rail DC) and in 1915 the Shildon–Newport section of the line to Middlesbrough was electrified on the overhead 1,500 volt DC system. He planned the electrification of the York–Newcastle main line on the same overhead system and had built an 1,800hp 2-Co-2 electric locomotive in 1922 which was never utilised as the LNER after the 1923 Grouping aborted the electrification scheme.

In 1915, Raven was appointed by Lloyd George as Superintendent of the Royal Woolwich Arsenal and immediately raised the output from 60 to 80 per cent in the production of munitions for the war, for which he received a knighthood in 1917. At the Grouping and the appointment of Gresley as LNER CME, he became, with Robinson, Gresley's technical adviser but he resigned in 1924, possibly in frustration at the abandonment of his electrification plans. He was then appointed with Sir Sam Fay to the Royal Commission on the New South Wales Government Railway in Australia.

He had married Gifford Allan Crichton in 1883 with whom he had four children, two girls and then two boys. Edward Thompson, later LNER CME, was his son-in-law when Raven's daughter Guendolen married him in 1913. He died of heart failure whilst on holiday with his wife in Felixstowe on 14 February 1934, aged 74.

Douglas Earle Marsh, Chief Mechanical Engineer, LB&SCR, 1905–11

Douglas Marsh was born on 4 January 1862 at Salle in North Norfolk, the second son of the local rector. At the age of sixteen he attended Brighton College and in 1879 was trained at University College London in pure and applied mathematics, engineering and mechanical technology. In 1881 he became an apprentice pupil of William Dean on the Great Western at Swindon. There he became initially a draughtsman, then an inspector of materials.

In 1889 he was appointed Assistant Works Manager, but this was not a happy or successful time as he clashed with the Works Manager and they failed totally to communicate. He sought a post elsewhere and in 1895 became the chief assistant to the Mechanical Engineering Manager, H.A. Ivatt, of the GNR at Doncaster. He had the delegated authority to supervise the Works and despite his prickly manner was an efficient manager of the Plant. He oversaw the construction of the Ivatt Atlantics and travelled widely in Europe on railway business.

By 1904 Robert Billinton on the LB&SCR was becoming seriously ill and had to resign, and Marsh was appointed in his place at a salary of £1,500 p.a. on the first of January 1905. He found a large number of locomotives out of action requiring repair, so he gave the Works the priority of maintenance over new construction until the backlog had been addressed. He was also involved with early electrification schemes of the South London line, Battersea Park and Brixton. He had a wide interest with his continental experience of steam railcars, petrol railcars and motor trains (push-pull working). Because of the need for new construction whilst dealing with the repair situation, he used his GNR contacts to obtain drawings of the Atlantics as a model for the H1 and H2 LB&SCR engines for which he is best known.

He did build the C3 0-6-0 goods engines in 1906, having briefly considered compounding, but despite the large boilers, they were badly flawed and extremely unsuccessful. Whatever the flaws in this design, the fitting of the large boiler to the earlier C2 0-6-0s forged a successful C2X which lasted well into BR days. His engineering accomplishments apart from the C3s were praiseworthy – the Atlantics, the splendid I3 4-4-2Ts, the rebuilding of the A1 0-6-0Ts, the C2Xs, the E6 0-6-2Ts, electrification, the rebuilding of Brighton Works – but his overall management style attracted much criticism. He had a turbulent relationship with the men under his supervision which suggests that the clash of personalities at Swindon in the 1890s might have been caused by his character and attitude. He was unpopular on arrival, a common response from a conservative workforce to a newcomer, but his brusqueness and unpredictable temper made things worse. He was officious and early on stopped overtime working at the Works which did not endear him to the staff there. Labour relationships dogged him for most of his time at Brighton and he seems to have had a long-running feud with the boilersmiths which led to strikes in 1909 and a full staff strike in 1911 that cost the company £20,000.

The financial problems of the company were reflected in his own personal circumstances and it seems to have been common knowledge that he struggled to pay his debts. He was involved in a libel case in 1913 after he stopped helping a man to whom he'd given some earlier support and although exonerated in court, the affair damaged his reputation. The result of the 1911 strike caused the company many problems in 1912 with a backlog of repairs – nearly 30 per cent of the 535 locomotive fleet were out of action under repair and a further 20 per cent were stopped awaiting repair. He was also accused by the company of minor irregularities involving the sale of scrap metal, and all these issues caused him to suffer from stress. He took leave and went abroad to convalesce, but never fully recovered and in his absence the LB&SCR appointed L.B. Billinton on the first of January 1912. Marsh left Brighton, therefore, under a cloud although any suggestions of dismissal were covered up, as reasons of poor health were given for his retirement at the age of fifty. In fact, despite continuing poor health, he became an engineering consultant to the Rio Tinto mining company for twenty years and died on 25 May 1933 and was buried at Batheaston Parish Church. He had married in 1906 and was survived by a son and daughter.

William Paton Reid, Locomotive Superintendent, NBR, 1903–19

William Reid was born in Glasgow on 8 September 1854, the son of Robert Whyte Reid. He was apprenticed at Cowlairs Works in 1879 and by the early 1880s was in charge of the locomotive depot at Balloch. He stepped up to Dunfermline in 1889 and Dundee in 1891. Matthew Holmes, the previous Locomotive Superintendent, had had two Assistants, Robert Chalmers, a very experienced man who also acted as Chief Draughtsman, and John Soutar who had been manager at St Margaret's, Edinburgh. In 1900 Soutar died and Taylor of Burntisland was offered the post of depot manager at St Margaret's, but declined to move there for domestic reasons and Reid was appointed in his place. A new senior post was then created of Outdoor Running Assistant Locomotive Superintendent which he held until he took on the Locomotive Superintendent's post on the retirement of Matthew Holmes in 1903. His promotion over the head of Robert Chalmers was unpopular, although because of the urgent need to replace Holmes he was initially only placed 'in charge'. After the first six months he was given a further six months 'on probation' and was only permanently appointed in June 1904 and then only after an 8-6 vote by the Board. His salary had risen from £173 p.a. in 1901 to £750 by 1904. Reid initially had a difficult time with the Board and Locomotive Committee directing policy and Reid being informed of decisions he had to implement by letter from the General Manager. Initial problems with his new Atlantic engines and his relationship with James Bell, the Civil Engineer, who resented the impact of Reid's Atlantics on his track, caused a troubled couple of years but eventually confidence in him grew and he remained as Locomotive Superintendent until well after the end of the First World War, retiring in 1919, when he was 65. He died on 2 February 1932, aged 75.

Chapter 1

THE LANCASHIRE & YORKSHIRE 'HIGHFLYERS'

The last design made by John Aspinall before he resigned from his mechanical engineering role to become the railway's General Manager was of a very unusual 4-4-2, class L1, with inside cylinders, huge driving wheels of 7ft 3in diameter and a high-pitched boiler, engines that proved to be fast runners and because of this and their appearance, became nicknamed 'Highflyers', an epithet that stuck throughout their lives. They were only the second design of an Atlantic in Britain, the first L & Y example, 1400, appearing only a few months, in February 1899, after the GNR's 990. Twenty were built at Horwich between February and October 1899, numbered 1400, and then 1392–1399, and 1401 -1404 and 700, 702, 708, 711, 718, 735 and 737. A further twenty were authorised by Aspinall and his Board in his new managerial role in 1901 and they were constructed between January and July 1902. They resumed numbers in the 14XX series, 1405–1424. Their dimensions were:

Cylinder diameter (2 inside): 19 x 26in
Coupled wheel diameter: 7ft 3in
Bogie wheel diameter: 3ft 0½in
Trailing wheel diameter: 3ft 7½in
Boiler pressure: 175lbs psi

Joy motion with slide valves
Heating surface: 1,928sqft
Grate area: 23sqft
Weight (engine): 58¾ tons
Tractive effort: 15,535lb

They were the first engines on the L&Y to be fitted with Belpaire fireboxes. The chimney and

***Below left*: L1 Atlantic** 1395 as designed by John Aspinall and constructed in April 1899, withdrawn in 1926 as LMS 10304. The high pitched boiler to clear the large coupled wheels was a significant feature of this class. (Real Photographs/MLS Collection)

***Below right*: 1395 as** seen from the rear at Manchester Victoria station in 1902. The 7ft 3in diameter driving wheels are very impressive seen from this angle. (Millbrook House/MLS Collection)

***Above*: 1424, the** last 'Highflyer' to be built in July 1902, seen the following year. (J.B. Hodgson/MLS Collection)

***Right*: The startling** and imposing front end of 1419 at Low Moor shed, c1905. 1419 was based at Fleetwood. (MLS Collection)

***Below left*: 700, built** in July 1899 and later fitted with a shorter chimney, seen c1910. (MLS Collection)

***Below right*: 700 again,** at Agecroft, c1910. (MLS Collection)

A pair of Atlantics, 735 and 1406, on shed, c1910. (MLS Collection)

708 with flat smokebox door and short chimney, c1920. (MLS Collection)

An official LMS photograph of 10327 (formerly 1412) as renumbered at the Grouping, 1923. (LMS/MLS Collection)

10303, formerly 1394, at York, c1924. (A.C. Roberts/MLS Collection)

***Right*: 10300, the** prototype former 1400, built in February 1899 and withdrawn in 1933, seen here c1932. (Real Photographs/MLS Collection)

***Below*: 10307, (ex-1398)**, coaled ready for its next turn, on shed ahead of a Hughes 'Dreadnaught' 4-6-0, c1925. 10307 was one of the last withdrawn in 1933. (Real Photographs/MLS Collection)

blastpipe were very near the front of the short smokebox and vacuum brake cylinders were provided. 737 was fitted with a low degree superheater or 'steam drier' and five more were equipped later, not too successful but an early innovation. In later years the trailing wheels were altered to outside bearings, although the reason for this is unknown – possibly liable to overheating when inside close to the firebox, or to improve the riding. Adams bogies replaced the earlier swing-link type, also to improve the riding. Some were fitted with short chimneys and others had a flat smokebox door.

Operation

They were fast and free-running engines and rode well after the modifications mentioned earlier, and drivers were prepared to use this capacity. 100mph is reputed to have been reached on at least one occasion on the level road between Liverpool and Southport. The L&YR route from Liverpool to Manchester, 36½ miles, was hilly with climbs to the tunnel between Upholland and Orrell, some 7 miles eastbound from Kirby at 1 in 200-300 range at first, steepening to 1 in 114 to 1 in 118 over the last three miles. Westbound the gradient was shorter, under four miles, but steeper at 1 in 92 for most of the distance. Eastbound, after the descent through Pemberton, the line rises to Hindley and Crow's Nest Junction with patches of 1 in 90 and 1 in 98 and then undulates through Atherton and Walkden to Pendlebury. The line then drops steeply to Pendleton at 1 in 80/99, providing an early obstacle for westbound trains, the gradient starting just 2½ miles from Manchester Victoria. The

40 minute schedule for the non-stop expresses between the two cities was tight, but loads were light, usually only three or four vehicles. Typically, a 'Highflyer' would start energetically out of Manchester on a Liverpool train, to get a run at Pendlebury bank which was usually surmounted at 40-45mph. It was quite usual to touch 75mph on the undulating stretch, but speed restrictions after Hindley prevented a run at the bank to Orrell Tunnel. Their major weakness was their lack of adhesion with only 35 tons available – most Atlantics suffered from poor adhesion compared with 4-4-0s or 4-6-0s, but the 'Highflyers' were noted in particular for the wheels spinning when accelerating trains at the start of their journeys

A timed run with 1423 clocked 48mph at the top of the 1 in 92 at Orrell, though with only three coaches. On another run 1416 achieved 54mph in the short level out of Manchester Victoria and topped the 1 in 80 at Pendlebury at 48½mph, Atherton was passed at 76mph, but after that p-way slacks around Hindley meant a slow start to Orrell Bank, the summit being passed at 42½mph. Another 76 on the descent meant Liverpool was reached well inside the schedule. However, with the addition of a fourth coach the schedule was tight and 1392 with four coaches dropped a couple of minutes although it had extra p-way slowings. The 4.30pm from Manchester to Liverpool, a through train from Newcastle, was a 7-coach 200 ton train and was normally hauled by a Hughes 4-6-0 after their introduction in 1908. On one occasion a 'Highflyer', 1407, substituted. A signal check prevented a fast start and the train fell to 37mph on Pendlebury bank, but hard running then produced 72½mph before Atherton, and the normal slack-infested dip after Hindley was, for once, free of checks and was rushed at 72 with the speed at Orrell only falling to 43mph. Down through Rainford the speed rose to 80½mph, averaging 76.8mph over the following seven miles to Fazakerley. This enabled the 40 minute schedule to be kept with this load, one of the best runs recorded with an Atlantic 'Highflyer', a time often not achieved by the heavier but somewhat sluggish saturated 4-6-0s. The fastest runs I can find with the light 3-coach trains on the 40-minute schedule are in the tables below and overleaf.

Liverpool Exchange–Salford, November 1912
1403, 95 tons
10.40am Liverpool

Miles	Location	Times	Speed		Gradients
0	Liverpool	00.00			
1.75	Sandhills	02.49			
3.75	Preston Road	05.03	53		1/440 R
5	Fazakerley	06.18	60		L
12.1	Rainford Jcn	12.28	72½		1/316, 1/277 R
14.25	Upholland	14.30	57½		1/114 R
15.5	Orrell	15.53			
17.25	Pemberton	17.28	76		1/92 F
21.8	Crow's Nest Jcn	21.35	59		1/90 R
25.5	Atherton	24.51	77		1/150, 1/116 F
30.5	Swinton	29.46	sigs 50*		
33.25	Pendleton	32.04	73		1/80, 1/99 F
35.75	Salford	34.19	(33¾ net)	2¾ E	

Manchester Victoria–Liverpool Exchange, November 1912
1403, 95 tons
11.45am Manchester

Miles	Location	Times	Speed		Gradients
0	Manchester	00.00			
0.75	Salford	02.15			
2.25	Pendleton	04.10			1/99 R
5	Swinton	07.23	51½		1/80 R
11	Atherton	12.38	77		1/129, 1/150 F
12.75	Daisy Hill	14.04			
	Crow's Nest Jcn	-	55*		
19.25	Pemberton	19.36	76		1/154 F
21	Orrell	21.22	53½		1/92 R
22.25	Upholland	22.46			1/114 F
24.4	Rainford Jcn	24.32	74		1/118 F
31.5	Fazakerley	29.36	85		1/316, 1/247 F
32.75	Preston Road	30.40	72		L, 1/340 R
34.2	Kirkdale	31.57	sigs		
36.5	Liverpool	36.10	(35 net)	3¾ E	

Rous-Marten died suddenly in April 1908 and his monthly article in the *Railway Magazine* was continued by R.E. Charlewood. He published an article at the end of the year which described runs with 'Highflyers' on heavier loads. 1399 had 160 tons and cut the 40 minute schedule to 38½ minutes, with speeds of 37½mph on the initial climb to Pendlebury, 67 before Atherton, 62-63 maintained over the undulating line to Hindley and then 78mph down the 1 in 90 to Pemberton Junction, rushing the 1 in 92 three mile climb to Orrell Tunnel with 40mph at the summit. A final 72½ on the descent into Liverpool saw the train complete the punctual run. 1398 had 200 tons and bad weather to contend with and completed the Manchester–Liverpool run in 41 minutes 21 seconds, after a signal check outside Liverpool. The initial climb to Pendlebury was excellent with 40½mph sustained, but in the gale and wet weather, 1398 slipped badly on the climb to Orrell, falling to 31mph at the summit. The maximum downhill speed was 72mph. Little mention was made of their exploits on other routes although they were regularly diagrammed to work to Leeds and York – the 47¾ miles over the Pennines from Manchester to Wakefield were scheduled in 58 minutes. The only run I can find on the Manchester–Southport route was a brief mention of a run by 1397 which ran the 34½ miles to St Luke's in 44 minutes with 205 tons – the first 16 miles to Pemberton Junction using the main Liverpool route. The 'Highflyers' were working regularly from Manchester with trains to Blackpool and Fleetwood via the LNW/L&YR joint line from Preston, but I can trace no logs of their performance on those routes. This is a shame because it would be good to have authenticated the rumoured 100mph allegedly achieved on the gently falling line between Pemberton Junction and Southport.

The engines were all passed to the LMS in 1923 and renumbered 10300–10339 in order of construction. They continued working their traditional routes in the 1920s. However, they were non-standard and the first

***Above left*: L1 Atlantic 1417 on test at an unknown location, c1903.** (MLS Collection)

***Above right*: 1412 picks** up water on the troughs between Lea Road and Salwick with a Manchester–Fleetwood express, c1905. (MLS Collection)

An unidentified 'Highflyer' leaving Queen's Road carriage sidings with stock for a Manchester–Blackpool express, 28 July 1905. A Midland Johnson 4-4-0 is in the carriage shed. (J.A. Peden/MLS Collection)

to be withdrawn were 10304 (the former 1395) and 702 (10314) in 1926. 10301-10303, 10306, 10308, 10318, 10326, 10332-10334 and 10338 (1392-1394, 1397, 1399, 735, 1411 and 1423) followed in 1927. By 1933 only 10307, 10309, 10310, 10316, 10320, 10322 and 10335 were left and only 10316 (the former 711 built in September 1899) lasted into 1934. There were ideas of preserving one, but it came to naught.

***Above left*: 1404 passing** Manchester Exchange and an LNWR 'Precursor' 4-4-0 with the 4.55pm Manchester Victoria–Blackpool, c1908. (J.F. Thomas/ MLS Collection)

***Above right*: 1411 leaving** Manchester Victoria with a Leeds express, passing LNWR 'Precedent' 2-4-0, 2148, 1908. (MLS Collection)

711 on a Hull Boat Train at Middleton Junction, c1912. (MLS Collection)

An unidentified L1 Atlantic at the Sowerby Tunnel, c1910. (MLS Collection)

***Below left*: An unidentified** 'Highflyer' at Hopwood, c1920. (MLS Collection)

***Below right*: A pair** of 'Highflyers', 1423 and 1420, at Leeds Central having arrived from Manchester, c1920. (W.H. Whitworth/MLS Collection)

1403 leaving York with a Manchester express, c1920. (R.E. Gee/ MLS Collection)

***Below left*: No. 1405** passing the Holgate platform, York, with a Manchester express, c1920. (H. Gordon Tidey/ MLS Collection)

***Below right*: 10303 on** the 3.50pm York - Manchester near Middleton Junction, 25 May 1925. (N. Fields/MLS Collection)

***Above left*: 10336 on** a Liverpool Exchange – Blackpool train leaving Ansdell & Fairhaven station, 6 October 1926. (F. Dean/MLS Collection)

***Above right*: 10320 at** Stockport, c1930. (MLS Collection)

***Below left*: 10316, the** last survivor of the 'Highflyers' on a lightweight express at an unknown location, 1932. (MLS Collection)

***Below right*: 10320 entering** Huddersfield station, c1932. (MLS Collection)

Chapter 2

THE GREAT NORTHERN ATLANTICS

The GNR C1 'Klondyke' (LNER C2)

By the mid-1890s the weight of GNR trains had increased considerably – both the weight of the individual carriages and the length of trains to accommodate the increasing number of passengers. For example, a train that could seat 248 passengers in 1880 weighed only 116 tons tare, whilst a train that could accommodate a similar number of passengers weighed 237 tons by 1896. Schedules had also been accelerated from an average for main line expresses of just under 50mph in 1880 to 55 over the same period. The Stirling 'singles', wonderful engines in their day, were not coping with the heavier trains and the GN Board was dissatisfied and persuaded Patrick Stirling to retire (he was already 75) and he died a few days later before his retirement took effect. Henry Ivatt was recruited as Locomotive Engineer from Inchicore Works in Dublin and Douglas Earle Marsh, Works Manager Swindon, as Assistant Locomotive Engineer and Works Manager at Doncaster, both in March 1896.

Ivatt's first designs were a 2-4-0 and a 4-4-0, but by February 1897 he had the backing of the Board to build an experimental 4-4-2. 990 was constructed at Doncaster and completed in May 1898, and immediately was given the nickname 'Klondyke' after the gold-rush that year on the Yukon River. This nickname stuck to the whole class, ten more, numbered 949, 950 and 982-989, being built in 1900. 990 was named *Henry Oakley* after the GNR's General Manager who had retired in 1896. Further examples were constructed in 1903, numbered 250 and 252–260, 251 being the first of a new class of Atlantic, to be described later. Their key dimensions were:

Cylinders (2-outside):	18¾ x24in
Coupled wheel diameter:	6ft 8in
Bogie wheel diameter:	3ft 8in
Trailing wheel diameter:	3ft 8in

Stephenson motion with slide valves

Boiler pressure:	175lb psi, 170lb psi after superheated
Heating surface:	1,442.1sqft
Grate area:	24.5sqft
Axleload:	16 tons 12 cwt
Weight (Engine):	60 tons
(Tender):	43 tons 2 cwt
(Total):	103 tons 2 cwt
Water capacity:	3,500 gallons
Coal capacity:	5 tons
Tractive effort:	15,649 lb

Ivatt, like his contemporary Churchward, took a great interest in boiler design and his first Atlantic had a large boiler, a great advance on Stirling's practice, though he did not use the high pressure of the GW engines. He liaised closely with Aspinall and borrowed one of his L&YR 4-4-0s with Joy's valve gear, but both men decided in the end that neither that nor the Stephenson motion gave the free running gear they wanted for fast running. For such a large boiler, the cylinders seemed small, but the new locomotive's axleweights had to be kept as light as possible as Ivatt had discovered the poor quality of the GNR track. He had in fact walked the 156 miles from King's Cross to Doncaster and was apparently appalled at its state and until the civil engineering improved, he refrained from designing a locomotive with a heavier axleload. Perhaps this is why he went for an express Atlantic rather than 4-4-0 development as the weight would be better spread. His first 4-4-0s (the '400' class, LNER D3) had a light axleload of only 14½ tons but his larger '1321' class (LNER D2) had a 17 ton load. 990 was balanced with just 15 tons on the bogie and first coupled axle, 16½ tons on the rear coupled axle and 12 tons borne by the trailing axle. 990 rode well despite the poor track, but drivers

The first 'Klondyke' 990, as built in 1898 before naming. (MLS Collection)

***Below left*: 984, one** of the first production series of 'Klondykes' built in 1900, c1905. (Loco Publishing Co./MLS Collection)

***Below right*: 252 of** the second series built in 1903, seen here c1905. (MLS Collection)

The 4-cylinder 'Klondyke', 271, built experimentally in 1902, seen here c1905. (Loco Publishing Co./MLS Collection)

were encouraged to push, indeed thrash, the engine uphill and on the level – the boiler could cope – but restrain running downhill to around 70mph.

In 1902 Ivatt built a 4-cylinder version, number 271, and its different dimensions were:

Cylinders (4): 15x20in

Stephenson motion with 8″ piston valves and, later, Walschaerts valve gear for the outside cylinders.

Heating surface:	1,303sqft
Axleload:	16 tons 16 cwt
Weight (Engine):	58 tons 13 cwt
(Tender):	40 tons 18 cwt
(Total):	99 tons 11 cwt
Water capacity:	3,670 gallons
Tractive effort:	16,071lb

However, it was unsuccessful and was rebuilt in 1911 with two inside cylinders of 18½x26in diameter, rebored to 19inx26in in 1923. It was equipped with a Schmidt superheater in 1911.

271 as rebuilt in 1911 with two larger inside cylinders, seen at King's Cross, c1912. (MLS Collection)

***Above left and above right*: The rebuilt** 271 seen at Doncaster in LNER livery but not yet renumbered 3271, 1923. (N. Fields/MLS Collection)

***Below left*:** The prototype, 3990 *Henry Oakley*, rebuilt with enlarged cylinders and piston valves in 1922, at Hitchin, c1925. (MLS Collection)

***Below right*:** 258 with the suffix 'N' added to GNR engines after the Grouping before renumbering as 3258, at King's Cross station, 1924. (MLS Collection)

From 1909 onwards the 'Klondykes', starting with 988, were fitted with superheaters and mechanical lubricators and eleven of the class were rebuilt with new enlarged cylinders (20inx24in) and 8in piston valves. The rebuilt engines had an improved tractive effort of 17,340lb, and the whole class, given the official identity as C1s by the GNR, was reclassified as LNER C2, the later wide firebox Atlantics being C1. They all had 3000 added to their numbers after the Grouping in line with other ex-GNR locomotives. They were repainted in LNER green livery from 1923 and LNER black with red lining from 1928 as an economy measure. The rebuilt C2s with larger cylinders were 3250, 3253, 3255, 3257, 3258, 3949, 3985-3988 and 3990.

By the mid-1930s they were considered too weak to be of much value and as some were due for reboilering, withdrawals started in 1935. 3982 was the first to be withdrawn in November and 3988 followed it to the scrapheap in December. Six were withdrawn in

***Above left*: 3252, superheated** in 1924 and with mechanical lubrication, at King's Cross, 1925. (F. Moore/ MLS Collection)

***Above right*: 988 was** fitted with an American style bogie with the frame outside the wheels from 1903 until 1909 when it was transferred to 983 until its withdrawal in 1936. Here it is seen on 3983, c1927. (MLS Collection)

3990 *Henry* *Oakley* in LNER post-1928 black livery at York in the early 1930s. (H. Gordon Tidey/ MLS Collection)

1936 including the inside cylinder 3271, six more in 1937 including 3990 *Henry Oakley,* and three more in 1938, before the oncoming war slowed down withdrawals of all classes. Five remained, 3254, 3256 and 3259 being withdrawn in 1943, 3250 in 1945 and the last survivor, 3252, was withdrawn in July 1945. 3250 and 3252 were allocated the numbers of 2893 and 2892 respectively, but neither were carried as withdrawals took place before the renumbering scheme was implemented. 3259 was used between 1943 and July 1946 as a stationary boiler at Doncaster Wagon Works. Some other C2 boilers were also used as stationary boilers. The boiler carried by 3254 survived at Doncaster Carriage Works until November 1964.

3252 at Cambridge, 10 June 1938. It would become the last survivor of the class, but one of the class retaining its original cylinders and slide valves, withdrawn in July 1945. (MLS Collection)

3989 with original cylinders and slide valves at Boston, c1937. It was withdrawn in April 1938. (MLS Collection)

Operation

990 was extensively tested on the Doncaster–King's Cross main line for a couple of years being stationed at Grantham, before the building of ten in 1900. Rous-Marten was invited to observe its working on an early run and he noted that 990 was pushed hard on the 1 in 200 to Potters Bar, maintaining 47mph requiring an edhp of around 700. On the descent through Stevenage to Hitchin, no more than 70mph was claimed and the maximum speed on the journey was 73mph near Connington at the foot of the 1 in 200 from Abbots Ripton. The main interest was in the climbing with 55mph at Leys box at the summit of the 3 mile climb at 1 in 200 from Huntingdon and the 100 miles to Stoke Box were passed in 108½ minutes, an average of 55.2mph from King's Cross.

Another early run timed by Rous-Marten was on the up *Flying Scotsman,* which ran non-stop from York to Grantham, slipping a coach at Doncaster. 990 had 293/315 tons from York, 271/290 from Doncaster. It covered the 82.7 miles in 94 minutes 26 seconds with much running in the mid-60s. The 1 in 200 climb to Markham Box brought the speed down to 51mph and the descent through Dukeries Junction got the speed up to its maximum of 69 before the long climb from Newark to Peascliffe Tunnel dropped the speed to 43mph – however, speed had slackened to 44mph over Muskham troughs before Newark and the train was running early so 990 was taken relatively easily over this last section. In 1903 990 worked the 9.45am King's Cross–Leeds under management scrutiny to see if acceleration was possible to compete with the Midland Railway service. The load was 212 tons and 990 was driven very hard on the initial 1 in 200 passing Potters Bar at 53½mph requiring an estimated 900 edhp. Peterborough was passed in 76 minutes 24 seconds, almost exactly 'even time', and the climb to Stoke was going well at 57mph just four miles from the summit when, despite official instructions, the train was brought to a 3 minute signal stop. Grantham was reached in 112¾ minutes (104 net) for the 105 miles

After the second ten were built in 1903, the 'Klondykes' were allocated to the main East Coast sheds for main line work between King's Cross and York. In 1905 the allocation was:

King's Cross:	252-254
Peterborough:	255, 256, 987, 988
Grantham:	257-259, 949, 950, 989, 990
Doncaster:	250, 260, 271, 982-986

The Leeds service was duly accelerated in July 1903 with the 9.45 down non-stop to Doncaster and the 2pm Leeds non-stop from Wakefield (176 miles) booked in 190 minutes. The train was, however, a lightweight four coach train but new 12-wheel vehicles, the set weighing 145 tons. Rous-Marten logged 253 coming up in 181 minutes, 173 net with a maximum of 85mph coming down from Stoke. Ivatt must have got the Civil Engineer to do something about the track!

In the down direction, 257 had a gross load of 290 tons on the *Flying Scotsman* and got to Peterborough in 80¾ minutes and Grantham in 119, a minute early. After initially falling to 38mph on the climb to Potters Bar, the engine was opened out and accelerated to 42 on the gradient, requiring an edhp of around 780-800 to achieve this. The maximum speed was 80mph through Three Counties and time was so well in hand by Peterborough that speed was allowed to fall to 36mph on the climb to Stoke Tunnel. 985 on the 1.30pm King's Cross–Leeds ran from Peterborough to Grantham in 31½ minutes net for the 29½ mainly uphill miles, speed falling gradually from the 66mph attained by Tallington to 63½ at Essendine, 60 at Little Bytham and 53 at Corby Glen on the 1 in 178 where the train was checked severely before the tunnel.

Runs with heavier trains on the King's Cross–Newcastle express, leaving Grantham at 2.20pm and allowed 97 minutes for the 82.7 miles, were booked for a D1 4-4-0 or 'Klondyke' and 257 with 350 tons made it exactly on time including two p-way slacks at Muskham troughs and Bawtry and a signal check outside York (90 minutes net). 949 and 355 tons took 106 minutes 25 seconds, passing Retford nearly twelve minutes late after a lengthy signal stop at Muskham troughs. Arrival at York was 9½ minutes late (93½ minutes net).

The 'Klondyke' allocation changed little in the first decade of the twentieth century, the only movement being that of 988 after its superheating in 1909, the first of the class, to Doncaster. As the Ivatt Atlantics with the wide fireboxes were increased in number the 'Klondykes' gradually lost their main line express work on which they had coped rather than excelled, the schedules not being unduly demanding. They were reputed to be somewhat sluggish on the banks. By 1913 the C1 wide-firebox Atlantics had reached 94 in number and had all but displaced the 'Klondykes' on main line express work, apart from covering relief trains, excursions and failures. Cecil J. Allen felt that drivers were not prepared to work their engines hard unless there was a special reason. The crews were allocated their own engines and reliability and economy of maintenance was of as much importance to them as punctual running. CJA summed up his experience of them in 1914 after innumerable runs on the East Coast carrying out his inspection of materials role, as 'curiously variable, sometimes record-breakers of the first water, but on other occasions unaccountably sluggish'. As well as good runs, he encountered a couple of shockers. The 4.12pm Doncaster was a heavy train but had a relatively easy schedule, allowed 93 minutes from Doncaster to Peterborough (79.6 miles) and 90 minutes to King's Cross (76.4 miles). One 'Klondyke' took 104 minutes from Doncaster to Peterborough, admittedly with 420 tons, whilst another with 405 tons eked out 102 minutes to get from there to King's Cross. Speed was falling to around 30mph on the long 1 in 200 gradients.

After the rebuilding of 271 with two inside cylinders, its performance was transformed. It was based at Doncaster and

King's Cross's 254 passing Holloway with an up East Coast express shortly after its construction, c1904. (H. Gordon Tidey/ MLS Collection)

252 on a down express at an unidentified location, somewhere between King's Cross and Hitchin, c1910. (Colling Turner/ MLS Collection)

254, still at King's Cross, relegated to a stopping Cambridge–King's Cross train at Greenwood, c1914. (MLS Collection)

3990 at Great Ponton with a Grantham–Peterborough stopping train, c1936. (Colling Turner/ MLS Collection)

3990 *Henry Oakley* departing from Sheffield Victoria with the 8.30am Liverpool–Hull, 1 August 1934. (MLS Collection)

was used frequently on express turns to London working turn and turn about with the large Ivatt Atlantics. It was reputedly a free-running machine and was kept on such work until around 1919. During the First World War the 'Klondykes' were called on for the heavier trains. 950 took 350 tons to Peterborough in 80¼ minutes net, top speed 77½ at Arlesey. 982 brought the Up *Flying Scotsman* – a 490 ton gross train – from Grantham to King's Cross in 135 minutes for the 105 miles, gaining four minutes on an admittedly slow schedule. The 2.20pm King's Cross–Edinburgh was a turn for a Grantham D1 4-4-0 or a 'Klondyke' (as reported in my previous book on LNER 4-4-0s) and Grantham's 257 with 360 tons just held the 97 minute schedule for the 82.7 miles despite incurring three bad checks. After the war the 'Klondykes' lost most of their remaining express work as more C1 large Atlantics were transferred to Grantham. The allocation in 1920 was:

King's Cross:	252-254, 949
Peterborough:	255-259, 982, 985, 987-990
Doncaster:	271, 986
York:	250, 260, 950, 983, 984

At York they were replacements for Ivatt D1 4-4-0s working stopping trains between York, Doncaster and Grantham. The allocation had changed again by the Grouping, the 1923 distribution being:

King's Cross:	3254
Cambridge:	3252, 3253, 3949
Peterborough:	3250, 3255-3260, 3982, 3985, 3987-3990
Doncaster:	3271, 3986
York:	3950, 3983, 3984

3271, the former 4-cylinder Atlantic rebuilt in 1911 as an inside 2-cylinder engine, on an up stopping train near Grantham, c1935 (MLS Collection)

Between 1923 and 1925 a number of C2s, as the 'Klondykes' were now identified, were allocated to Starbeck, Harrogate, working to Doncaster and back on Leeds–London expresses, but by 1925 they had been replaced by NER D20s and D21s. The remaining York C2s were used on similar turns to the NE engines working to Leeds, Hull, Scarborough and Harrogate. Between 1923 and 1928 the Peterborough engines worked slow trains to King's Cross, and in Lincolnshire to Boston, Lincoln and Grimsby. The next influx of new engines to affect the C2 allocation was in the late 1920s when the Gresley Pacifics were available in decent numbers and the B17s commenced construction. The Cambridge C2s were dispersed, 3949 to March where it remained until its demise. A couple went to Mexborough shed in 1928/9 and 3254 and 3990 stayed there for several years, 3990 being particularly popular and well cared for, often working that depot's main turns from Sheffield to Hull. Doncaster's C2s worked to Nottingham on Leeds and York services to Bournemouth as well as a variety of stopping passenger and parcels trains.

The Cambridge engines worked Cambridge–King's Cross slow services and occasionally deputised for a larger Atlantic on the semi-fast tightly timed 'Beer Trains' which were introduced in 1932. Logs of C2s in the Rail Performance Society's archives are nearly all on these trains and some by Mr M.H. Cobb are in the tables below:

		King's Cross–Cambridge 'Beer Trains' 1936											
		3257 7 chs 192/205 tons 2.05pm King's Cross 14.1.1936			**3257 6 chs 190 tons 11.40am King's Cross 28.1.1936**			**3257 6 chs 185/195 tons 11.40am King's Cross 8.2.1936**			**3257 6chs 200 tons 8.10pm King's Cross 29.2.1936**		
Miles	**Location**	**Times**	**Speed**		**Times**	**Speed**		**Times**	**Speed**		**Times**	**Speed**	
0	King's Cross	00.00			00.00			00.00			00.00		
2.6	Finsbury Pk	06.05	36		05.55			06.00			05.55	48	
3.4	Harringay	07.20			07.15			07.10	50		07.10	50	
4	Hornsey	08.05	50		08.00			07.55	56		08.00	56	
5	Wood Green	09.05	56/54		09.00	56/53		08.55	56/53		09.00	58/53	
9.2	New Barnet	13.50	50/53/50		14.10	47½ /50		14.30	to SL pws		14.20	pws 10*	
10.6	Harold Wood	15.30	51½		15.50	50		19.25	SL		18.15	39/44	
12.7	Potters Bar	18.00	60		18.30	56/60		23.10	43/56		21.15	56	
17.7	Hatfield	22.55	69/sigs 40*		23.30	64/75		30.25	sigs /53		26.00	75	
20.3	Welwyn G-C	26.25		1½ L	26.40		1¾ L	34.15		9¼ L	29.10		4¼ L
		00.00		2 L	00.00		1½ L	00.00		9¼ L	00.00		4 L
1.7	Welwyn North	04.00	26/45		03.40	48½		03.30	47½		03.30	50	
3.2	Woolmer Gn	06.15	50/56		05.35	50/56		05.20	50/ 60		05.23	60	
4.7	Knebworth	08.00	60/64½		07.20	60/65		07.05	60		07.10	60	
6.4	Langley	09.35	66½		08.50	69		08.48	69/66½		08.40	69/65	
8.3	Stevenage	11.20	72		10.20	78½		10.20	75		10.25	75	
11.6	Hitchin	15.20		3¼ L	14.25		2 L	14.20		9½ L	14.30		4½ L
0		00.00		4 L	00.00	slipping	2¼ L	00.00		9½ L	00.00		4 L
2.6	Letchworth	05.20	37	4 L	06.05		3 L	05.20	41	9½ L	05.20		4 L
0		00.00		4¼ L	00.00		3¼ L	00.00		9¼ L	00.00		5 L
2.1	Baldock	03.40	50/60		03.25	60/47½ /56		03.25	50/53/60		03.25	60/50	
6.5	Ashwell	08.30	72		08.30	64*		08.10	66½ *		08.25	66½	
10.4	Royston	12.25		3¼ L	12.20	36*/64		11.45	32*/56		12.10	45*/64	
13.4	Meldreth	03.40	50/60		15.35	69		15.00	67/60*		15.20	66½	
18.3	Shepreth	06.15	56		17.15	60		16.35			17.00		
19.4	Foxton	07.25	56		18.25	60/56		18.20	53		18.00	65	
23.8	Shepreth B Jn	12.05			23.20	58/32*		23.30			22.25	41/sigs*	
25.3	Trumpington	14.00	sigs		26.10	pws 10*		25.43	60		24.40		
26.4	Cambridge	17.25		5 L	29.20		5 L	27.55		9 L	27.40		4¾ L

These trains were tightly timed and the C2s were pushed to run fast where possible, reaching higher speeds regularly than in their early days when 70mph was rarely significantly exceeded. Despite their age, these Atlantics were said to ride well. The significant gradients affecting the above were the 8-mile 1 in 200 climb to Potters Bar, the descent to Hatfield, mainly at 1 in 200, another 1 in 200 climb to Knebworth and 1 in 200 descent from Stevenage to Hitchin. There is a nasty 1 in 161 bank from Hitchin to Letchworth, followed by a dip at 1 in 244 to Baldock with undulating track to Ashwell and then a descent all the way from there to Meldreth varying from 1 in 183, 1 in 163 and finally 1 in 120, after which it is broadly level. There is a speed restriction through Royston and at Shepreth Branch Junction. Mr S.P.W. Corbett timed some up trains a couple of years earlier, logs that appeared in the March 1934 *Railway Magazine*:

Cambridge–King's Cross Beer Trains, 1933/4

		3252			**3257**			**3252**			
		5 chs, 147/155 tons			**5 chs, 153/160 tons**			**5 chs, 153/160 tons**			
Miles	**Location**	**Times**	**Speed**		**Times**	**Speed**		**Times**	**Speed**		**Gradients**
0	Cambridge	00.00			00.00			00.00			
2.6	Shepreth B Jn	04.36			04.28			04.30			
5.3	Harston	08.12			07.58			08.01			
8.1	Shepreth	10.55	62		10.52	59		10.40			L
10	Meldreth	12.37	67		12.46	65/52		12.18	73½/61		L, 1/120 R
13	Royston	15.37	55½		16.31		1 L	15.39		T	
16.9	Ashwell	19.35	62		06.30			06.21	51		1/163, 1/183 R
21.3	Baldock	23.33	74½		11.40	70		10.42	70½		1/197 F
23.4	Letchworth	25.51		2 E	13.42		2 L	12.58		T	
0		00.00		T	00.00		2 L	00.00		T	1/161 F
2.6	Hitchin	05.03		T	04.45		1¾ L	04.53		T	
0		00.00		T	00.00		2 L	00.00		T	
3.3	Stevenage	06.18			05.42			05.21			1/200 R
6.2	Knebworth	10.10	45		09.00	55		08.36	56½		1/330 F, 1/200 R
9.9	Welwyn North	13.09	74		11.36	75		11.10	69/75		1/200 F
11.6	Welwyn G C	15.19		1¼ L	13.37		1¾ L	13.09		¾ E	
0		00.00		1 L	00.00		1¾ L	00.00		T	
2.6	Hatfield	04.06	sigs	1 L	03.53		1½ L	03.46	60	¼ E	1/200 F
7.6	Potters Bar	10.02			09.00	59		08.34	65		1/200 R
11.1	New Barnet	13.45	sigs		12.14			11.44			1/200 F
15.3	Wood Green	17.25			15.38	74		15.11	75½		1/200 F
17.8	Finsbury Pk	19.59			17.42			17.24	sigs		
20.3	King's Cross	24.30	(22 net)	3½ L	22.03		1½ L	22.47	(21½ net)	¼L	
		(68½ net)			(70½ net)			(68 net)			

3255 at Brookmans Park with a King's Cross–Peterborough stopping train, June 1937. (Colling Turner/MLS Collection)

Eight C2s were still working around London in 1935 on both Cambridge buffet ('Beer') trains and stoppers to Cambridge and Peterborough. However, withdrawals were taking place and the B17s would soon take over the Cambridge faster services from the Atlantics although the C1s would remain a while longer. At the end of 1938 there were only five left, 3252 at Cambridge and four – 3250, 3254, 3256 and 3259 – at Peterborough New England shed. Then just before the war 3254 and 3256 were transferred to Lincoln, followed by 3252 from Cambridge in 1941. Peterborough's last two were transferred away in April 1940 – 3250 to Boston and 3259 to Retford. Lincoln's engines were seen on workings to Manchester via the Woodhead line during the war, but when 3254 and 3256 were withdrawn in 1943, the others were all based at Retford working trains to Sheffield, Cleethorpes and Lincoln.

3983, the C2 with the American style outside framed bogie, on a down freight near Ruddington on the GC main line, 9 May 1935. (W. Potter/MLS Collection)

Preservation

990 was built in 1898 at a cost of £2,522 and named *Henry Oakley* after the GNR General Manager. Renumbered 3990 at the Grouping,

it was withdrawn in October 1937 after running 1,296,000 miles and restored to the GNR livery as 990, but in its final re-cylindered condition with piston valves. It was placed in the LNER Queens Road museum adjacent to York station in January 1938 and remained there until it was overhauled to running condition to pilot C1 251 on special trains to celebrate the 100th anniversary of Doncaster Works in 1953 (see log of Leeds – King's Cross run on 27.9.53 on page 76). It took part in the Stockton & Darlington Railway 150th anniversary parade in 1975 and in the summer of 1977 was hired to work on the Keighley & Worth Valley heritage railway. Subsequently it was displayed in the Bressingham Museum for a number of years before finally residing in the National Rail Museum.

Left*: 990 *Henry Oakley as prepared for preservation in 1937 underneath York City Walls. (NRM/MLS Collection)

***Below left*: 990 double-heads** C1 251 with the 1953 *Plant Centenarian* nearing Stoke summit with the King's Cross–Doncaster special, 20 September 1953. (MLS Collection)

Below right*: 990 *Henry Oakley and 251 take water at Grantham a week later with the special train carrying enthusiasts to Doncaster to celebrate the anniversary of the Doncaster Plant, 27 September 1953. (MLS Collection)

The '251' GNR C1 Class (LNER C1)

In the middle of the construction of the 'Klondykes' Ivatt produced 251, an Atlantic with similar wheel arrangement and spacing and cylinder/valve motion but with a significantly larger boiler. The most striking aspect of the new engine was the adoption of the wide firebox, which looked as though its concept stemmed from American practice with which Ivatt, like Churchward, was familiar. Ivatt was known to view the ability of a locomotive to boil water quickly as all important and the capacity of the old GWR broad gauge engines to steam with the width of their fireboxes allowed by the gauge is said to have been well known by Ivatt and an influence in his decision. What was more surprising, having conceived a locomotive that had such a large heating surface and grate capacity, was that he did not match it with larger cylinders to use the steam efficiently and in their early days before superheating and fitting with piston valves, they had to be worked very hard – some say 'thrashed' – to put up some of the exceptional performances ascribed to them. Later modifications with ever increasing superheating and rebuilding of the cylinders with piston valves increased their day to day efficiency and operation and their reputation stems more from their later rather than early years. Early dissatisfaction was apparent in the degree of experimentation that took place to test alternative modifications.

251 appeared in December 1902 and no more appeared until the construction of the 'Klondykes' had been completed in the middle of 1903. Twenty were constructed at Doncaster very rapidly in May and June 1904 and were numbered 272–291. Their key dimensions were:

Cylinders (2-outside):	18¾x24in
Coupled wheel diameter:	6ft 8in
Bogie wheel diameter:	3ft 8in
Trailing wheel diameter:	3ft 8in

Stephenson motion with slide valves

Boiler pressure:	175lb psi
Heating surface:	2,478sqft
Grate area:	30.9sqft
Axleweight:	20 tons
Weight (Engine):	68 tons 6 cwt (with slight variations for those built after 1908)
(Tender):	43 tons 2 cwt
(Total):	111 tons 8 cwt
Water capacity:	3,500 gallons
Coal capacity:	6½ tons

The dimensions of the exceptionally large boiler were a width of the boiler barrel increased from 4ft 8in to 5ft 6in, the distance between the tube-plates was increased to 16ft and the diameter of the tubes increased from 2 to 2¼in. There were 248 tubes

The prototype 'Large Atlantic' 251 as built with Stephenson gear and slide valves, 1902. (MLS Collection)

and the wide firebox length was 6ft 6in. The heating surface was 65 per cent greater than that of the 'Klondykes' but cylinder size and arrangements were unchanged. The length of the boiler barrel and the need to increase the volume of the smokebox meant that it was extended at the front ahead of the chimney in the form that was adopted for the 4-4-0s later. 293–301 and 1400–1410 were constructed to the standard design in 1905, 1411-1420 in 1906 and 1422–1451 in 1907/8.

Dissatisfaction with the initial batch of the large boilered Atlantics was compounded by the fact that the wide firebox prevented the fitting of screw reversing gear and the operation of lever reverse at speed was difficult, so drivers tended to use long cut-offs and drive on the regulator, giving the locomotives a reputation for being heavy on coal and water. Ivatt therefore set in motion a series of experiments. In 1905 he built a 4-cylinder compound Atlantic, 292, and at the same time commissioned a 4-cylinder compound, 1300, designed and built by the Vulcan Foundry to the de Glehn system. The original Vulcan design had a boiler pressure of 225lb psi and weighed 72 tons, but the GN Board decreed that its weight must not exceed 70 tons and the boiler pressure was dropped to 200lb psi. 1300 cost £4,000 but payment was withheld for a time until initial defects and problems had been solved. In 1907 he constructed 1421 as another 4-cylinder compound engine, incorporating lessons learned from 292 and 1300. The key dimensions of the two 1905 designs were:

1450 built to the original standard design in August 1908, in photographic grey. (MLS Collection)

292		**1300**	
Cylinders (4)	13x20in high pressure (outside)	(4)	14x26in high pressure (outside)
	16x26in low pressure (inside)		23x26in low pressure (inside)
Coupled wheel diameter:	6ft 8in		6ft 8in
Bogie wheel diameter:	3ft 8in		3ft 2in
Trailing wheel diameter:	3ft 8in		3ft 8in
Boiler pressure:	200lb psi		200lb psi
Valve gear:	Walschaerts with slide valves (outside)		Walschaerts with piston valves
	Stephenson with slide valves (inside)		
Heating surface:	2,500sqft		2,514sqft
Grate area:	31sqft		31sqft
Axleweight:	20 tons		20 tons
Weight (Engine):	69 tons		70 tons 5 cwt
(Tender):	40 tons 18 cwt		43 tons 2 cwt
(Total):	109 tons 18 cwt		113 tons 7 cwt
Water capacity:	3,670 gallons		3,500 gallons
Coal capacity:	5 tons		6½ tons
Tractive effort:	8,994lb (compound)		14,869lb
	20,070lb (simple)		

1421, the 4-cylinder compound built by Ivatt in 1907, the most powerful of all the GN Atlantics. (Kingsway Real Photographs/MLS Collection)

1421 'built a couple of years later' had much larger cylinders, the low pressure inside cylinders being 18x26in and the outside high pressure cylinders identical to the standard C1 Atlantics at 18¾x24in. The valve gear for both inside and outside cylinders was the Walschaerts motion. As a result, it was the most powerful of any of the GN Atlantics with a theoretical tractive effort of 23,620lb. However, surprisingly the design of the boiler seemed to go backwards, with the distance between tube-plates reduced from 16 to 14½ ft, and the narrow rather than extended smokebox utilised. The heating surface reduced from 2,500 to 2,351.6sqft. The boiler pressure was 200lb psi like 292 and 1300.

A deeper grate was designed in 1906 with a slope to 6in instead of 3in at the front – each referred to later as the 'deep' or 'shallow' grate. This made firing easier as coal shook down to the front and it increased the heating surface by a small margin. In 1910 Ivatt built a further ten standard Atlantics, 1452-1461, which were fitted with Schmidt superheaters and piston valves. The diameter of the cylinders was increased to 20in. The heating surface was reduced to 2,053sqft plus the 392.2sqft of the superheater. The last GN Atlantic was built in 1911. Successive improvements in design and size of superheaters were made. Initially they were 18-element superheaters, enlarged to 24-element from 1912 for both Schmidt and Robinson type and in 1918 1403 was equipped with a 32-element Robinson superheater, followed then by several others. Only eleven C1s were still working with saturated steam at the Grouping and all bar 1433 were superheated by the end of 1924. The superheating of that locomotive appears to have been overlooked until a Works visit in 1926. The boiler pressure in the superheated engines was initially reduced from 175 to 150lb psi and to compensate the cylinder diameter was enlarged slightly to 19in.

However, this loss of power in a locomotive whose tractive effort was low compared with other Atlantics was temporary and Gresley, who had followed Ivatt in 1911, restored the standard boiler pressure to 170lb psi from 1912. All the C1s were eventually fitted with the 32-element superheater which could achieve 800 degrees Fahrenheit when working hard. 3274 was the last to be so converted in 1934. Mechanical lubrication was introduced to the class in 1912, mostly the Wakefield type although other types were tried

1421, seen here at King's Cross Yard, c1908. It was rebuilt in 1920 as a standard 2-cylinder C1 Atlantic. (F. Moore/MLS Collection)

1300, the 1905 Vulcan Foundry 4-cylinder compound, rebuilt as a 2-cylinder simple engine in 1917, seen here, c1923. (Real Photographs/ MLS Collection)

in GN days. Gresley undertook a further experiment in 1915, partly as a trial for the Pacific that he intended to build, when he rebuilt 279 as a 4-cylinder simple engine with piston valves and Walschaerts valve gear and rocking shafts to the inside cylinders. All four cylinders measured 16½x26in (later reduced to 15in) but boiler pressure was only 170lb psi. The engine was heavy at 73½ tons, 116 tons 12cwt with tender. Tractive effort was calculated at 21,128lb. In 1917 the Vulcan compound 1300, which had never performed to Gresley's satisfaction, was rebuilt as a simple machine with two cylinders, retaining the 200lb psi boiler and had Walschaerts motion with 10in piston valves. Finally, 1421 was rebuilt in 1920 as a standard 'Large C1 Atlantic'. The remaining compound, 292, stayed in that form until it became an early withdrawal in 1927.

At the Grouping, 3000 was added to their numbers and the 'Large-boilered' Atlantics retained their GNR classification of C1. They were given the LNER lined green livery but unlike other LNER 4-4-0s and 4-4-2s, they retained their green livery after 1928 when the other classes were painted black. In 1923 a further engine was selected for experimentation, 1419, which was fitted with a booster to augment its starting and hill-climbing power. Gresley was aware of the fitting of a booster to a locomotive on the New York Central Railroad in 1919 and 1419's booster was ordered from the Franklin Railway

279 as rebuilt in 1915 as a 4-cylinder 'simple' locomotive with Walschaerts valve gear and rocking shaft, c1923. (N. Fields/MLS Collection)

4419 fitted with a booster to its trailing wheels, after various modifications, July 1926. Note the enlarged cab with side windows and the live-steam pipe running to the booster above the running plate. (F. Moore/MLS Collection)

Supply Co. of New York in October 1922. It consisted of a 2-cylinder steam engine to drive the trailing wheels and the claim was that it could boost the engine's power by 50 per cent when operated. The frame was lengthened by 2ft 1in to accommodate the cylinders whose diameter were 10x12in and gave an additional 8,500lb traction effort. The weight of the engine was increased to 74 tons 2 cwt. The live steam-pipe passed along the left-hand side of the engine to the booster and the exhaust steam-pipe on the right-hand side to a cowl of the chimney inside the smokebox (in 1924 changed into a new blastpipe arrangement). After various tests, the booster was removed in July 1924 for modifications to the gears and control system and it was refitted at Darlington Works in February 1925 – in particular this allowed the booster to be cut in at higher speeds, but it also reduced the additional power to 4,970lb rather than the 8,500 initially claimed. Initial poor steaming was resolved when a standard blastpipe top was fitted. 4419 was often the subject of complaints about poor riding and although used successfully for a number of years, the booster was removed in 1935.

The first withdrawals were two of the experimental engines – the rebuilt 1300 (4300) in 1924 and the 4-cylinder compound 3292, in 1927. The rest of the class were still subject to modifications to improve their performance, notably the fitting of the Robinson 32-element superheaters and the replacement of the balanced slide valves by new cylinders of 20x24in and 8in piston valves, a process that had begun as early as 1914 and had continued right through that decade and the 1920s and even as late as 1942 (4428). In 1936 there was a proposal to streamline a C1 to a few members of the class in the style of the A4s at a time when streamlining was the fashion and C1s on occasions had replaced failing A4s on streamlined trains, but the scheme was not progressed. 3279, the 4-cylinder 'simple' engine, was rebuilt as a 2-cylinder engine in 1938, with 20x26in diameter cylinders, Walschaerts valve gear and 10in piston valves. The engine weight was reduced from 73 tons to 70 tons 14 cwt and the tractive effort was reduced from 21,128 to 18,785lb. It was renumbered 2808 in 1946 and withdrawn in 1948.

4419 from the right-hand side with the exhaust steam pipe above the running plate. The frame extension is more obvious in this photograph. It is also fitted with Westinghouse brake pump. It is seen on King's Cross shed, c1926. (H. Gordon Tidey/MLS Collection)

***Top left*: Standard C1** 1427N at King's Cross shed in the LNER lined green livery, c1923. (N. Fields/MLS Collection)

***Top right*: 3283 at** Grantham in 1931. (J.G.A. Coltas/MLS Collection)

***Above left*: 4411 at** King's Cross, c1930. (MLS Collection)

***Above right*: 3251, the** first large boilered GN Atlantic, at King's Cross shed, May 1937. (G. Harrop/MLS Collection)

***Left*: 3274 at** King's Cross shed, 25 April 1937. In the background is N2 4744, now preserved. (MLS Collection)

3274 again from the other side at Cambridge shed, 6 September 1938. (MLS Collection)

The first withdrawals of the standard C1s commenced in 1943 (4459) and 1944 (4407, 4414, 4426, 4430, 4431 and 4437), twenty-one in 1945, eighteen in 1946 and no less than twenty-nine in 1947, with so much of their work being performed by the Thompson B1 4-6-0s. In 1946 they were renumbered in the 2800 series and seventeen became British Railways assets in 1948 and were allocated 628XX although only 62822 (the last survivor, withdrawn in November 1950) and 62885 (withdrawn in January 1950) ever bore the BR numbers. Many of the boilers survived for a number of years as stationary boilers, some as long as twenty years after withdrawal from traffic.

***Below left*: 3272 on** Hitchin shed, 10 June 1938. (MLS Collection)

***Below right*: 4424 in** wartime black livery at Sheffield Darnall depot, 17 April 1945. (MLS Collection)

***Above left*: Early withdrawals** 4457 and 3284 in the scrapyard at Doncaster Works, 1 September 1946. Both were withdrawn in the previous winter. (N. Fields/ MLS Collection)

***Above right*: 2829, formerly** 301, built in 1905 at Doncaster, 8 May 1948. It appears to have suffered minor collision damage to the buffer beam and front running plate. It was withdrawn just two months later. (MLS Collection)

2885, the former GNR 1455 built in 1910 and one of the last two survivors that received a BR number, 62885, at Doncaster shed after what looks like a Works repair, 8 June 1947. (H.D. Bowtell/MLS Collection)

***Above*: 2833, formerly** 1403, in its last gasp of life at Grantham shed, 11 May 1947. It was withdrawn in July. (N. Fields/MLS Collection)

***Below left*: 2830, formerly** 1400, with a J50 tank at Doncaster shed, 21 September 1947. It was withdrawn in December, one of the twenty-two C1s that were withdrawn still with their original cylinders and slide valves. (MLS Collection)

***Below right*: 2870, formerly** 1440, built in April 1908 and withdrawn in February 1948, seen here at Doncaster Plant awaiting dismantling, 14 March 1948. (J.D. Darby/MLS Collection)

Operation

For the first few months only 251 was in operation and subject to extensive testing, but the building of twenty more in 1904 led to their allocation at the principal GN East Coast depots, King's Cross and Grantham, and their use on the main East Coast expresses between London, Leeds and York. They were allocated to regular crews and initially timekeeping was poor as drivers were reluctant to work their locomotives too hard. They steamed well enough but their power was relatively weak because of their small cylinders. Only when they were under official scrutiny did they rise to the occasion as when Charles Rous-Marten made the crews aware that he was timing them and publishing the results in the *Railway Magazine.* The working timetable for the fastest trains required uneven performance with a very tight timing of 23 minutes for the 17.7 miles to Hatfield which meant 18 minutes to clear Potters Bar with rising gradients most of the way from King's Cross. The timings thereafter did not require speeds higher than maintaining an average speed of the low 60s, so much easier running was in order to get to Peterborough in 83 minutes for the 76.4 miles. The load of the fastest services was around 300 tons.

Rous-Marten apparently primed the drivers to make a number of experiments, the results of which he published in his articles for the *Railway Magazine* in 1906. He used the 1.30pm King's Cross–Leeds for his 'trials', which was timed to Peterborough in 83 minutes and on to Doncaster from there, 79.6 miles, in 88 minutes. He logged four different engines – the standard 251 and 275, the compound 292 and 294, the boiler pressure of which had been raised to 200lb for official tests in comparison with the compounds. The engines were thrashed to meet the tight booking to Potters Bar and Hatfield, the four engines passing Potters Bar respectively in 18 minutes exactly, 17 minutes 53 seconds, 19 minutes 2 seconds, and 16 minutes 23 seconds. The compound was slowest, the C1 with 200lbs the fastest. All then could take it easily over the following 63.7 miles to the Peterborough stop, making the following average speeds – 61, 60.8, 60.7 and 59.7mph. All arrived in Peterborough early. The schedule then required the train to pass Grantham in 35 minutes which meant clearing the 1 in 200/178 to Stoke summit in 30 minutes with speed thereafter requiring nothing more than averages in the mid-50s. The four crews once again showed off their skills and their engines by flailing them up the long gradients to Stoke Tunnel, passed by the four engines in times of (in the same loco order) 26 minutes 46 seconds, 26m 51s, 27m 10s and 26m 14s. 251 and 292 were thereafter taken under light steam to Doncaster arriving on time, but 275 and 294 were kept hard at it and recorded times of 81m 43s and 83m 3s. Both of these engines were sustaining around 52-53mph on the long 1 in 200s requiring a power output of around 1,050 edhp, rather more than 40 per cent of the locomotive's nominal tractive effort. The locomotives must have been driven 'all-out' most of the way – the large boiler undoubtedly would have produced the steam but at what cost in efficiency (and to the fireman!)?

More typical was a run in 1907 on the 1.5pm Doncaster–Peterborough with a later built Atlantic, 1424, which with a heavier load of 380 tons dropped four minutes on the easier 93 minutes schedule averaging less than 50mph. Normally they were slow starters and weak on the banks but could run fast once under way. Rous-Marten timed the *Flying Scotsman* in 1907 with 1414 and nearly 400 tons but the 'Large Atlantic' could only sustain 36mph on the climb to Potters Bar, taking 28½ minutes to passing Hatfield, 5½ minutes late. To compensate, the Atlantic rushed down through Hitchin and Three Counties touching just over 80mph, but speeds of only 40mph on the 1 in 200 climb past Abbots Ripton to Leys summit and 36mph on Stoke Bank meant that the train was two minutes late at Grantham in 125 minutes for the 105 miles from King's Cross. The maximum edhp calculated by Rous-Marten was around 800 compared with the 1,050 experienced on his 'test' runs., but the steam generation was much more even. He commented that the Atlantic was blowing off steam for much of the way but the small diameter cylinders could not use the steam to full advantage on the climbs – he reckoned these Atlantics could just about time the trains with 350 tons but could not exert the necessary power to maintain time with 400 tons. It would be a different story in the 1930s when the Atlantics were equipped with 32-element superheaters, 20in cylinders and piston valves. The train was taken forward from Grantham by nothing better than a D2 4-4-0 which lost more time to York. Rous-Marten and his successor in the *Railway Magazine* articles published comparative runs with C1 Atlantics, an Ivatt 4-2-2 and a D2 4-4-0 between 1903 and 1911. A summary of the logs is below:

King's Cross–Grantham

		269 4-2-2		**1388 4-4-0**		**1426 4-4-2**		**300 4-4-2**		**1414 4-4-2**		**287 4-4-2**	
		275 tons		**280 tons**		**325 tons**		**365 tons**		**275 tons**		**325 tons**	
0	King's Cross	00.00		00.00		00.00		00.00		00.00		00.00	
12.7	P.Bar	24.42		22.22		21.43		22.09		19.36		20.06	
17.7	Hatfield	30.18	7¼ L	27.49	4¾ L	27.05	4 L	27.47	4¾ L	24.56	2 L	25.06	3 L
31.9	Hitchin	44.37	6½ L	42.14	4¼ L	41.49	3¾ L	42.20	4¼ L	42.29*	4½ L	38.29	½ L
58.9	Hunt'don	69.35	3½ L	67.07	1 L	65.15	¾ E	67.44	¾ L	68.29	2½ L	61.55	4 E
76.4	P'boro	87.55	3 L	85.04	T	82.04	3 E	87.03	2 L	85.58	1 L	79.25	5½ E
100.1	Stoke Bx	119.15		116.28		111.22		117.42		29.39		108.25	
105.5	G'tham	125.44	5¾ L	120.59	1 L	118.40	1¼ E	124.17	4¼ L	35.47	¾ L	114.28	5½ E
* P-way slack													
Ave speeds (mph)													
Potters Bar		36.4		36.0		38.5		37.6		42.3		42.3	
Three Counties		69.1		73.8		76.5		76.0		50.7*		77.7	
Abbots Ripton		51.1		48.9		52.8		45.6		51.1		52.7	
Stoke Box		37.9		36.5		41.0		38.3		46.0		45.7	

The 4-2-2 and 4-4-0 failed to keep time on the uphill gradients though the 4-4-0 was run hard downhill to minimise the loss. 1427 was able to keep to the schedule without any intermediate delay. 365 tons was clearly too much for the C1 300, but 287, the best run in the table, showed what could be achieved with a 325 ton load. It was probably the best run noted with an unsuperheated 'Large Atlantic'. In September 1906 the infamous accident at Grantham took place involving Atlantic 276 and its crew of regular Driver Fleetwood and Doncaster pupil Ralph Talbot. It was on the 8.45pm night express to Edinburgh and inexplicably passed all signals which were at danger approaching Grantham and derailed at around 50mph on points set for the Nottingham route. No satisfactory explanation of the accident was ever established and 276, after stripping down and repair, gained the reputation of being a 'jinxed' locomotive.

In 1905 the GNR had built the 4-cylinder compound and had commissioned the Vulcan Foundry to design and build a compound also. These two engines were tested with a standard Atlantic in October 1905 on Leeds–King's Cross trains and, as mentioned earlier, Rous-Marten had conducted his own comparative trials on the 1.30pm King's Cross–Leeds. The authorities conducted a series of more thorough tests over nine weeks in 1906, comparing the performance of 292, 1300 and a standard Atlantic, 294, which had its boiler upgraded to 200lb psi to be of similar theoretical power to the two compounds. Coal and oil consumption for the three engines were carefully monitored and records of timekeeping with causes of delays being taken into account. A summary of the results conveyed to Ivatt recorded that:

	1300	292	294
Train miles run	11,405	11,415	11,415
Average speed	49.02mph	49.9mph	49.58mph
Average train weight	230 tons	238 tons	234.3 tons
Coal used per train mile	45.84lb	43.98lb	45.31lb
Oil used per 100 train miles (pints)	7.34	7.18	6.22
Cost or repairs per engine mile	0.56d	0.45d	0.37d
Total cost per engine mile	3.125d	2.91d	2.88d

No time was lost on any of the trains in the tests for engine causes. As seen above, there was little difference between 292 and 294, with the compound slightly more economical on fuel consumption whilst 294 needed less oil than the 4-cylinder engines. One outcome was the building of another compound Atlantic in 1907, 1421. The key difference was that 292 when running in compound mode had a very low tractive effort of 8,994lb, but 20,070lb in simple expansion, so it would run as a simple from King's Cross to Potters Bar and from Peterborough to Stoke summit, and 1421, similarly more powerful at 23,620lb when working as a simple, whereas 1300, working on the de Glehn system could only use the simple expansion system on starting. No contemporary logs of 1421 or 1300 can be found in the articles of the *Railway Magazine,* but 1421 was involved in a test run of the royal train stock of 302 tons in February 1909. 1421 achieved 60mph in less than the five level miles from the Doncaster start, reaching 73mph before the Selby slowing, passed in 19½ minutes for the 18.4 miles. A brand-new NER R1 (LNER D21) took over at York and took 21 minutes to cover the first 18 level miles, only reaching 65mph working at 27 per cent cut-off and full regulator. The controls used on the GN engine were not recorded.

In the autumn of 1909 there was a locomotive exchange trial with the London & North Western Railway, GN Atlantic 1449 working between Euston and Crewe and LNWR 'Precursor' 4-4-0 412 *Marquis* between King's Cross and Doncaster. Both engines ran over 4,000 miles in the exchange. The loads were similar, 236-237 tons, as were the average speeds (53.12mph for 1449 and 52.73 for 412). The GNR engine did show a slight advantage in fuel economy (both coal and oil). Another 'Precursor', 510 *Albatross,* was tested at the same time on the LNWR route but with 290 tons against the average of 320 for the GN engine. Actual coal consumed by the 'Precursor' was less, but if calculated per ton-mile, was 0.14lb compared with the Atlantic's 0.128lb. The general conclusion about the early years' performance of the GN Atlantics was that they performed well when under close supervision and test conditions but running in everyday traffic was often not so good and fell short of expectations. Cecil J. Allen made an analysis of 25 runs that he had made in the first three months of 1910 which showed frequent loss of time when starting on time and failure to make up time if starting late. This compared poorly with his experience of LNWR 4-4-0s on a similar number of journeys he made between Euston and Crewe.

1444 on a down East Coast express, c1909. (MLS Collection)

***Above left*: 1402 on** a down East Coast express, c1907. (F. Moore/MLS Collection)

***Above right*: 1441 with** a down Scottish express at Oakleigh Park, 1 April 1911. (G.M. Shoults/MLS Collection)

***Below left*: The Vulcan** Foundry 4-cylinder compound 1300 at Holloway & Caledonian Road with a heavy East Coast express, c1912. (F. Moore/MLS Collection)

***Below right*: 1427 on** arrival at Skegness with an excursion from King's Cross, c1914. (MLS Collection)

The allocation of these Atlantics in 1912 which reflected experience from when the whole fleet of 94 had been completed was:

King's Cross:	22
Peterborough New England:	22
Grantham:	16
Doncaster:	34

The last series of Atlantics built in 1910 were fitted with 18-element Schmidt superheaters and a reduction of boiler pressure to 150lb psi (160 for 1454). Cecil J. Allen, as part of his role as Inspector of Materials, frequently travelled to Darlington or Newcastle and was enthusiastic about the difference in performance achieved by the superheated engines, even though their tractive effort was only 15,250lb. The 1.03pm Doncaster–Peterborough was a heavy train, usually at least 360 tons and sometimes loading to over 400 tons and he published seven runs with the 1452-1461 superheated series which all beat the 93 minute schedule for the 79.6 miles apart from 1456 with 405 tons which missed it by 25 seconds only. Speed at Stoke summit coming south ranged from 30mph to 36mph. Speed down the bank was usually in the 75-80mph range. A couple of runs with this series were timed in January 1912 and March 1913.

		Wakefield–King's Cross, 1912/13						
		1459, 165 tons			1461, 190 tons			
		2pm Leeds–King's Cross			2pm Leeds–King's Cross			
Miles	**Location**	**Times**	**Speed**		**Times**	**Speed**		**Gradients**
0	Wakefield	00.00			00.00			
5.5	Nostell	08.20			07.15			1/100 R, 1/100F
13.3	Hampole	15.49	77		14.08	77½		1/150 F
19.9	Doncaster	21.39		¾ L	19.56		1 E	
24.6	Rossington	26.38	63/60		24.54			L, 1/198 R
32	Ranskill	33.55	69		31.35	69		L
37.3	Retford	39.01		T	36.46		2¼ E	L
	Markham	-	56		-	53		1/178, 1/200 R
44	Tuxford	46.10			44.09			
49.5	Carlton	50.27	83		48.44	75		1/200 F
55.8	Newark	57.11		1¾ E	54.30		4½ E	L
66.2	Barkston	67.57	58		65.23	56		1/200 R
70.4	Grantham	72.36		2½ E	70.25		4½ E	
75.8	Stoke Box	79.07	42		76.46	41		1/200 R
83.7	Little Bytham	86.15	sigs		84.04	77½		1/178, 1/200 F
91.1	Tallington	94.04			90.43	sigs		
99.5	Peterborough	104.52		T	100.59		4 E	
106.5	Holme	112.46	pws		109.20			L
112.4	Abbots Ripton	119.35			115.03	59		1/200 R
117	Huntingdon	124.12	77		119.52	69 eased		1/200 F
124.2	St Neots	130.05	68		126.43			1/200 R
134.8	Biggleswade	139.08	72		137.19			L
140.2	Three Counties	144.02			142.48			1/400 R
144	Hitchin	147.34	60	4½ E	146.44			1/200 R
147.3	Stevenage	151.14	45/40		150.55	47		1/200 R
158.2	Hatfield	162.14	72	4¾ E	161.49	68	5¼ E	1/200 F
163.2	Potters Bar	167.45			167.05			
170.9	Wood Green	176.29	easy		-	eased (fog)		1/200 F
173.3	Finsbury Park	179.35			179.08	sigs		
175.9	King's Cross	184.18		2¾ E	183.03		4 E	

1459, having been delayed by signal checks on the descent from Stoke to Peterborough and encountering a p-way slack at Yaxley, was driven hard to Hitchin and then eased to avoid being too far ahead of time. 1461, already nearly five minutes early by Grantham, ran under relatively light steam on to King's Cross, coming up in just under 113 minutes. These are decent performances with the new superheated series of Atlantics but with very moderate loads only.

The rebuilding of 279 in 1915 with four cylinders, 170lb psi boiler pressure, piston valves and Robinson 24-element superheater provided a locomotive with nearly 40 per cent increase of its tractive effort compared to the 1452-61 series. A couple of runs with 279 shortly after its rebuilding on the 2.20pm King's Cross–Edinburgh, which it worked to Grantham, gave a significantly improved performance especially on the banks, sustaining 45mph with 350 tons on the 1 in 200 to Potters Bar.

This was no better, though, than some of the earlier Atlantics which, since 1912, had been rebuilt with 24-element Robinson superheaters. 1404 on the 2.20pm King's Cross in 1915 had 335 tons and despite two p-way slacks, one before Potters Bar and the other before Hitchin, and signal checks at Welwyn and Sandy, only lost 3½ minutes to Grantham on its 122 minute schedule (net 116½ minutes). Actual speeds at key locations were 45mph at Potters Bar, 76 at Hatfield, 75 at Arlesey, 42½ at Abbots Ripton and 37½ at Stoke Box. During these war years, as express passenger train services were reduced, the loads on the remaining trains increased significantly, reaching 450-500 tons on occasions. After a number of incidents with Atlantics stalling on the climb through the tunnels out of King's Cross two Ivatt 4-4-0s, 1314 and 1346, were kept at King's Cross to assist Atlantics with heavy loads out to Potters Bar. For example, 1407 with a gross load of 575 tons, assisted by 1314, took 22 minutes 40 seconds to reach Potters Bar. Restarting from there, it took 24½ minutes to clear Hitchin, 19.9 miles and then got away, touching 75mph through Arlesey and getting to Peterborough well inside the very slack wartime schedule of 103 minutes for the 76.4 miles. Despite the reduction of services, the Atlantics were called on to run heavy troop trains, and fast freights until they were relieved towards the end of the war by the larger boilered Gresley 2-6-0s (the LNER K2s). Some other typical wartime runs with very heavy loads are given below:

		King's Cross–Peterborough, 1916				
		298		**1416**		
Pilot to Potters Bar:		**1314**		**1346**		
		500 tons		**545 tons**		
		2pm King's Cross		**1.30pm King's Cross**		
Miles	**Location**	**Times**	**Speeds**	**Times**	**Speeds**	**Gradient**
0	King's Cross	00.00		00.00		
2.6	Finsbury Park	06.20		06.45		
12.7	Potters Bar	20.30		22.00		1/200 R
5	Hatfield	08.05	61½	08.35	62½	
	Woolmer Green	-	46½	-	44	1/200 R
19.2	Hitchin	23.30		24.25		
	Arlesey	-	74	-	67	1/200, 1/400 F
46.2	Huntingdon	49.35		54.55		
63.7	Peterborough	70.15 (pass) (arrived Grantham 1 E)		76.40	T	

Other typical performances at the latter years of the war were analysed from logs provided by R.A.H. Weight as well as CJA. The 5.30pm King's Cross–Grantham with five members of the 1452-61 series and loads ranging from 425-475 tons on a 125 minute schedule took between 129 and 146 minutes (net 128–133, apart from 1454 on a very stormy evening taking 143 minutes unchecked with 475 tons). Engines changed at Grantham and four runs with

1401 at Ganwick with an East Coast express, c1920. (H. Gordon Tidey/ MLS Collection)

272, 273 (twice) and 298 ran the 50½ miles on to Doncaster in 55, 57½ and 59½ minutes, losing no more time. The 2.20pm King's Cross–Grantham, from eight logs, all with standard superheated Atlantics, and loads between 345 and 425 tons ranged from 121 to 134 minutes against the 122 minute schedule, but net times were no more than 118½-121 minutes for four of the runs, the other three in 127¾, 128¼ and 129¼ minutes. It would seem, even with wartime schedules, that the Atlantics struggled with anything over around 380 tons.

The Ivatt Atlantics had come through the war in reasonable condition, unlike the locomotives of many other railways. Their maintenance had been upheld and they still bore the green GN passenger livery. The introduction of an eight-hour working day for train crews in 1919 caused the reduction of some of the longer turns, with more engine changing required at Grantham. As a result, the 1920 allocation saw a transfer of four New England and eight Doncaster engines to Grantham and one from King's Cross, so that Grantham then had a fleet of twenty-nine large Atlantics. A couple of the Atlantics were at sub-sheds – 299 of King's Cross spent time at Hitchin and 1440 of Doncaster at York. They continued to be in charge of most East Coast expresses south of York until the first Gresley Pacifics came onto the scene in 1922/23. In the immediate aftermath of the war loads were still heavy and the Atlantics still required assistance to Potters Bar, but the pilot was then usually an N2 0-6-2 tank engine.

There was a lengthy coal strike from April 1921 until well into the summer and a number of trains were cancelled and others combined. With the availability of the new Gresley '1000' class moguls (LNER K3) and their power (tractive effort 30,031lb), most of the heaviest trains during the strike period were handled by these locomotives, though the Atlantics also found themselves in charge of very heavy loads on occasions. The train schedules were not relaxed during this period despite the loads. On one occasion Cecil J. Allen caught the 8am from Newcastle which was combined with the 9.35am from Leeds at Doncaster. The load was 526 tons tare but with an estimated 800 passengers and luggage the gross load was approximately 600 tons. For this superheated Atlantic 295 was provided, relieved by 290 from Peterborough.

		Doncaster–King's Cross, 1921 **295 to Peterborough, 290 to King's Cross** **18 chs, 526/600 tons** **8am Newcastle/9.35am Leeds**			
Miles	**Location**	**Times**	**Speeds**		**Gradients**
0	Doncaster	00.00			
4.7	Rossington	08.40	47½		L
6.6	Pipers Wood Box	11.25	39		1/198
8.3	Bawtry	13.35	slack*		1/198 F
12.1	Ranskill	17.30	60		L
17.4	Retford	23.40		1¾ L	
0		00.00		2 L	
4.9	Markham Box	11.55	26		1/178, 1/200 R
6.7	Tuxford	14.25			
12.2	Carlton	19.45	69		1/200 F
18.5	Newark	23.45	60		L
23.2	Claypole	30.40	48		1/330, 1/220 R
28.9	Barkston	37.40	37½		1/300, 1/200 R
33.1	Grantham	44.20		2¼ L	
0		00.00		3 L	
5.4	Stoke Box	13.30	30½		1/200 R
8.4	Corby Glen	17.15			1/178 F
13.3	Little Bytham	21.35	72½		1/200 F
16.9	Essendine	24.30	75		1/264 F
20.7	Tallington	27.40	70½		1/440 F
26	Werrington Junction	32.25	65		L
29.1	Peterborough	36.05		3 L	
0		00.00	295 off/290 on	3L	
3.8	Yaxley	08.05			
7	Holme	11.40	58½		L
12.9	Abbots Ripton	18.30	39		1/200 R
17.5	Huntingdon	24.05	68		1/200 F
24.7	St Neots	31.00	55		1/200 R (1 mile)
32.3	Sandy	39.00	62½		1/330 F, L, 1/264 R
39.4	Arlesey	47.00			
44.5	Hitchin	53.35	47		1/200 R
47.8	Stevenage	59.30	33		1/200 R
58.7	Hatfield	72.25	69		1/200 F
63.7	Potters Bar	78.00	51		1/200, 1/330 R
67.2	New Barnet	81.35	67		1/200 F
71.4	Wood Green	85.50	pws		1/200 F
73.8	Finsbury Park	88.25			
76.4	King's Cross	92.35	(91 net)	2½ L	

For locomotives with such a low tractive effort compared with most of their contemporaries, this was a phenomenal effort by these two locomotives and their crews – I suspect particularly by their firemen!

At the Grouping with the first Gresley Pacifics in action and some Great Central locomotives being trialled on the GN main line, further transfers took place. In 1923 the distribution was (compared with 1920):

King's Cross:	16 (-5)
Hitchin:	2 (+2)
Cambridge:	1 (+1)
New England:	16 (-2)
Grantham:	33 (+4)
Doncaster:	24 (-2)
Copley Hill:	1 (+1)
York:	1 (+1)

In the late summer of 1923 dynamometer tests were carried out on the former NER, GN and NB Atlantics between Newcastle and Edinburgh. The trials were carried out on two regularly heavily loaded trains, the 3.26pm Newcastle and the 10.35pm Edinburgh return. The first week of the tests, from August 20, NER C7 733 was tested, and GN C1 1447 with its own King's Cross driver, the following week. The NB representative was 878 *Hazeldean.* All three locomotives had problems during their test week, 733 suffering a hot box, 1447 needing attention at Gateshead to leaking tubes on two occasions and 878 breaking a bogie spring. The trials were inconclusive, so further runs were made in October with a special test train loaded to 405 tons. Again, there was little to choose between the running performance of the three engines, though there was some surprise that the coal consumption of the GN Atlantic on the special test train was slightly higher than the other two. The GN fireman also complained that 1447 was an indifferent steamer, an unusual complaint of a GN 'Large Atlantic'. The reports do not say how the locomotives were worked to achieve these results and it is probable, given the comparative tractive efforts, that 1447 had to be worked harder than the other two to achieve similar train performance times. This appears to have been the only time a GN superheated Atlantic was given dynamometer tests and it is unfortunate that the results were unrepresentative of the best that these engines had shown that they could do.

The LNER introduced new Pullman services in 1923. The *Harrogate Pullman* actually ran from King's Cross to Newcastle, but via Leeds, Harrogate and Ripon. With Robinson as consultant to Gresley at the time, it was no surprise that four of the Great Central 4-6-0s (LNER B3 class) were transferred to King's Cross to work the new service. In 1924 a second Pullman service was introduced, to Sheffield via Grantham and Nottingham, scheduled non-stop to Nottingham over the 128¾ miles in 143 minutes. This train was worked by selected GN Atlantics and their regular crews. The Up working was booked for one of two GC B2 4-6-0s. The train timings were altered after a few weeks and the Gorton diagrams were stopped, the trains now covered by King's Cross C1s only. In April 1925 it was extended from Sheffield to Manchester but was withdrawn as commercially unsuccessful in September 1925. The Pullman cars were then used on a new service to Leeds and Bradford named the *West Riding Pullman.* From 1925 also the *Harrogate Pullman* was extended to Edinburgh. At first GC 4-6-0 engines were used, based at both King's Cross and Leeds Copley Hill. In 1927 the unpopular 4-6-0s returned to the GC section and King's Cross C1s were the mainstay supported by some GC 4-4-0 D11 'Directors' based at Copley Hill. In May 1928 the *Harrogate Pullman* was further extended to Glasgow and became *The Queen of Scots.* From May 1928 until September 1935 the *West Riding Pullman* train was worked entirely by King's Cross Atlantics and men and the King's Cross–Leeds portion of the *Queen of Scots* was shared between King's Cross Atlantics and Copley Hill D11 'Directors'. On Sundays the Pullman cars were used for a *Harrogate Pullman* again worked to Leeds and back by King's Cross Atlantics and men.

One of the celebrated King's Cross drivers was W. Sparshatt and a couple of fine runs by him and a superheated Atlantic were recorded, the first in 1928 with the Up Sunday *Harrogate Pullman.* With 4442 he covered the 156 miles from Doncaster to King's Cross in 149 minutes, arriving six minutes early despite encountering twelve minutes of delays en route from Leeds. The load was 240 tons. A colleague, W. Barnes, with 4436 and a heavier load, 295 tons, passed Peterborough thirteen minutes late after earlier delays but arrived in King's Cross on time, having run the 76.4 final miles in 68 minutes. In 1931 significant accelerations were made to the schedules of many of the principal East Coast expresses and Sparshatt with an afternoon relief train, 2.48pm off Peterborough, with 3295 and 235 tons ran up in 71 minutes 10 seconds (67½ net) start-to-stop, inclusive of a severe slack for a bridge renewal at New Southgate. I would have been pleased to experience such a run with a double chimney A3 or A4 in the early 1960s.

O.S. Nock recorded two exceptional runs on the up *Queen of Scots Pullman,* although unfortunately he did not publish the date of either. He was a guest on the footplate of the second run made some three years after the first, after further acceleration of the Pullman services, and that provides us with some information about how the Atlantics were worked to achieve some remarkable runs in this 1928-1935 period, a time when the Atlantics, most now with 32-element superheaters, were at their zenith, performing at a level way above that of their earlier years.

Leeds Central–King's Cross, *The Queen of Scots Pullman*

		3284			**4456**			
		8 chs,314/325 tons			**7 chs, 277/290 tons**			
		Driver Payne			**Driver Worboys**			
Miles	**Location**	**Times**	**Speeds**		**Times**	**Speeds**		**Gradients**
0	Leeds Central	00.00			00.00			1/50 R
2.5	Beeston	06.47	41½		06.12	45		1/100 F (short), 1/100 R
5.6	Ardsley	12.07	31		10.52	39		1/100 R
7.5	Lofthouse	14.17	60		13.12	59		1/122, 1/100 F
9.9	Wakefield	16.55	40*	1 E	15.52	35*	2 E	
15.4	Nostell	23.40	56/48½		22.10	59/50		1/150 R
25.8	Carcroft	33.25	pws 35*/78		31.26	76½		1/200, 1/400 F
29.8	Doncaster	38.10	sigs/30*	¾ E	36.05	sigs	2 E	
34.5	Rossington	43.15	62/55		41.48	59/52½		L, 1/198 R
41.9	Ranskill	50.00	75		49.15	69		1/198 F, L
47.2	Retford	54.25	70½	2½ E	54.00	73	2 E	L
52.1	Markham Box	58.55	60		58.33	60		1/178, 1/200 R
59.4	Carlton	64.42	85/sigs 66*		64.20	82		1/200 F
65.7	Newark	69.50	60	5¼ E	69.30	64	4½ E	L
70.4	Claypole	74.22	64½		73.52	68		1/330, 1/220 R
76.1	Barkston	79.45	55½		79.10	58		1/200 R
80.3	Grantham	84.10	62	5¾ E	83.24	64	4½ E	L
85.7	Stoke Box	90.00	48½		88.55	55		1/200 R
88.7	Corby Glen	92.55	72		91.38	77½		1/178 F
93.6	Little Bytham	96.35	87½		95.10	90		1/200 F
97.2	Essendine	99.02	88		97.32	93		
101	Tallington	101.40	86½		100.03	92		1/440 F
106.3	Werrington Junction	105.30	81		104.91	pws 35*		L

		Leeds Central–King's Cross, *The Queen of Scots Pullman*						
		3284			**4456**			
		8 chs,314/325 tons			**7 chs, 277/290 tons**			
		Driver Payne			**Driver Worboys**			
Miles	**Location**	**Times**	**Speeds**		**Times**	**Speeds**		**Gradients**
109.4	Peterborough	109.20	20* / sigs	9¾ E	109.40/114.25 water **		7¼ E/2½ E	
113.2	Yaxley	115.40	52½		121.00	54		L
116.4	Holme	119.00	66		124.07	68½		L
122.3	Abbots Ripton	124.42	53		129.44	57		1/200 R
126.9	Huntingdon	129.13	77½	7¾ E	133.58	79	1 E	1/200 F, L
134.1	St Neots	134.57	69		139.40	71		1/200 R (1 mile)
138.4	Tempsford	138.30	76½ / sigs 40*		143.11	76½		1/330 F, L
141.7	Sandy	141.35			145.58	72		1/264 R
150.1	Three Counties	150.47	55/64½		153.24	65/69		1/264, 1/400 R
153.9	Hitchin	154.35	56	7½ E	156.56	62½	3 E	1/200 R
157.2	Stevenage	159.25	49½		160.29	53½		1/200 R
168.1	Hatfield	169.00	56/75	7 E	170.23	64/82	3½ E	1/200 F
173.1	Potters Bar	173.55	54		174.40	69		1/200, 1/330 R
176.6	New Barnet	177.22	69		177.40	74		1/200 F
180.8	Wood Green	180.45	79/sigs		181.09	70		1/200 F
183.2	Finsbury Park	183.45	-/sig stop		183.25	sigs		
185.8	King's Cross	191.15		¾ E	189.35		3½E	
			(net 181¼)			(net 176)		

(** Werrington troughs – under repair)

3274 on the first run was checked by the 3.10pm from Leeds which stopped at Peterborough due only ten minutes ahead and therefore 3274's driver took it easily out to Holme until it was clear that the latter's Gresley Pacific was making good time also. Nock makes a number of interesting observations about the run with 4456 which was a hastily substituted engine after the failure of the booked King's Cross Atlantic. 4456 was a Doncaster engine, not in good condition outwardly, but mechanically strong although as

4419, the booster –fitted Atlantic, on a heavy 17-coach East Coast express in the London area, c1923.

1460, still in GNR livery, heads a down Pullman train past Belle Isle Box, King's Cross Goods Yard in the background, while GC 4-6-0 1167 *Lloyd George* waits to back down to King's Cross for another Pullman working, c1923. (H. Gordon Tidey/MLS Collection)

Nock describes it, 'she pitched, corkscrewed and tail-wagged at the cab-end – one of the wildest things I have ever ridden'. Heaven knows what the experience was coming down from Stoke at 93mph, although the track there was in excellent condition and Nock says it rode surprisingly smoothly over this section. Leaving Leeds and climbing to Ardsley, the cut-off was 50 per cent and full regulator. The cut-off was then set at 35 per cent all the way to Peterborough and driven on the regulator.

In 1932 C1 Atlantics replaced the Copley Hill D11 'Directors' and three Atlantics and their crews were in the Pullman link – 3280, 4423 and 4433. More exciting runs were recorded including a down run on the *Queen of Scots* with 4433 when it reached Leeds, 185.7 miles, 185 minutes 40 seconds (175 minutes net), against the schedule of 194 minutes. Hatfield–Doncaster was covered at an average speed of 70.3mph. Highlights were an average of 82.8mph over 18.9 miles from Stevenage to Tempsford, top speed 85, and a minimum of 64mph at Leys summit (Abbots Ripton) and 84mph down the bank at Connington. The King's Cross Atlantic Pullman era finally came to an end in September 1935 and the Copley Hill Atlantics were replaced by Pacifics in 1937. Thus finished a remarkable period when the performance of the 32-element superheater Atlantics outshone their work of previous decades. To compensate for their low tractive effort, their regular men got the best out of them. They were clearly maintained in excellent condition and the men were not afraid to work them hard, leaving the cut-off fixed at 35, 40 or even 50 per cent and using the adjustments of the regulator to match the gradients. The distribution of the whole class of 92 (the two compounds had been withdrawn) during this period (1933) was:

King's Cross:	24
New England:	19
Grantham:	16
Doncaster:	12
Copley Hill:	4
York:	2
Sheffield:	7
Hitchin:	3
Cambridge:	5

Below left: **Four-cylinder 279**, repainted in LNER livery but not yet renumbered, pilots a D3 4-4-0 on an East Coast down express, July 1924. (MLS Collection)

Below right: **1459, in** LNER livery but still with GN number, on a down Pullman service, c1924. (Real Photos/MLS Collection)

***Above left*: 1459 arrives** at Leeds Central with one of the Pullman trains, c1924. (MLS Collection)

***Above right*: 4411 passing** Doncaster with an up Pullman train from Leeds, c1928. (MLS Collection)

4444 accelerates up the grade past Belle Isle with a Newmarket race special, c1928. (MLS Collection)

4419, the booster-fitted Atlantic, passing Greenwood Box with a down Pullman train, c1928.

***Below left*: 4460 near** Hadley Wood with a down Pullman train, c1928. (Railway Photographs/ MLS Collection)

***Below right*: 4461 climbing** Holloway Bank with a down Pullman express, c1928. (MLS Collection)

Above left: **Copley Hill** C1 4433 climbing Holloway Bank with the down *Queen of Scots Pullman*, 1936. (Kelland/MLS Collections)

Above right: **3280 at** Copley Hill shed after working the *Queen of Scots Pullman* from King's Cross as late as May 1939. (MLS Collection)

Below: **4457 and** 3274 double-head an express out of York, bound for King's Cross, 14 July 1928. (MLS Collection)

By 1938 the work of the Atlantics was significantly changed with their main work being secondary and stopping services on the main line, the Cambridge 'buffet' trains, and semi-fast and local services in the Sheffield and Doncaster areas. This was reflected in their allocations that year:

King's Cross:	17 (-7)
New England:	23 (+4)
Grantham:	11 (-5)
Doncaster:	12 (no change)
Copley Hill:	6 (+2)
York:	2 (no change)
Sheffield:	7 (no change)
Colwick:	3 (+3)
Hitchin:	8 (+5)
Cambridge:	3 (-2)

However, the occasional failure of Pacifics on main line expresses enabled the Atlantics to still show their capabilities. There are three recorded instances where an A3 Pacific failed at or near Grantham with overheated middle big-end trouble and was replaced at short notice by an Atlantic – in each case with a heavy load of over 500 tons. In 1934 4415 took over the 545-ton 1.20pm King's Cross at Grantham and although the log was submitted to Cecil J. Allen, he never published it in his monthly *Railway Magazine* as he did not believe it, although later he accepted its veracity after he'd had a similar experience.

Grantham–York, 1934

4415, 16 chs 506/545 tons

1.20pm King's Cross–Edinburgh

Driver Samwells, King's Cross

Miles	Location	Times	Speeds		Gradients
0	Grantham	00.00			
4.2	Barkston	08.22	61		1/200 F
6	Hougham	10.05	71		1/300 F
9.9	Claypole	13.22	74		L
14.6	Newark	17.13	68	2¼ L	1/330 R/ 1/300 F
21.9	Crow Park	23.18	73		L
25.8	Dukeries Junction	27.01	57½		1/200 R
28.2	Markham Box	29.41	53		1/200 R
33.1	Retford	34.16	72½	¾ E	1/178 F
38.4	Ranskill	38.52	69/71½		L
42.2	Bawtry	42.04	72/67		1/198 R
47.7	Black Carr Junction	46.56	70½		L
50.5	Doncaster	49.34	59½	3½ E	
57.5	Moss	56.24	64		L
64.3	Templehurst	63.05	65		L
68.9	Selby	67.35	24*	5½ E	
73	Riccall	75.08	50		L
78.5	Naburn	81.11	58		1/390 R
80.7	Chaloners Whin Jcn	83.33			
82.7	York	86.56		3 E	

The losses and gains shown are compared to the schedule over this section. The schedule, of course, was from passing Grantham at 60mph plus, not from a standing start as here. The train in reality was presumably late because of the forced engine change, though the amount is unknown. Then in 1936 there was almost a replica of this run. The 1.20pm King's Cross-Edinburgh, with 17 coaches, 585 tons gross, failed at Grantham once more and its Pacific was replaced by the Grantham pilot, 4404. After struggling to get the train restarted, it passed Retford, 33.1 miles, in 36 minutes 15 seconds at 77½mph and maintained 72-75mph on the level after Retford. The 1 in 198 to Piper's Wood was cleared at 61mph and Brayton Junction, just before Selby, 67.5 miles, passed in 67 minutes 41 seconds. The 82.7 miles to York were completed in 87 minutes 40 seconds, over two minutes less than the schedule. The run was timed by Cecil J. Allen who was travelling by chance on that day. 4404 continued to Newcastle piloted by a Z Atlantic from York despite Driver Walker insisting that they did not need assistance. There was a third occasion in 1938 when 3285 was called on at Grantham and ran its 540 ton load to York in 89 minutes, 86 net, though full details of the run were not given. Another famous occasion was the exploit of 4452 on the up *Silver Jubilee.* Its A4 failed at York and was replaced by the poppet valve Z Atlantic 732, but the driver, Samwells, realised it was not up to the task and stopped at Doncaster in the expectation of obtaining a Pacific. He was given C1 4452

***Above left*: 3300 on** Langley troughs with an up Newcastle express in the 1930s. (MLS Collection)

***Above right*: 4455 arriving** from the south at York with a mixed bag of coaching stock, c1928. (G.M. Shoults/MLS Collection)

4446 assists an A1 Pacific with a heavy East Coast express in the late 1920s or early 1930s. (MLS Collection)

which took the 235-ton *Silver Jubilee* from Doncaster to King's Cross, 156 miles, in 139 minutes start-to-stop, not quite maintaining the streamliner's schedule, but not far off. On another occasion the same driver had to replace the *Silver Jubilee* A4 at Peterborough with 4446, the Peterborough pilot, for the 76.4 miles to London. And as late as 1939, 4401 took over the up *Yorkshire Pullman* at Grantham and ran the 380-ton train to King's Cross in 104 minutes 35 seconds for the 105.5 miles.

4409 on a northbound express leaving Peterborough on Werrington troughs, c1930. (MLS Collection)

Below left: The 4-cylinder 3279 on a down East Coast express just beyond Greenwood Box, c1928. (Railway Photographs/MLS Collection)

Below right: Sheffield's 3280 at Sheffield Victoria with a Liverpool–Hull train, 25 April 1932. K2 4637 stands on the centre track awaiting its turn of duty. (MLS Collection)

3287 with a Hull–Liverpool train near Bredbury Junction, 2 June 1934. (MLS Collection)

***Below left*: 3276, the** so-called 'jinxed' C1 that was involved in the unexplained train accident at Grantham in 1906, at Godley Junction, Manchester, with the 8.55am Hull–Liverpool express, 29 March 1935. (R.D. Pollard/MLS Collection)

***Below right*: 3276 again** on the Woodhead route at Torside, with the 1.18pm Liverpool–Hull train, 2 August 1937. (MLS Collection)

3299 at Sheffield Victoria with a Liverpool–Hull train, 30 May 1938.

4420 at Cheadle with a Hull –Liverpool express, June 1939. (W. Potter/ MLS Collection)

By 1938 their main line work was much reduced with an abundance of A3 and A4 Pacifics now available, although as noted earlier, they could be brought into use for emergencies. Occasionally they would still be allocated to an express, if there was a shortage of Pacifics at the right place and time. Interestingly they seemed to be first reserve in the pre-war years rather than a V2 or B17 4-6-0 (the latter of course confined to the GE and GC lines). As an example, in February 1939 4429 was allocated to an express due off Peterborough at 3.04pm and with 255 tons it ran up to King's Cross in 76 minutes

4429 with an up Cambridge –King's Cross express at Bell Bar, Hertfordshire, 1937. (H.W. Pontin/MLS Collection)

***Below left*: 3289 with** an express standing at Newark station, 27 August 1938. (G.A. Barlow/MLS Collection)

***Below right*: 4419, the** former booster-fitted locomotive (removed in 1935), at Hatfield with a Down local stopping train, c1938. Note the retention of the side-windowed cab. (Photomatic/MLS Collection)

42 seconds (73 net) with 54mph minimum at Abbots Ripton, 75 at Tempsford, 57 minimum at Stevenage and a final 81 at Wood Green. They were by then more often employed on local and outer suburban runs from King's Cross, and stopping trains around Peterborough and Grantham into the Fen Country and westwards to Nottingham and Sheffield, or further north from Doncaster to Leeds or Hull.

One of the routes on which they were still timed by enthusiasts was the Cambridge–King's Cross runs on the famous 'Beer' trains, the lightly loaded buffet car expresses. O.S. Nock timed 4402 on 7 coaches, 230 tons gross, after joining one such train at Hitchin. It surmounted the 1 in 200 past Stevenage at 50mph, 65 at Knebworth and 75 in the dip before stopping at Welwyn Garden City in 14 minutes 10 seconds, a loss of ten seconds on the sharp 14-minute booking for the 11.6 mainly uphill miles. Then followed the dash to King's Cross, reaching 76½mph down the long 1 in 200 descent from Potters Bar to Wood Green, but signal checks approaching the terminus caused a 1½ minute late arrival, in 23½ minutes for the last 20.3 miles.

M.H. Cobb was obviously a frequent traveller between Cambridge and London in the 1930s and the Railway Performance Society has a large number of his logs on the 'Beer' trains. I have picked a couple of fairly typical examples of locomotive performance, though these were mercifully mainly free of excessive signal or p-way checks which seem to plague many of his runs.

		Cambridge–King's Cross						
		4440			**3297**			
		6 chs, 183/195 tons			**6 chs, 195 tons**			
		5.25pm Cambridge			**9.25am Cambridge**			
		15.3.1935			**8.2.1936**			
Miles	**Location**	**Times**	**Speeds**		**Times**	**Speeds**		**Gradients**
0	Cambridge	00.00		T	00.00			
1.1	Trumpington	02.35	47½		02.30	47½		L
2.3	Shepreth Bch Jcn	04.45	33*		04.40	26*		
5.3	Harston	08.25	60		08.20	56		1/132 F
7	Foxton	10.05	64½		09.55	64½		1/440 F
8.1	Shepreth	11.10	66½		11.00	65		L
10	Meldreth	12.50	66/53		12.50	50		L, 1/100 R
13	Royston	15.55	53	T	16.25		T	1/120, 1/175 R
		-			00.00		T	
16.9	Ashwell	20.05	58		06.15	54/64		1/163, 1/412, 1/183 R
21.2	Baldock	24.25	69		10.25	72		1/197 F
23.4	Letchworth	26.40		2 E	12.35		2 E	
0		00.00		½ L	00.00		T	1/161 F
2.6	Hitchin	04.50		¼ L	04.43		¼ E	
0		00.00		½ L	00.00		T	
3.3	Stevenage	06.00	47½		06.00	50		1/200
5.2	Langley	08.10	60		08.05	60		1/330 F
6.9	Knebworth	09.45	64½		09.40	64½		1/200 R

		Cambridge–King's Cross						
		4440			3297			
		6 chs, 183/195 tons			6 chs, 195 tons			
		5.25pm Cambridge			9.25am Cambridge			
		15.3.1935			8.2.1936			
Miles	**Location**	**Times**	**Speeds**		**Times**	**Speeds**		**Gradients**
8.4	Woolmer Green	11.10	64/69		11.05	64½		1/330 R
9.9	Welwyn North	12.35	75		12.25	69		1/200 F
11.6	Welwyn Gdn City	14.35		1 L	14.35		½ L	
0		00.00		1 L	00.00		¼ L	
2.6	Hatfield	03.55	56/60		03.45	60		1/200 F
7.6	Potters Bar	09.00	62/60		08.38	64/69		1/330, 1/200 R
11.1	New Barnet	12.10	75		11.50	72/75		1/200 F
15.3	Wood Green	15.30	78½		15.12	78½		1/200 F
17.7	Finsbury Park	17.35	sig stop		17.28	sigs		
20.3	King's Cross	24.50		3½ L	21.55		T	

At the commencement of the Second World War, some of the C1s were nearing forty years of age and withdrawals would have begun, but as with many classes, they were required for the war effort which had increased transport needs significantly. Their work would now include freight and military traffic, troop trains and the haulage of heavier passenger services as loads increased while a number of passenger services were cut to increase the route capacity and resources for the essential war traffic. In the early days of the war their performance held up, as was recorded in June 1940 when 4413 brought the 570-ton *Aberdonian* into King's Cross having dropped only four minutes on the schedule. The Leeds fleet were kept busy with heavy loads between Leeds and Doncaster and they began to appear more frequently in other areas where they were comparatively rare before. They were seen in the Tyneside area and even in Scotland, and more frequently on the former GC routes stemming from Sheffield, both south to Nottingham and on the Woodhead route. One common use was the piloting of A3s and V2s on some of the exceptionally heavy remaining East Coast expresses.

However, the difficulties of locomotive maintenance during the war with the shortage of skilled staff and materials began to affect the Atlantics and their condition deteriorated. In 1943 the first standard C1 Atlantic was withdrawn, one of the 1910 built King's Cross stalwarts, 4459, followed by a further six in 1944. At the end of the war mass withdrawals took place with twenty-one taken out of stock in 1945. At the same time the Thompson B1s were appearing in large numbers and took on many of the residual mixed traffic duties of the Atlantics of all former LNER companies. At nationalisation in 1948 only seventeen remained, allocated as follows (1946 numbers with previous numbers in brackets):

King's Cross:	2817 (3288), 2821 (3293)
New England:	2808 (3279), 2839 (4409), 2871 (4441)
Grantham:	2810 (3281), 2822 (3294), 2870 (4440), 2876 (4446)
Doncaster:	2854 (4424), 2877 (4447), 2885 (4455)
Ardsley:	2828 (3300), 2829 (3301), 2849 (4419)
Copley Hill:	2875 (4445), 2881 (4451)

C1 4454 assisting ex-GC B1 4-6-0 5195 on the Woodhead line, c1945. (W. Potter/MLS Collection)

4400, in poor post-war condition, descending under easy steam from Woodhead Tunnel, near Crowden, on the 1.18pm Sheffield–Manchester, 17 August 1946. It was renumbered 2830 a month later and withdrawn in December 1947. (J.D. Darby/ MLS Collection)

Their remaining activity as BR machines was very limited. Seven were withdrawn quickly in 1948. 2817 and 2828 had a short last few months at Hitchin, but were gone by mid-1949. Just five remained in 1950, 2839 of New England working stopping trains from Peterborough to Grantham. Sheffield had acquired three, 2817 from Hitchin, 2854 and 62885 from Doncaster, which worked stopping services to Doncaster, Lincoln and Cleethorpes. The last survivor was 62822 of Grantham which had been working to Nottingham and Boston on local passenger and pick-up freight duties. The finale

2839 of New England on the 3.55pm Peterborough–Grantham stopping train near Great Ponton, 12 June 1948. (R. Gee/MLS Collection)

2885, recently transferred from Doncaster to Sheffield, turning on the Dinting triangle after assisting a B1 on the Woodhead route, c1948. It was renumbered 62885 in May 1948 and was the penultimate withdrawal of the class in January 1950.

The last survivor '62822' arriving at Doncaster on its last run on 26 November 1950, standing at the station and then on display with the preserved 251 and an A4 at Doncaster Plant. (All MLS Collection, the photo at the Plant by J.D. Darby)

2877, ex-1447, seen in store at Doncaster, as observed by me during a 3-week holiday near the railway town with a school friend in August 1950. It had been withdrawn several months earlier in November 1949 and was used as a stationary boiler at the Wagon Works from February–July 1950 and then in the Carriage Works until April 1952. (MLS Collection)

came on Sunday 26 November 1950 when 62822 worked the *Ivatt Atlantic Special* from King's Cross to Doncaster. The train was delayed heavily by thick fog in the London area, but it was clear after Huntingdon and 62822 accelerated its train to 75mph at Connington, and only fell from 62 to 42½mph on the climb to Stoke Tunnel with its 330-ton load. It was then displayed at Doncaster Plant before the special returned to King's Cross appropriately behind A1 60123 *H.A.Ivatt.*

Some of the Atlantics were retained to act as stationary boilers, some just the boilers, but seven as the complete engine, all at Doncaster in the Loco, Carriage or Wagon Works. They were:

3274	1946-1952
3285	1946-1952
2812	1947-1952
2821	1948-1950
2829	1948-1953
2849	1948-1953
2877	1950-1952

Some of the boilers lasted even longer, six staying until 1965. The frames of 4461 and 2854 were retained at Doncaster Works as boiler carriers until the early 1950s and one unidentified example was still in use in 1961. Darlington used the frames of 2825 and 2845 for a similar purpose.

Preservation

The prototype, 251, was built in December 1902, superheated in 1918 and its slide valves replaced by piston valves in 1923. It was renumbered 3251 in March 1925 and 2800 in December 1946. It was withdrawn in July 1947 and restored to its original GN condition with slide valves and Ramsbottom safety valves and the superheater was removed. It is on record that the boiler used came from 3278 withdrawn in 1945 and that the frame used was from 2868 (ex-4438), so how much of the original 251 is preserved is conjecture. It was then painted in GN livery and was exhibited at King's Cross in 1952. In September 1953 it was paired with the restored 'Klondyke' 990 *Henry Oakley* to run the *Plant Centenarian* special train to Doncaster, the return once again using A1 60123. A second special was run a week later from Leeds to King's Cross and recorded just over 80mph descending Stoke Bank (see log below). 251 was used again for a special working in September 1954 organised by Alan Pegler for the Northern Rubber Company, working in tandem with D11 62663 *Prince Albert* to Liverpool and a week later to Farnborough, with 62663 again, to the air display there.

Grantham–King's Cross, 27 September 1953
'The Plant Centenarian'
990 *Henry Oakley* + 251
11 chs, 409/435 tons

Miles	Location	Times	Speeds	Gradients
0	Grantham	00.00		
5.4	Stoke Box	09.41	42	1/200
8.4	Corby Glen	12.50	68	1/178 F
13.3	Little Bytham	16.52	78	1/200 F
16.9	Essendine	19.35	80	
20.7	Tallington	22.37	75/68	1/440 F
26	Werrington Junction	27.19		L
29.1	Peterborough	31.32		
0		00.00 water for 251		
3.8	Yaxley	06.56		L
7	Holme	10.10	64½	L
12.9	Abbots Ripton	16.07	51½	1/200 R
17.5	Huntingdon	20.55	66	1/200 F, L
24.7	St Neots	27.50	57	1/200 R (1 mile)
28.9	Tempsford	31.52	67½	1/330 F, L
32.3	Sandy	34.52	65/69	1/264 R
35.3	Biggleswade	37.31	65	1/330 R
40.7	Three Counties	42.47	57/64½	1/264, 1/400 R
44.5	Hitchin	46.32	55½	1/200 R
47.8	Stevenage	50.57	40½ /eased	1/200 R
58.7	Hatfield	64.02	56/pws	1/200 F
63.7	Potters Bar	71.13		1/200, 1/330 R
71.4	Wood Green	81.20	62	1/200 F
73.8	Finsbury Park	84.09	sigs	
76.4	King's Cross	89.35		2¼ E

In between these runs 251 was stored in the paint shop at Doncaster Plant until moved to the LNER York Queens Road Museum in 1957 and in 1975 it was transferred to the National Railway Museum. It then moved to the Bressingham Museum in April 2005 and on further to the Barrow Hill Roundhouse in April 2012 and then to Locomotion Museum at Shildon. In January 2021 it became the first locomotive exhibit at the new Danum Gallery & Museum at Doncaster where it still resides in 2024.

Chapter 3

THE GREAT WESTERN FRENCH & CHURCHWARD ATLANTICS

Churchward had worked alongside William Dean from 1897 when the latter's mental health began to fail and whilst he continued during that time to maintain the construction of Dean's 4-4-0 passenger engines, he began experimenting with boiler design and took great interest in locomotive developments in both the USA and France. There was much interest in the best wheel arrangement for express passenger locomotives, as will be appreciated from perusal of copies of the *Railway Magazine* of the time and particularly in articles on locomotive practice and performance by Charles Rous-Marten. Rous-Marten himself was a staunch supporter of the trusted 'singles' especially the Dean and Stirling 4-2-2s and the Johnson Midland engines, but acknowledged that heavier train loads at the turn of the century were making the 4-4-0 a more practical solution. Then in 1898 Ivatt had designed and Doncaster had constructed a 4-4-2, the L&YR's 'Highflyers' following the next year, the wheel arrangement seen as an enlargement of the 4-2-2s. In 1902 the wide firebox Great Northern Atlantic 251 came upon the scene and the debate raged – 4-4-0 or 4-4-2? Another topic of discussion in learned railway journals and papers was the subject of compounding and the improved efficiency set against the extra complexity and maintenance costs.

Churchward, however, shook the established thinking by unveiling in 1902 a stark powerful 4-6-0, numbered 100, with a parallel boiler, Belpaire firebox and piston valves. He followed it with another 4-6-0 numbered 98, with an improved front end, enlarged piston valves and part tapered boiler and Belpaire firebox. When Dean had finally retired in 1902, Churchward was ready with the specification of six standard locomotive types constructed as far as possible with interchangeable parts, six types that would provide comprehensive cover for the company's traffic requirements, and numbers 98 and 100 were his solution to the express passenger requirement. A third locomotive, 171, developed from 98, immediately showed great promise, and this locomotive formed the basis of the famous 'Saint' class which were the pioneers and basis of the 2-cylinder 4-6-0s that became the most common British type for traffic that ranged from express passenger to fast freight haulage.

Despite this success, Churchward's engineering curiosity was not satisfied and he had been impressed with the Nord compound Atlantic, 2.642, which had been displayed at the Paris Exhibition in 1900. It, and its sister 2.641, which had been building a fine reputation in efficient fast train haulage at the same time, were 4-cylinder compounds designed by du Bousquet, motive power superintendent of the Nord, and de Glehn, the director general of the Societé Alsacienne. Churchward managed to persuade his Board to purchase a similar Atlantic, to be constructed by the

Societé Alsacienne de Construction Méchanique. The purchase, around £4,000, was of the locomotive minus tender, shipped to the UK in thirteen large packing cases and assembled at Swindon in 1903, and was matched with a GWR standard tender. Its key dimensions were:

Cylinders (high pressure outside):	13⅜x25 3/16in driving the front axle
(low pressure inside):	22 1/16 x25 3/16in driving the rear coupled axle
Coupled wheel diameter:	6ft 8½in
Bogie wheel diameter:	3ft 0in
Trailing wheel diameter:	4ft 8in
Walschaerts motion and valve gear	
Boiler pressure:	227lb psi
Heating surface:	2,455 .77sqft
Grate area:	29½sqft
Weight (Engine):	64 tons 18 cwt
(Tender):	43 tons 3 cwt
(Total):	108 tons 1 cwt
Water capacity:	3,500 gallons
Coal capacity:	5 tons
Tractive effort:	23,710lb

The GWR official photograph of the du Bousquet/de Glehn compound 102 *La France*, after assembly at Swindon Works in 1903 and matched with a standard GW 3,500 gallon tender. The steam-pipes to the cylinders are clearly visible, curved above the boiler in front of the dome. (MLS Collection)

Churchward decided in February 1904 to convert his third 4-6-0, 171, to the 4-4-2 wheel arrangement and the rear coupled axle was replaced by supplementary frames with outside bearings for trailing wheels of 4ft 1½in diameter to compare the performance of his own design with that of the French locomotive. It was named *Albion* at the same time. 171's dimensions were:

Cylinders (2-outside):	18x30in
Coupled wheel diameter:	6ft 8½in
Bogie wheel diameter:	3ft 2in
Trailing wheel diameter:	4ft 1½in

Stephenson motion & 10in piston valves	
Boiler pressure:	225lb psi
Heating surface:	1,640.9sqft
Grate area:	27.22sqft
Weight (Engine):	70 tons 10 cwt
(Tender):	43 tons 3 cwt
(Total):	113 tons 13 cwt
Water capacity:	3,500 gallons
Coal capacity:	5 tons
Tractive effort:	24,395lb

The prime purpose of the conversion was to test the efficiency and performance of the 4-cylinder compound engine against that of his own 2-cylinder simple engine without the bias of the difference in wheel arrangement. In fact, 171 performed well enough for the Board to authorise a further nineteen of Churchward's locomotives, thirteen as Atlantics (172 and 179-190) and six as 4-6-0s (173–178). 172–180 were built as Swindon Lot 154 in 1905 and 181-190 as Lot 158 later in the year. The Atlantics were named:

***Above*: 102, now** painted black and seen at Stafford Road shed, Wolverhampton, c1905. (F. Moore/MLS Collection)

Below*: 171 *Albion as rebuilt in 1904 as a 4-4-2 for comparison with the French compound, 102. (F. Moore/MLS Collection)

171	*Albion*
172	*Quicksilver* (*The Abbot* after 1907)
179	*Magnet* (*Quentin Durward* after 1907)
180	*Coeur de Lion*
181	*Ivanhoe*
182	*Lalla Rookh*
183	*Red Gauntlet* (*Redgauntlet* after 1915)
184	*Viscount Churchill* (*Guy Mannering* after 1907)
185	*Winterstoke* (*Peveril of the Peak* after 1907)
186	*Robin Hood*
187	*Robertson* (*Bride of Lammermoor* after 1907)
188	*Rob Roy*
189	*Talisman*
190	*Waverley*

172 *Quicksilver*, the first Churchward large passenger engine to be built as a 4-4-2 after the conversion of 171. It was renamed *The Abbot* in March 1907. (Bob Miller/ MLS Collections)

Churchward had not completed his experiments with compounding, however, and in 1905 two further French compounds were purchased, larger locomotives of the Paris-Orleans Railway's 3001 class. They were numbered 103 and 104 and named *President* and *Alliance* (the 'Entente Cordiale' between Britain and France was signed in 1904). The dimensions of the two larger French compounds that differed from 102 were:

Cylinders (high pressure outside):	14¼x25¼in driving the front coupled axle
(low pressure inside):	23 5/8x25¼in driving the rear coupled axle
Coupled wheel diameter:	6ft 8½in
Bogie wheel diameter:	3ft 2in
Trailing wheel diameter:	4ft 8½in
Boiler pressure:	227lb
Heating surface:	2,757sqft
Grate area:	33.35sq ft
Weight (Engine):	71 tons 14 cwt
(Tender):	40 tons
(Total):	111 tons 14 cwt
Water capacity:	3,500 tons
Tractive effort:	27,174lb

The other Churchward 4-4-2s built in Lots 154 and 158 had a boiler pressure of 200lbs psi (Churchward had raised 171's to 225 to maintain comparability with 102), reducing the tractive effort to 20,530lb. However, 225lb psi became the standard pressure for the Swindon No.1 boiler and that was carried by all the 4-6-0s. 171 was converted back to 4-6-0 in 1907 and all the other Swindon built 4-4-2s were rebuilt as 4-6-0s in 1912 and became identical to 2901-2910 which had been built in 1906 as 4-6-0s and 2911-2930 in 1907. 2901 was the first locomotive in Great Britain fitted with a modern superheater. A new GW 4-4-2 of Lot 154 was tested against 4-6-0 178 *Kirkland* in June 1905 on the steep 1 in 42 of Hemerdon Bank, a few miles east of Plymouth. Both were successful but the drivers

190, the last of Churchward's Atlantics from Lot 158, built at Swindon in the Autumn of 1905. It was named *Waverley* in 1906, rebuilt as a 4-6-0 in 1912 and renumbered 2990. (F. Moore/MLS Collection)

were more confident with the 4-6-0 arrangement on such gradients. The Atlantic wheel arrangement allowed a wide firebox to be placed on the Great Northern Atlantic, but the narrow Belpaire box of the GW standard No.1 boiler was designed to burn good quality Welsh coal. The GW Atlantics were merely 4-6-0s with the rear coupled wheels replaced by a bolted-on mini frame for the trailing wheels. The GW Atlantics were generally freer running and better riding than the 4-6-0s, but with 50 per cent greater adhesion weight, the 4-6-0s were considered more suitable for the GWR terrain.

The larger French de Glehn compounds were powerful enough to achieve Churchward's aim of sustaining a two-ton drawbar pull at 70mph. 104 was rebuilt, however, as early as 1907 during its first major overhaul, with a GW standard No.1 unsuperheated boiler. 103 then received 104's French boiler until 1909 when it returned to 104, 103 then receiving an unsuperheated GW standard boiler in February 1910. 103 was superheated in 1914. Clearly if the repair of boiler and motion proceeded at a different speed during major overhauls, boilers were exchanged as was

***Below left*: 103 after** being named *President*, the Paris-Orleans de Glehn compound purchased by the GWR in 1905, seen at Old Oak Common, c1906. (MLS Collection)

***Below right*:**
103 *President*, at Old Oak Common, c1906. (Bob Miller/MLS Collections)

***Above left*: 186 of** Swindon Lot 158, built in the Autumn of 1905, as yet unnamed, at Taunton in early 1906. (Bob Miller/ MLS Collections)

***Above right*: 186, now** named *Robin Hood*, at Old Oak Common, c1907. (F. Moore/MLS Collection)

Right and below*: 104 *Alliance as rebuilt with a Swindon No.1 boiler by Churchward in 1907, in photographic grey livery. (Loco Publishing Co. & Real Photographs/ MLS Collection)

the practice with other GW locomotives and with only the two French boilers available for 103 and 104, a standard GW boiler was used whilst the French boiler was repaired and put on 103 or 104, whichever was next in Works needing boiler repair. 102 received top feed and new steam pipes in 1913 and was rebuilt with a standard No.1 boiler in 1916 which it then retained until its withdrawal. All three engines finished their careers with the GW superheated standard boiler.

Churchward, after the initial experiments and tests of 1905, went one better, designing a 4-cylinder simple expansion locomotive of his own, another Atlantic, No. 40, authorised by the Board in July 1905 at an estimated cost of £3,600 – it actually cost £3,210 with an extra £1,036 for a 3,500 gallon tender. In a report to the Board, Churchward stated, 'It is designed with four simple cylinders with a view to see if the same smoothness of running and economy can be obtained as with the de Glehn compounds without the same

103 *President* as rebuilt by Churchward with standard No.1 boiler in 1910. (MLS Collection)

amount of complication and cost.' More 2-cylinder 4-6-0s were built while the 4-cylinder engine was tested in comparison with the compounds. No.40 combined the tapered domeless No.1 boiler and 225lb psi pressure with large diameter long-travel piston valves and streamlined internal steam passages. It was delivered from the Works in April 1906 and after initial tests was allocated to Old Oak Common where it was put to work on the *Cornish Riviera Express* through to Plymouth. It was an exceptionally free and smooth running locomotive which could run economically with cut-offs between 15 and 20 per cent unlike most British locomotives at the time which worked on much longer cut-offs varying the power output with the regulator open.

In June 1906 Churchward further reported to the Board, 'This engine has now been at work for a week or two and the result is very promising indeed.' He went on to give his reason for eventually abandoning the 4-4-2 wheel arrangement:

> 'It (No.40) is reported to be more powerful than any of our other engines and to run with remarkable steadiness at high speeds. If we build more of them, I think it will be necessary on account of its great power to couple six wheels, as the amount of slipping with four wheels is more than it

***Below left*:**
103 *President* at Old Oak Common, c1912. (Bob Miller/MLS Collection)

***Below right*:**
104 *Alliance* at Old Oak Common with Swindon No.1 boiler in 1908 before receiving its former French boiler again in 1909 which had been on 103 for a couple of years. (MLS Collection)

104 *Alliance* at Westbourne Park, c1908.
(F. Moore/MLS Collection)

102 *La France* was not rebuilt with a Swindon boiler until 1916. It is seen here at Westbourne Park around 1920.
(F. Moore/MLS Collection)

should be for good practice. From our experience now with engines of this power it is clear we must couple six wheels and this limits the possible types to 4-6-0 or 4-6-2.'

The fact that the fluted coupling rods were replaced by standard rectangular rods as they were not strong enough was evidence of his change of policy, following damage from bouts of slipping.

In September 1906 it was named *North Star.* It was indeed the most powerful British Atlantic by a considerable margin, both when it was built and then of any built later. It could be strongly argued that it was also the most economical, although the initial construction costs were probably higher than most others. It was initially fitted with scissors type valve gear similar to that of the French Atlantics, but its setting at the Works was extremely difficult and protracted and whilst it proved good and reliable in service, future builds of the 'Star' class reverted to Walschaerts valve gear between the frames. Its key dimensions were:

Cylinders (4):	14¼x26in
Coupled wheel diameter:	6ft 8½in
Bogie wheel diameter:	3ft 2in
Trailing wheel diameter:	4ft 1½in
Boiler pressure:	225lb psi
Heating surface:	2,142.9sqft
Grate area:	27.07sqft
Axleweight:	19 tons 16 cwt

Weight (Engine):	74 tons 10 cwt
(Tender):	40 tons
(Total):	114 tons 10 cwt
Water capacity:	3,500 gallons
Coal capacity:	6½ tons
Tractive effort:	25,090lb

Operation

The first du Bousquet/de Glehn Atlantic was numbered 102 and named *La France* and painted lined black, changed to standard GW green after its initial overhaul in 1905. Its inaugural run to Swindon in early 1904 was observed by a mass of interested spectators at Paddington station. This first run was unspectacular but very efficient and stress free, reaching Swindon eight minutes early. It was then rostered to haul the

***Above*: Churchward's 4-cylinder** Atlantic, No.40, as built in 1907, with the same rear axle arrangements as the 2-cylinder engines. (Bob Miller/MLS Collection)

***Below left and below right*: The Atlantic** No.40 now named *North Star,* at Old Oak Common, c1908. (F. Moore/MLS Collection)

Above: **102 *La France*** speeds westwards with a Paddington–Bristol–Plymouth express, c1905. (Loco Publishing Co./MLS Collection)

Below: **102 *La France*** with a light up express between Taunton and Bristol, c1912. (MLS Collection)

Cornish Riviera Express and Rous-Marten published his experience when it hauled 160 tons through to Exeter. The 193¾ miles via Bristol were completed in 203 minutes 14 seconds, 6¾ minutes early, despite signal stands at Milton Crossing and Wellington – a standing time of 3¾ minutes in total, plus further p-way slacks, the net time being only 182½ minutes. 102 achieved a steady 85mph on the level, the 56 miles from Paddington to the stop at Milton Crossing taking just 52 minutes 39 seconds. After the dead stand at Wellington, 102 accelerated its train to 48mph at the summit of the 1 in 80 at Whiteball Tunnel. Rous-Marten returned on a different date on the 12.07pm Exeter when 102 had 270 tons, and completed the run to Paddington in 197¾ minutes net, with 53mph on the 1 in 115 from Burlescombe to Whiteball Tunnel. This was not surprising as the twenty of the class by then running on the Nord railway in France were sustaining 75mph (120kph) on the level between Paris and Calais with 300 tons, and 64-70 with 360 tons, surmounting the 1 in 125 of Caffiers bank at 62mph with the former tonnage. On another occasion 102 with a train of 350 tons completed the Exeter–Paddington run in 198 minutes including an eight minute stop at Bristol Temple Meads, that is a running time of 190 minutes for the 193¾ miles.

Charles Rous-Marten published the logs of two runs with 171 on the 10.50am Paddington *Cornish Riviera Express*, which 171 worked to Bristol, first as a 4-4-2 and then later as a 4-6-0 (it had been converted back to a 4-6-0 in 1907).

		Paddington–Bristol, 1905 & 1907					
		10.50am Paddington–Plymouth *Cornish Riviera Express*					
		171 ***Albion***			**171** ***Albion***		
		320 tons			**320 tons**		
		as 4-4-2			**as 4-6-0**		
Miles	**Location**	**Times**	**Speed**		**Times**	**Speed**	
0	Paddington	00.00			00.00		
5.7	Ealing Broadway	07.58			07.18		
7.3	Hanwell	09.35			09.00		
9.1	Southall	11.19	62		10.41	62	
13.2	West Drayton	15.25			14.53		
18.5	Slough	20.19	65		19.55	63½	
22.5	Taplow	24.04	65		23.51	61	
24.2	Maidenhead	25.48	65		25.41	63	
31	Twyford	32.33	60		32.36	58	
36	Reading	37.29	61		37.40	59	
41.5	Pangbourne	42.47	63		45.41	sigs to stand, Scours Lane	
53	Didcot	53.36	64	1 E	57.57	55	3 L
60.4	Wantage Road	60.30	63/69		65.41	58	
71.6	Shrivenham	71.04	65		77.15	57	
77.3	Swindon	76.29	pws (bridge)	3½ E	83.17	57	3¼ L
82.9	Wootton Bassett	83.33			87.58		
94	Chippenham	92.37	75		96.54	77	
106.8	Bath	105.18			108.28		
118.35	Bristol Temple Meads	117.03	(113 net)	3 E	121.14	sigs (114½ net)	1¼ L

The 4-6-0 accelerated hard from Paddington over the first five miles, but thereafter the honours went to the 4-4-2. After the delay at Scours Lane, 171 as a 4-6-0 might have been expected to have the edge over the 4-4-2 but speed stayed low until after Swindon when the driver piled on steam and would have made right time at Bristol had not signals intervened at Saltford and between St Anne's Park and Temple Meads. From 1 July 1904 the *Cornish Riviera Express* became non-stop in both directions between Paddington and Plymouth apart from the non-advertised stop at Newton Abbot to attach a pilot over the steep Devon banks. As mentioned earlier, 102 hauled this inaugural run and then worked turn and turn about with the 'Atbara' 4-4-0s and the GW Churchward Atlantics on this long non-stop working.

Rous-Marten took an early opportunity to see for himself the capability of the new 4-cylinder Atlantic, No.40, and reported glowingly in his monthly article for the *Railway Magazine* in December 1906. He had selected the Down *Cornish Rivera Express,* the 10.30am Paddington–Penzance, on which No.40 had a 250 ton load from London and after slipping coaches, at Westbury

103 before naming at Hayes & Harlington with a down express, c1905. (E. Pouteau/MLS Collection)

Below left: **104, also** still unnamed, with a down express at West Drayton, c1905. (Bob Miller/MLS Collections)

Below right: **103 *President*** at Kensal Green with a Paddington–Oxford train, c1920. (Railway Photographs/MLS Collection)

180, as yet unnamed, passing Old Oak West with an express for Cardiff and West Wales, c1906. (Bob Miller/MLS Collections)

Below left: **184** ***Guy*** *Mannering*, waiting to depart from Paddington with a down express, c1907. (Bob Miller/ MLS Collections)

Below right: **180** ***Coeur de Lion*** runs beside the sea wall between Dawlish and Teignmouth with the down *Cornish Riviera Express,* c 1906. (MLS Collection)

***Above left*: 183, unnamed,** with a down Bristol express at Bathampton, c1906.
(MLS Collection)

***Above right*:**
185 *Winterstoke*, renamed *Peveril of the Peak* in 1907, passing Old Oak Common West with an express for Ilfracombe in the summer of 1906.
(Bob Miller/MLS Collections)

and Exeter 220 tons, then 160 tons over the South Devon banks. After an easy start passing Slough in 20¾ minutes, the train suffered a bad p-way slowing at Ruscombe and took nearly 39 minutes to clear Reading. The next 60 miles took 56 minutes 42 seconds and the first coach was slipped at Westbury, passed in 95 minutes 39 seconds for the 95½ miles from London. The 1 in 112/107 climb to Brewham summit reduced the speed only to 55mph and the 3½ miles descent to Castle Cary took just 2 minutes 38 seconds, an average speed of 80.8mph, so maximum was not far short of 90. Taunton was passed in 146 minutes 4 seconds (142 net) at 64mph, passed Wellington at 57½mph and cleared Whiteball summit at 43mph, but a fast descent was spoiled by another p-way slack at Collumpton. Exeter was cleared in 178 minutes 24 seconds (170 net), and after another p-way slack at Starcross, Newton Abbot in exactly 200 minutes. The minimum at Dainton was 23.7mph and at Rattery, 25mph and the train was halted outside Plymouth in 4 hours 1 minute and 18 seconds from

179 *Magnet*, renamed *Quentin Durward* in 1907, at Bath Spa, 1906. Rebuilt as a 4-6-0 in 1912, it would survive until January 1951, the penultimate of the former Atlantics to remain in service.
(Loco & General/MLS Collection)

Paddington, and into the platform to a stand in 4 hours 3 minutes 58 seconds, 3 minutes early. Net time was 3 hours 51 minutes.

In an article in the December 1910 *Railway Magazine* J.F. Gairns tabled the comparison of a couple of runs he had experienced from Paddington to Exeter, firstly with a 2-cylinder 4-4-2 and secondly with a 4-6-0 'Star'. He published passing times only but described his opinion of the performance. I have calculated averaged speeds between the locations given and have estimated speeds at key locations based on these.

No.40 on a down express at Old Oak Common West, c1907. (F. Moore/MLS Collection)

40 ***North Star***, seen at Plymouth North Road after arriving with the *Cornish Riviera Express*, c1908. (Bob Miller/MLS Collection)

		Paddington–Exeter, c1910				
		188 *Rob Roy*		4008 *Royal Star*		
		7 chs, 265/280 tons		8 chs, 280/305 tons		
		11.30am Paddington		*Cornish Riviera Express*		
Miles	**Location**	**Times**	**Speed**	**Times**	**Speed**	**Gradients**
0	Paddington	00.00		00.00		
5.7	Ealing Broadway	08.30		08.00		
9.1	Southall	11.50	61 (ave)	11.30	58 (ave)	L
18.5	Slough	20.30	65 (ave)	20.05	66½ (ave)	
	Ruscombe	-	68 (est)	-	70 (est)	L
36	Reading	37.05	63½ (ave)/ 10*	36.05	65½ (ave)/10*	
44.7	Aldermaston	47.30		47.30		L
53.1	Newbury	55.50	62 (ave)	55.40	63 (ave)	
70.1	Savernake	73.45	57 (ave)	73.00	59 (ave)	
	Savernake summit	-	52 (est)	-	55 (est)	1/175 R, 1/106 R
86.9	Lavington	88.45	67 (ave)/80 (est)	88.15	66 (ave)/75 (est)	1/222 F
95.5	Westbury	96.15	30*	95.30	10* (1 coach slipped)	
101.3	Frome	103.15		104.00	10* pws	
	Brewham Box	-	52 (est)	-	48 (est)	1/112 R, 1/107 R
115.3	Castle Cary	117.25	(59 ave)	119.30	(54 ave)	1/98 F, 1/358 F
125.7	Somerton	127.20	(63 ave)	128.40	(68½ ave)	
	Langport	-	70 (est) pws40*	-		1/264 F
142.8	Taunton	145.15	(57 ave) 1 ch slipped	146.00	30	
150	Wellington	152.25	(60 ave)	155.00	(48 ave)	1/174 R
	Whiteball Tunnel	-	40 (est)	-	42 (est)	1/90 R, 1/80 R
154.5	Burlescombe	158.45	(42 ave)	161.15	(43 ave)	
158.7	Tiverton Junction	162.30	(67 ave)	165.00	(67 ave)	1/115 F
170.2	Stoke Canon	172.30	(69 ave)	173.45	(79 ave)	varying F
173.6	Exeter St David's	177.55		178.05	pass 30*	

The 4-6-0 accelerated more rapidly from Paddington, but eased and then was slightly faster between Slough and Reading. The Atlantic, however, accelerated faster from the Reading slack though the 4-6-0 had a slight advantage on the long climb to Savernake. I estimate that *Rob Roy* probably exceeded 80mph on the 1 in 222 from Patney to Lavington and 4008 nearer 75. 4008 had 10mph slowings at Westbury and Frome, affected by station rebuilding and slowed again at Taunton whilst 188 slipped a coach there at around 60mph. 4008 probably touched 80mph on the descent from Whiteball whereas 188 'running early' took it easily down to Exeter. With moderate loads both engines showed complete mastery over the task. The Atlantic 2-cylinder engine more than held its own against the 4-6-0 'Star'.

180 was timed on a heavy 2-hour Bristol express and its log published in the December 1914 *Railway Magazine* – the run was in 1912 just a few months before it was rebuilt as a 4-6-0.

Paddington–Bristol Temple Meads, c1912
180 *Coeur de Lion*
355 tons

Miles	Location	Times	Speed		Gradients
0	Paddington	00.00		T	
1.3	Westbourne Park	03.28			
5.7	Ealing Broadway	09.38			
7.3	Hanwell	-	pws 10* (bridge rebuilding)		
9.1	Southall	14.28			L
18.5	Slough	24.18	65		
22.5	Taplow	-	sigs 30*		L
24.4	Maidenhead	-	52		
31	Twyford	37.39	65		
36	Reading	42.27	65/62		L
44.8	Goring	50.43	63		L
53	Didcot	58.34	64	3½ L	
66.5	Uffington	71.33	66/64		1/754 R
77.3	Swindon	81.28	60	1½ L	
87.7	Dauntsey	-	85		1/100 F
94	Chippenham	95.30	60*		
104.6	Bathampton	-	sigs 15*		
106.8	Bath	108.43	30*	3¾ L	
113.8	Keynsham	-	72		L
118.6	Bristol Temple Meads	121.36	(115 net)	1½ L	

102 had completed a successful 30,000 miles in traffic by the end of 1904 and was certainly more powerful and more economical than the GW Dean and Churchward 4-4-0s. The problem was that its adhesion weight was only 33 tons compared with the Churchward 4-6-0's 54 tons. His conclusion was that his own engines could more than match the performance of the compounds with cheaper initial construction and maintenance than that of the much more complex locomotives. He also realised that the extra adhesion of the 4-6-0s gave better initial acceleration and was certainly more suited to the heavily graded banks in South Devon, so as well as the conversion of the 2-cylinder Atlantics, all the 29XX 'Saints' and 40XX 'Stars' were built as 4-6-0s. No. 40 was converted to a 4-6-0 in 1909, retaining its name *North Star.*

All three French compound Atlantics were transferred to Oxford in 1926, 102 being withdrawn that year after accumulating 728,031 miles in traffic. 103 and 104 worked to Worcester and Paddington, both being withdrawn in 1928. The Churchward 2-cylinder

The die was cast and by 1907 Churchward had decided that the future lay with his 4-6-0s rather than with his Atlantics. Despite the building of the 4-cylinder Atlantic in 1907 to further develop lessons learned from the French Atlantics, the pioneer test Atlantic, 171 *Albion*, was converted back into a 4-6-0 in 1907. It is seen here at Old Oak Common after its re-conversion, c1908. (E. Pouteau/MLS Collection)

Below left*: 171 *Albion after rebuilding as a 4-6-0 in 1907 and renumbering in 1912 as 2971, on a Great Western express between Reading and Paddington, c1920. (Railway Photographs/ MLS Collection)

Below right*: 2971 *Albion at Swindon shortly before withdrawal in January 1946. (MLS Collection)

4-4-2s were all converted to 4-6-0s by the beginning of 1913 and ran as members of the 'Saint' class, being renumbered in the 29XX series from 1912 and most lasted into the 1940s and early 1950s, the last survivor of the former Atlantics being 2979 (ex-179) *Quentin Durward* which was withdrawn in January 1951 with a final mileage in traffic of 1,802,144 and 2981 (ex-181) *Ivanhoe* which lasted until March 1951 having accumulated 1,838,884 miles. The highest mileage former 2-cylinder Atlantic

was 2980 (ex-180) *Coeur de Lion* which clocked up 1,901,031 miles before its withdrawal in 1948. No. 40 ran 119,888 miles as a 4-4-2, 918,804 miles as a 'Star' (both as 4-4-2 and 4-6-0) and a further 1,426,356 miles as a 'Castle' after it was rebuilt as the latter with a new larger boiler in 1929. It thus achieved a total mileage of 2,345,160 before its withdrawal in 1957, the second highest mileage of any Great Western engine (the highest was Castle 4037, also a rebuilt Star).

The final years for the French Atlantics are approaching – 102 *La France* at Moreton Cutting near Didcot, c1925. It was withdrawn the following year. (H. Gordon Tidey/MLS Collection)

104 *Alliance*, by now looking tired and uncared for, at an unidentified location, c1927, a year before its withdrawal. (F. Moore/MLS Collection)

Above*: *North Star, as rebuilt as a 4-6-0 in 1909 and renumbered 4000 in 1912, at Old Oak Common, c1920. (MLS Collection)

***Below left*: The ultimate** form of Churchward's No.40, rebuilt as a Collett 'Castle' in 1929 and seen here in 1935, still identified as 4000 *North Star*. It was not withdrawn until 1957, its lifespan just reaching fifty years. (Real Photographs/MLS Collection)

***Below right*: 4000 *North* ***Star* with the 11.45am Bristol–Paddington train at Temple Meads, 1949. It finished its days, after a spell at Stafford Road, at Landore from where it was withdrawn in 1957. (G.G.A. Coltas/MLS collection)

Chapter 4

THE GREAT CENTRAL ATLANTICS

The '8B' Atlantics (LNER C4)

Churchward was not the only Chief Mechanical Engineer to try out both 4-4-2 and 4-6-0 designs in the early years of the twentieth century. J.G. Robinson of the Great Central Railway ordered four locomotives from Beyer, Peacock & Co. in 1903, designed by that company but based on Robinson's earlier 6ft wheel diameter 4-6-0 design (LNER B5 class) – two Atlantic 4-4-2s and two 4-6-0s. The Atlantics were delivered in December 1903, numbered 192 and 194 and were classified by Gorton as class '8B'. They were deliberately designed to be as identical as possible with the 4-6-0s (which were GC class '8C') so as to make comparison based purely on the wheel arrangement. The 4-6-0s had a shallow firebox to encompass the wheel arrangement, and these first two Atlantics were similarly equipped, though all later Atlantics had deeper fireboxes and the first two were subsequently fitted with deeper ones also. One reason for the initial design was the ease then of conversion to 4-6-0 should the latter engines show advantages in traffic in the first few months.

The Great Central was expecting an increase in traffic and therefore heavier train loads on their main line to London at this time, but in fact traffic grew more slowly than hoped for and loads of the main Great Central expresses remained light which meant that the cheaper Atlantics could perform all that was required. Unlike Churchward, Robinson and his Board decided that Atlantics rather than 4-6-0s were the future engines for GC expresses over the London Extension and a further twenty-five were built between 1904 and 1906, five numbered 263-267 by Beyer, Peacock, then twelve numbered 1083-1094 by the North British Locomotive Company and finally eight by the GC's own Gorton Works, numbered 260-262, 358 and 360-363. Their principal dimensions were:

Cylinders (2-outside):	19x26in
Coupled wheel diameter:	6ft 9in
Bogie wheel diameter:	3ft 6in
Trailing wheel diameter:	4ft 3in

Stephenson motion with slide valves

Boiler pressure:	180lb psi
Heating surface:	1,972sqft (the two shallow firebox engines initially had 1,911sqft)
Grate area:	26.24sqft
Axleload:	18½ tons
Weight (Engine):	71 tons 18 cwt
(Tender):	48 tons 6 cwt
(Total):	120 tons 4 cwt
Water capacity:	4,000 gallons (192 & 194 had 3,250 gall tenders for a short while)
Coal capacity:	6 tons
Tractive effort:	17,729lb

In 1908, Robinson rebuilt 1090 as a 3-cylinder engine using saturated steam to compare with both the 2-cylinder versions and the four 3-cylinder compound Atlantics (classes 8D & 8E) built in 1905/6 (see next section). It was selected for the experiment as its frames and cylinders had been badly damaged in the overheating and disintegration

***Above left*: 192, the** original Beyer, Peacock designed prototype, at Neasden, 4 June 1904. (K. Nunn/LCGB/MLS Collections)

***Above right*: 361 of** the 1906 Gorton built Atlantics in photographic grey livery as built that year. (GC official/ MLS Collection)

361 again, in GC lined green livery, at Leicester, 22 April 1911. (W. Bradshaw/ MLS Collection)

of the big end whilst travelling at speed. Rebuilt and back into traffic in December 1908, 1090 was classified as '8J'. It had three sets of Walschaerts valve gear, but was rebuilt in 1922 back as a standard 2-cylinder Atlantic, the experiment not showing any advantage that led to the conversion of others.

Superheaters were first fitted in 1912, together with piston valves and larger cylinders of 21x26in cylinders, the first to be so equipped being 361.

All were eventually superheated, although it took until 1936 when the last was equipped, but the new enlarged cylinders with 10in piston valves were only fitted when new cylinders were necessary. Seven locomotives of the class were withdrawn before this happened. The tractive effort of the re-cylindered engines rose to 21,658lb. The superheated engines had a heating surface of 1,745sqft, including 242sqft of superheating. 361, 1086 and 1090 were provided with Wakefield mechanical lubricators, but twelve Atlantics superheated in 1920/21 had Robinson's own 'Intensifore' equipment located in the cab. The LNER fitted the remainder with Detroit or Eureka sight feed lubricators and changed the 1920/21 and the three earlier Wakefield lubricator engines to this system between 1930 and 1935.

They were elegant engines and were nicknamed 'Jersey Lilies' after the music hall star Lillie Langtry. They were of course initially turned out in the standard GC lined green livery and at the Grouping renumbered with the addition of 5000 as on other ex-Great Central engines. Some retained their GC livery for a while with L & NER on the tenders, but they were all eventually painted in the LNER lined green livery, reverting to black with red lining after 1928 – surprisingly as the GN and NER Atlantics retained their apple green liveries. The LNER classified the GC Atlantics as class C4 and the various modifications to superheating and cylinder size were not distinguished until 1929 when Gorton identified the original unrebuilt engines as C4/1, those still with slide valves, but superheated as C4/2 and the superheated re-cylindered piston valve engines as C4/3. This was not officially recognised by the Doncaster administration. After the Grouping, because of the larger height restrictions on the GC routes compared to the GN and GE ones, the Robinson chimneys and domes were replaced with lower

Beyer, Peacock 264, built in 1904, at Manchester Central station, c1911. (MLS Collection)

North British built 1088 still in the condition built, at Woodford shed, 9 August 1921. (W. Potter/MLS Collection)

Gorton built 262 as built, at Leicester in the initial 1923 LNER lined livery, 1923. (Loco & General/MLS Collection)

North British built 1085 in initial L&NER livery just before its rebuilding with superheater and piston valves, 1924. (Real Photographs/MLS Collection)

ones to conform to the general LNER gauge and route restrictions, the Robinson chimneys replaced by the smaller 'flowerpot' examples or reduced size GC outline ones. 6085 had its upper boiler fittings reduced in size to fit the LNER Composite Load Gauge in 1925, but when it was superheated and had new cylinders with piston valves in 1932, it was given the classification C4/4. From 1936 most had their upper boiler fittings reduced and those still working with saturated steam and slide valves were C4/2 and those superheated with enlarged cylinders and piston valves C4/4. 5267, the last C4/3, had its boiler fitting reduced in 1939 and then all the GC Atlantics were either C4/2 or C4/4.

6090 (ex-1090) seems to have been an unfortunate locomotive. After its damage and rebuilding in 1908 and its reversion to the standard 2-cylinder format in 1922, it became the first to be withdrawn in November 1939 after damage sustained in a shed collision at Banbury. However, the Second World War needs kept the remainder in active service with only 5266 in October 1943 and 6087 in November 1944 withdrawn during the war's duration. However, four went in 1947 just before nationalisation and the remaining twenty became British Railways stock, although they disappeared quickly thereafter, Thompson B1s largely covering their remaining roles. They were allocated and most renumbered 2900–2925 in 1946, with just 2905 and 2911 remaining vacant for the 1943/4 withdrawn two (6090 was never allocated a revised number).

The prototype 192 designed and built by Beyer, Peacock, at Nottingham Victoria, in the initial LNER livery and before renumbering to 5192, c1924. (Railway Photographs/MLS Collection)

North British 6084 with 'flowerpot' chimney, lower dome and Ross pop safety valves in LNER lined green livery, at Neasden, 1926. (F. Moore/MLS Collection)

The prototype 192 again, by now renumbered 5192 and class C4/3 and painted in the post-1928 black livery, c1930. It still retains a Robinson reduced height chimney and original dome but has Ross pop safety valves instead of the original Ramsbottom ones. (Photomatic/MLS Collection)

The superheated C4/3, Beyer, Peacock 5264 with 'flowerpot' chimney, at Leicester shed, 1932. Sister engine 5267 is in the background.
(J.A.G. Coltas/MLS Collection)

***Below left*: The last** 8B built at Gorton in August 1906, 363, renumbered 5363 and class C4/4, at Gorton in LNER black livery, April 1939.
(W. Potter/MLS Collection)

***Below right*: C4/4 2919,** the Gorton built ex-261, at Retford shed, 8 June 1947. It was one of the last survivors, withdrawn in November 1950.
(W. Potter/MLS Collection)

Two withdrawn C4s, including the prototype 2900 (ex-192), await their fate at Gorton Works, three months after withdrawal, 11 February 1951. (D. Carter/MLS Collection)

Six were left in 1950, 2900, 2901 (the original 192 and 194), 2908, 2909 and 2919 lasted until November and 2918, one month longer, when in December 1950 the class became extinct.

Operation

The initial allocation of the Atlantics was split between Gorton and Neasden but from 1906 many were stationed at Leicester and this became the principal depot of the Atlantics for many years. The Marylebone–Manchester and Bradford trains were still just four or five coaches and were easily handled by Atlantics, and as the Leicester contingent grew, engines were changed there. From 1904 they worked through from Leicester to the Great Western via Banbury to locations such as Weston-super-Mare, Weymouth and even as far as Plymouth although later they usually exchanged for a GWR engine at Bristol. On one earlier excursion to Plymouth, the GC driver had insisted that his heavy Atlantic, nearly 72 tons with 37 tons available for adhesion, would climb Hemerdon Bank without the offered assistance. The attempt, which failed, demonstrated the rightness of the GW decision to use the 4-6-0 wheel arrangement rather than 4-4-2 for its main express locomotives. In 1909 a new diagram was produced for a GC Atlantic to be based at the GW shed at Oxford, working Southampton–York trains between Oxford and Sheffield. 1093 was the first based there followed by 267. The diagram continued through the First World War and only ceased in 1919 when the eight hour crew roster was adopted and diagrams changed to fit.

A brief description of an early Atlantic run was described by Rous-Marten in a 1908 article in the *Railway Magazine.* The train was the 11.25am Manchester–Marylebone, scheduled to take 264 minutes for the 216½ miles, a long through working but the load was only four vehicles, 125 tons. The locomotive was 1905 North British built 1091. After a stop at Guide Bridge, the 36¼ miles to Sheffield took 46 minutes, the climb to Woodhead Tunnel made at a steady 45mph with nothing over 65mph down to

***Above left*:** A Great Central official publicity photograph of 1085 and a dining car express on the London Extension, c1906. (MLS Collection)

***Above right*: 362 on** a heavy London–Manchester express, c1910. (Real Photographs/MLS Collection)

260 with a London–Manchester express near Woodford, c1910. (W.A. Brown/MLS Collection)

Penistone. The 38¼ mile colliery slack infested route to Nottingham took 48 minutes 22 seconds and the 23½ mile section on to Leicester was completed in 25 minutes exactly. The train was routed via the GC/GW joint line and the 79½ miles to High Wycombe, scheduled to take 82 minutes, were completed in three seconds over 78 minutes (61.2mph average) with speeds of 80½, 82 and nearly 84 being clocked on the long 1 in 176 descents between Leicester and Grendon Underwood Junction. Arrival at Marylebone was three minutes early.

By the Grouping the entire class was divided between Leicester (16 engines) and Woodford (11 engines) and this remained so until the mid-1930s, the Gorton and Neasden turns covered by the D10 and D11 'Directors' and the two classes of large passenger 4-6-0s. One or two members were based at Neasden for short periods in the early 1930s including 5261 and 6091. The Leicester engines worked both north and south on expresses and the Woodford engines handled much of the traffic to the Great Western via Banbury. The Leicester stud including twelve engines that remained there until the advent of the B17 'Footballers' in 1936 – 5192, 5265-5267, 5361, 5363, 6083, 6086, 6087, 6089, 6090 and 6092. Three others spent most of that period there with only short absences – 5264, 5358 and 5360. The latter engine, 5360, was involved in a series of bridge tests throughout the country, set up by a committee led by academic, Professor Dalby, in 1925. The C4 was one of the four locomotives chosen because of its heavy axleload and hammerblow – the others were a former North

Above: 260 with a Sheffield–Great Western express which it will work to Banbury, c1912. (Real Photographs/MLS Collection)

Below: 1086 departing from Woodford with a Great Western–Sheffield express which it took over at Banbury, c1912. (W.A. Brown/MLS Collection)

Eastern Atlantic C6, a North Eastern Q7 0-8-0 and an L&YR Hughes 0-8-0. 52 bridges were tested and 5360 visited the Lune Viaduct and the Runcorn bridge on the West Coast Main line, based temporarily at Crewe with Leicester men, ex-GE infrastructure at Manningtree, Hilgay and Broxbourne and Great Western bridges at Stoke Canon, Langport East and Somerton and a Southern Railway bridge at Poole Harbour. 5360 was required to pass over the bridges at 75mph (something that the 0-8-0s were presumably not required to do!).

One train that was invariably hauled by a Leicester Atlantic in this period was the 6.20pm Marylebone–Bradford, routed via the GW/GC joint line via High Wycombe, the return working of a Bradford–Marylebone express that left Leicester at 12.49pm. Loads were usually around 300 tons but coaches were slipped at Finmere and Woodford until around 1935/6 after an incident when the slip coach collided at slow speed with the main train that for some reason had been brought to a halt. The schedule for the 107.6 miles via High Wycombe was 114 minutes and with restricted running until Northolt Junction, left just 94 minutes for the 96 miles on to Leicester. The schedule was tight for an Atlantic with 300 tons and a run with 6087 with 295 tons in 1926 dropped six minutes to the Finmere slip drop and a further 4½ minutes to Woodford when the conditional stop at Brackley was activated. The train arrived at Leicester nearly 15 minutes late. Here 6087 was exchanged for 5267 and additional vehicles were added, the load made up to 325 tons. Loughborough (9.8 miles) was passed in 11 minutes 50 seconds at 77½mph with a minimum of 61½ on the 1 in 176 to Barnston Box and 80½ down through East Leake to Ruddington, completing the 23.4 miles to Nottingham Victoria in 24 minutes 40 seconds. 5267 on another occasion, taking over late from one of the 3-cylinder compound Atlantics, had 340 tons and got to Nottingham in just over 26 minutes with 75mph at Loughborough, 57 at Barnston and 75 at Ruddington.

O.S. Nock timed the 6.20pm Marylebone as far as Leicester a number of times with more meritorious results, though the best runs only just achieved the schedule and 6090 with 340 tons and bad delays early in the run struggled. I table below three of his logs on the non-stop run with the slip coaches and one with the Finmere and Woodford stops in 1936.

The 3-cylinder 1090, rebuilt in 1908, at Chorlton Junction on a Liverpool–Harwich boat train, c1913. (G.M. Shoults/ MLS Collection)

Marylebone–Leicester via High Wycombe, 1927-1934

6.20pm Marylebone – Bradford

		5264			**5262**			**6090**			
Load	**to Finmere:**	**276/290 tons**			**285/300 tons**			**315/340 tons**			
	toWoodford:	**239/250 tons**			**248/260 tons**			**278/300 tons**			
	to Leicester:	**202/210 tons**			**211/220 tons**			**241/260 tons**			
Miles	**Location**	**Times**	**Speed**		**Times**	**Speed**		**Times**	**Speed**		**Gradients**
0	Marylebone	00.00			00.00			00.00			
3	Brondesbury	06.42	40		07.01	32		07.15			1/100 R
5.1	Neasden Junction	09.38	59/50*	½ L	09.34	63/45*	½ L	10.10	50*	1¼ L	1/90 F
8.8	South Harrow	13.43	50/58		14.23	43/57		15.05	43½		1/142,264 R
11.6	Northolt Junction	17.05	44*	T	17.41	49*	¾ L	20.25	sigs 0*	3½ L	
16.1	Denham	22.16	60		23.05	53		27.50	50		1/264 R
18.7	Gerrards Cross	25.10	51		26.26	46		31.30	sigs 35*		1/175 R
	Seer Green	-	55½		-	57½		-	43		1/254 R
23	Beaconsfield	30.05	66		31.23	69		37.55	60		1/225 F
27.8	High Wycombe	34.45	45*	¼ E	35.58	44*	1 L	43.15	42*	9¼ L	
32.8	Saunderton	41.25	45½		42.39	45		50.15	42		1/164 R
36	Princes Risborough	45.00	75	T	46.23	69	1¼ L	54.10	63½		1/100, 88 F
41.4	Haddenham	50.03	pws 50*		50.43	80½		58.50	74		1/176 F
45.4	Ashendon Junction	54.20	56		54.04	69		62.30	63½		L
51.3	Grendon Junction	60.28	61½	½ L	59.37	64/67	¼ E	68.25	57½	8½ L	
53.3	Calvert	62.28	56/62		61.34	58/66		70.30	54/61		1/176 R, 176 F
59	Finmere	68.30	50	½ L	67.13	54	¾ E	76.45	47	8¾ L	1/176 R
63.8	Brackley	73.38	66/60		72.00	69/62		82.15	62½		1/176F,R
67	Helmdon	77.10	53		75.18	57		86.00	50		1/176 R
71.8	Culworth Junction	81.47	70½		79.51	72		91.00	67		1/176 F
73.6	Woodford	83.22	67	1¼ L	81.24	66	½ E	92.35	64½	10½ L	
76	Charwelton	85.48	57½		83.46	60		95.00	58½		1/176 R
83	Braunston	91.40	80½		89.42	82		101.05	80½		1/176 F
87.7	Rugby	95.51	60/68		93.43	61/69		105.10	64/72		1/176R,F
91.3	Shawell	-	50		-	50½		-	57½		1/176 R
94.5	Lutterworth	102.49	60/53		100.33	60/51		111.20	66/		1/176 F,
98.4	Ashby	106.52	68		104.41	67		115.00	70½		1/176 F
102.9	Whetstone	110.30	81		108.23	75		118.30	82		1/176 F
107.6	Leicester	114.40		¾ L	114.00	sigs	T	122.45		8¾ L	
		(net 113½)			(net 112)			(net 116)			

Marylebone–Leicester via High Wycombe, 1936
6.20pm Marylebone – Bradford
5363, 241/260 tons

Miles	Location	Times	Speed		Gradients
0	Marylebone	00.00		T	
3	Brondesbury	06.38	32		1/100 R
5.1	Neasden Junction	09.20	56 /pws 22*	¼ L	1/90 F
8.8	South Harrow	16.07	43/56		1/142 R, 1/264 R
11.6	Northolt Junction	19.45	42*	2¾ L	
16.1	Denham	24.58	61½		1/264 R
18.7	Gerrards Cross	27.46	55		1/175 R
	Seer Green	-	60		1/254 R
23	Beaconsfield	32.13	72½		1/225 F
27.8	High Wycombe	36.48	42*	1¾ L	
32.8	Saunderton	43.31	47½		1/164 R
36	Princes Risborough	46.56	73	2 L	1/100F, 1/88 F
41.4	Haddenham	51.03	88		1/176 F
45.4	Ashendon Junction	54.06	78		L
51.3	Grendon Junction	59.08	67/69	¾ E	
53.3	Calvert	60.57	65/70		1/176 R, 1/176 F
59	Finmere	66.50	(64 net)	¾ E	
0		00.00		T	
4.8	Brackley	07.18	63/57		1/176 F, 1/176 R
8	Helmdon	10.48	54		1/176 R
11.6	Culworth	14.13	67/62		1/176 F, 1/176 R
12.8	Culworth Junction	15.15	76½	1¼ L	1/176 F
14.6	Woodford	17.11		¾ L	
0		00.00		1 L	
2.4	Charwelton	04.52	46		1/176 R
9.4	Braunston	11.09	82		1/176 F
14.1	Rugby	15.07	63/73		1/176 R, 1/176 F
17.7	Shawell	18.15	56		1/176 R
20.9	Lutterworth	21.31	66/61		1/176 F, 1/176 R
24.8	Ashby	25.08	74		1/176 F
29.3	Whetstone	28.27	87		1/176 F
33	Leicester South Goods	31.06	80½		1/264 F
34	Leicester	32.25		½ E	

It will be noted that the timings of the train, once the slip coach working had been replaced by station stops, were extremely tight, the Finmere–Woodford timing impracticable. 5363 and its driver did manage to cut a minute and a half off the mile-a-minute schedule from Woodford to Leicester, which included an exceptionally fast approach to Leicester itself, 80mph just a mile from the stop. A 1930 run recorded in the archives of the Rail Performance Society displayed an excellent meticulous punctual run at all timing points, arriving at Leicester one minute early on a run unchecked throughout. 6092 had eight coaches, 300 tons, passing Denham at 58mph, Gerrards Cross at 49½, Saunderton cleared at 43½, no more than 75mph at Haddenham and Grendon Underwood Junction was passed in 58 minute 50 seconds, just over a minute early. 49½ before Finmere and 52 at Helmdon, 82 at Braunston, 54 at Shawell and a final 75 at Whetstone was enough to just hold to the scheduled timings on the GC London Extension route.

The Leicester Atlantics also worked certain trains north of Leicester to Nottingham, Sheffield and Manchester, one renowned turn being the 2.32am Marylebone newspaper train that left Leicester at 4.10am. Initially engines were changed again at Nottingham, but in 1929 the diagram was changed and the Leicester Atlantic went through to Sheffield on the tightly timed train, although much of the load had been shed by then and the last section was usually reduced to just two or three vehicles. In 1930 the 4.55pm Marylebone was extended from Sheffield to Manchester, non-stop over the Woodhead route, due into Manchester precisely at 9pm. This had been worked north of Leicester by one of its Atlantics and that engine worked through to Manchester on the extended run. Despite the steeply graded route to Woodhead Tunnel, the Atlantics gained an enviable record for punctuality on this service. It then returned to Leicester with the heavy 10.30pm Manchester mail train. This diagram was one of the most testing for the Leicester Atlantics. Albert Mellor was a frequent traveller over the former GC routes in the 1930s and his records are held in the archive of the Rail Performance Society. Three logs of northbound runs on the 4.15pm from Leicester are of interest and are shown below. An unassisted Atlantic found the Leicester–Nottingham timing with over 300 ton loads too tight, but managed the 50 minute schedule over the difficult route through the coal mining area north of Nottingham, sufficient if not affected by too many extra p-way or signal slowings.

		Leicester–Nottingham–Sheffield, c1930									
		5262			**5194 + D9 5105**			**5362**			
		9 chs, 325 tons			**9 chs, 325 tons**			**9 chs, 325 tons**			
Miles	**Location**	**Times**	**Speed**		**Times**	**Speed**		**Times**	**Speed**		**Gradients**
0	Leicester	00.00		¼ L	00.00		T	00.00		3 L	
2.3	Belgrave	04.35			04.10			04.15			1/176 R
5	Rothley	07.40			07.00			07.40			1/176 F
7.8	Quorn	10.15	66 ave		09.25	70 ave		10.25	61 ave		1/264 F
9.9	Loughborough	12.20			11.40			12.40			
		14.35			13.30			14.45			
14.2	East Leake	21.50			20.00			22.00			1/176 R
15.4	Rushcliffe Halt	22.45			21.00			22.55			1/176 F
19	Ruddington	25.55	67½ ave		24.05	70½ ave		26.00	70½ ave		L
22.5	Arkwright St	29.20			27.25			29.15			
23.4	Nottingham	31.25	(30¼ net)	1¾ L	28.50	(28 net)	1¼ E	30.45	(29¾ net)	3¾ L	
0					00.00			00.00			
1.6	Basford				03.30			04.20			1/130 R
3.3	Bulwell Common				06.20			07.25			L 1/330F
5.8	Hucknall				09.30	45		10.50	37		1/130 R
10.8	Kirkby South Jcn				16.10	45		19.00	36		1/130 R
16.3	Tibshelf				22.45	50		26.05	pws		1/132 R
17.9	Pilsley				24.30	54		28.15	pws 40*		1/132 R
20.3	Heath				27.05			31.25			1/300 F
26.2	Staveley				32.40	75/pws		36.50	62/70		1/100 F
28.2	Eckington				35.00			38.45	pws		1/176 F
30	Killamarsh				36.50	60		40.25	70		1/176 F
32.1	Beighton				38.50	64		42.20	65		1/165 F
33.2	Woodhouse				40.45	pws		44.25	pws		
36.2	Darnall				45.25	sigs		49.20	sig stop		1/137 R
38.2	Sheffield				49.00	(45 net)	1 E	53.35	(49 net)	7½ L	

During this period the Woodford stud of Atlantics changed rather more frequently than the Leicester fleet. Only 5194 stayed there throughout the Grouping era until 1936, though 6093 and 6094 were there most of the time. They worked the services from Newcastle and York to both the Great Western and the Southern between Sheffield, Leicester and Banbury. Changes in the timetable and diagrams in 1930 reduced the number of Atlantics required at Woodford to seven and from that date Woodford were allocated 5194, 5261, 5362, 6084, 6088, 6093 and 6094. This created a problem on summer Saturdays when loads were heavy and trains to the south coast often ran in several portions. Loads on the Newcastle–Bournemouth service could reach over 400 tons and the relief portions were often run with GWR engines through to Leicester when no Woodford Atlantics were available. The Woodford engines also had long turns in the opposite direction on fast goods and fish trains to and from Grimsby. These were heavy van trains and punctuality was important because of the perishable nature of the traffic. By the early 1930s, the use of Atlantics ceased on these trains as Woodford received ex-GC B1 and B5 4-6-0s. A number of interesting observations were made by recorders whose logs were archived by the RPS. 6091 on the 2.37pm Oxford on 15 April 1929 took over from GW mogul 6376 and worked through to Leicester, the same C4 on the 10.50am ex-Oxford on 29 June 1929 took over its six coaches from GW 'Bulldog' 3370, and at Sheffield gave way to GN C1 Atlantic 4420. 5194 on 14 July 1931 took over at Leicester the 1.18pm Liverpool with seven coaches from 'Director' 5504 *Jutland* and handed the train over at Banbury to GW 4935 *Ketley Hall*. Albert Mellor timed a number of these runs between Leicester and Banbury, all having suffered delays in the run from Sheffield.

		Leicester–Banbury, 1934/5									
		6084			**5194**			**5362**			
		253 tons			**344 tons**			**313 tons**			
		31/3/1934			**21/7/1934**			**20/4/1935**			
Miles	**Location**	**Times**	**Speed**		**Times**	**Speed**		**Times**	**Speed**		**Gradients**
0	Leicester	00.00		9½ L	00.00		15¼ L	00.00		5 L	
4.7	Whetstone	07.10			07.20			07.15			1/176 R
9.2	Ashby	13.40	41½		13.25	44½		13.30	43/35		1/176 R
13.1	Lutterworth	19.00	48		18.45	48		20.10			1/176 R,1/176 F
16.3	Shawell	-			-			23.40			1/176 F
19.9	Rugby	26.30		9 L	25.35		13¾ L	27.15		5½ L	
0		00.00		9 L	00.00		14 L	00.00		5 L	
4.7	Braunston	06.40			06.20			07.00			1/176 FL
8.2	Staverton Rd Box	10.50	50		10.05	56		11.25	48		1/176 R
11.7	Charwelton	16.05	39		15.05	42		17.30	35		1/176 R
14	Woodford	20.00		8 L	18.25		11½ L	20.50		5¾ L	
0		00.00		8 L	00.00		11½ L	00.00		6 L	
1.8	Culworth Junction	03.15			03.30			03.25			
4	Eydon Road	06.35			06.50			06.50			L, 1/176 R
7.9	Chalcombe Road	11.15			11.25			11.45			1/100/132 F
10	Banbury Junction	14.55			38.05 sig stands*			14.40			1/183 F
11.5	Banbury	17.45		6¾ L	46.15 sig stands*		40 L	16.45		4¾ L	

* major congestion at Banbury following an incident – a pity after 5194 had displayed most energy with the heaviest load.

By the mid-1930s the passenger train loadings on the Marylebone–Sheffield/Manchester and Bradford expresses were getting too much for the Atlantics and double-heading became common until the B17s arrived in 1936/7. 6083 went from Leicester to Cambridge to infiltrate the GN and GE engines working the 'Buffet' expresses to King's Cross, though its axleload restricted its speed between Cambridge and Hitchin. 5358 went to March and was used on the Lowestoft–York train that ran via the GN/GE joint line. Both engines were transferred to Immingham in 1938. Six Leicester Atlantics – 5192, 5266, 5267, 5361, 6087 and 6089 – were transferred to Lincoln in 1936 and took over a number of services in the area previously performed by 4-4-0s. The most important train they worked was the York portion forward from Lincoln of the Harwich–Liverpool boat train. Most trains however were local stopping trains to March, Ely or New Holland and Cleethorpes. They were much used on summer Saturdays with holiday traffic to the East Coast resorts – Skegness, Yarmouth and Lowestoft. A couple were based at Colwick and another couple at Annesley for services in the Nottingham–Mansfield area. Woodford had lost all bar two Atlantics, 5261 and 6084, after 1937. These worked stopping passenger trains to Marylebone.

M.H. Cobb was fortunate in catching the one C4 that worked on the Cambridge 'buffet' trains for a short while alongside the GN C1 Atlantics.

		King's Cross–Cambridge, 1937/8						
		6083			**6083**			
		7 chs, 225 tons			**7 chs, 230 tons**			
		8.10pm King's Cross			**8.10pm King's Cross**			
		18/11/1937			**24/2/1938**			
Miles	**Location**	**Times**	**Speed**		**Times**	**Speed**		**Gradients**
0	King's Cross	00.00			00.00			
2.6	Finsbury Park	06.09			07.18	pws 20*		1/107 R
4.45	Hornsey	08.13	50		10.12	54½		
5	Wood Green	09.11	56/53		11.13	52½		1/200 R
9.2	New Barnet	14.03	50		16.14	47½		1/200 R
12.7	Potters Bar	18.23	48		20.48	45½		1/200 R
17.7	Hatfield	23.08	72		25.44	72½		1/200 F
20.3	Welwyn-Garden-City	25.54		1 L	29.54	(26½ net)	5 L	
0		00.00		¾ L	00.00		4½ L	
1.7	Welwyn North	05.16	sigs/42		03.56	46/ sigs sl.		
3.2	Woolmer Green	07.32	53		05.56	53		1/200 R
4.7	Knebworth	09.30	69		07.52	62½		1/330 F
8.3	Stevenage	12.46	72		11.32	67 easy		1/200 F
11.6	Hitchin	16.30	(15 net)	3¼ L	15.40	(15 net)	6¼ L	
0		00.00		3¾ L	00.00		4½ L	1/161 R
2.6	Letchworth	05.26		3¾ L	05.28		4½ L	
0		00.00		4¼ L	00.00		4¾ L	
2.1	Baldock	03.27	53/60		03.30	58		1/244 F
6.5	Ashwell	08.10	6½		08.21	69½		L, 1/183 F
10.4	Royston	11.53	43*/69		12.11	45*/67		1/163 F
13.4	Meldreth	15.05	67		15.23	69½		1/120 F
15.3	Shepreth	16.48	62		17.09	62		L
16.4	Foxton	17.54	61/56		18.15	59 easy		L
18.1	Harston	19.25	60/50*		19.59	55		
20.8	Shepreth Branch Jcn	22.27	43*/50		23.26	34*/47		
22.3	Trumpington	24.25	sigs		25.42	sigs 15*		
23.4	Cambridge	27.10	(26½ net)	3¼ L	28.18	(27 net)	5 L	

I have found a series of runs on the Cambridge buffet 'Beer Trains' in the RPS records with pre-war runs with 6083 and Ivatt C1 and C2 Atlantics and B17 Sandringhams post-war. The table below is the one Up run that was the only log of a C4 together with an outstanding run with a C1 – both were better than the post-war B2 and B17s in that article! The C4 achieved the best performance from Hitchin to Welwyn Garden City while the C1 achieved by far the highest speed of any run with its 84mph at Wood Green. Both runs were joined by the timer at Hitchin.

5363 entering Nottingham Victoria with a Sheffield–Great Western express, 1926. (MLS Collection)

		Hitchin–King's Cross, c1937						
		6083 C4			**4426 C1**			
		8 chs, 270 tons			**9 chs, 315 tons**			
		4.05pm Cambridge			**6pm Cambridge**			
Miles	**Location**	**Times**	**Speed**		**Times**	**Speed**		**Gradients**
0	Hitchin	00.00			00.00			1/200 R
3.3	Stevenage	06.21	47		06.40	43		1/200 R
5.2	Langley	-	60		-	59		1/330 F
6.9	Knebworth	10.10	60		10.30	60		1/200 R
8.4	Woolmer Green	-	64		-	58		1/330 R
9.9	Welwyn North	13.03	62 easy		13.25	69		1/200 F
11.6	Welwyn Garden City	15.24		½ E	15.25		½ E	
0		00.00		T	00.00		T	1/200 F
2.6	Hatfield	04.13	54		04.05	55		1/200 F
7.6	Potters Bar	09.44	58/56		09.40	57		1/330 R
11.1	New Barnet	14.14	64/pws 5*		12.49	74		1/200 F
15.3	Wood Green	19.17	68		16.00	84		1/200 F
17.8	Finsbury Park	21.33	63		18.03	sigs		
20.3	King's Cross	25.46	(23½ net)	1¼ E	24.53	(23 net)	2 E	

The C4 had the advantage in starting up the grade from Hitchin, the C1 being weaker away uphill with the heavier load but then let fly on the descent to King's Cross. The C4 was interrupted by a severe p-way slowing before New Barnet, so whether the King's Cross driver would have pushed 6083 downhill as hard as 4426's driver did is an unknown factor.

Most of the expresses on the former GC main line were curtailed during the Second World War to a few semi-fast services and from 1940 just four Atlantics were still required at Leicester, working mainly stopping trains in both directions. One of them was 6086 which was based at Leicester until its withdrawal in 1947 (as 2910) having spent twenty-six years at the depot. A third of the class was based in the Nottingham area

6093 with a Sheffield–Swindon train on Charwelton troughs, 1928. (H. Gordon Tidey/ MLS Collection)

***Below left*: 5362 departing** from Sheffield Victoria with a York–Leicester excursion, 3 September 1932. (MLS Collection)

Below right: 6083 at Sheffield Victoria with a Newcastle–Southampton express, 1 August 1934. (MLS Collection)

during the war at Colwick and Annesley. Immingham's 5358 was added to in 1940 with 5266 and 5267 and worked Cleethorpes–New Holland and Doncaster services. Retford had 5261, 5266 and 6089 in 1941 and served in particular the local service needs for the Royal Ordnance Factory opened at Ranskill. They remained there until 1947 working Cleethorpes–Lincoln and Sheffield stopping trains.

By the end of the Second World War and the introduction of the Thompson B1s, there was little remaining work for the Atlantics. They were now over forty years old . The surviving engines in 1947 were all removed from Woodford and Leicester and at the beginning of 1948 on

5363 with a heavy Marylebone–Manchester express at Rickmansworth, c1935. (F. Moore/MLS Collection)

Below left: 5265 finds itself still on express work despite its external condition in 1946 on a Marylebone–Manchester express near Wardsend. (MLS Collection)

Below right: A pair of Atlantics, C4 2914 and GN C1 2815, run light engines towards Sheffield, at Torside, 17 May 1947. (H.D. Bowtell/MLS Collection)

nationalisation twenty remained as follows:

Boston:	9
Lincoln:	9
Immingham:	2

The last transfers before withdrawal were 2909 from Lincoln to Boston to Immingham, whilst 2902 and 2903 left Immingham for Boston and Lincoln respectively. 2919 went from Boston to Immingham and 2915 from Lincoln to Boston. Several went to store in the winter but re-emerged for work in the summer of 1949. The final allocation in 1950 for the last six in traffic was:

Boston:	62900, 62901
Lincoln:	62908, 62918
Immingham:	62909, 62919

Five were withdrawn in November 1950 and 62918 in December.

2900 (the prototype 192) runs into Grantham station with a stopping train from Nottingham, March 1948. (Photomatic/ MLS Collection)

2923 on the 11.33am Sheffield Victoria–Manchester Central, at Torside on the descent from the Woodhead Tunnel, 28 September 1948. (MLS Collection)

Immingham's 2909 at Barton, c1949. This was the only GC Atlantic that the author ever saw, from the top window of a double-decker bus en route from Doncaster to Sheffield in August 1950. (W.A. Camwell/MLS Collection)

2909 again at New Holland, c1949. (W.A. Camwell/MLS Collection)

The '8D & E' compound Atlantics (LNER C5)

In the mid-1900s the possibility of compounding was causing increasing interest among locomotive engineers, primarily looking for reduction in fuel consumption. Not only had Churchward aroused interest by his purchase of three French compounds but the apparent success and multiplication of the Midland 4-4-0 compounds, the first five, using the NER engineer W.M. Smith's system, were also admired. Therefore in 1905 Robinson built a couple of 3-cylinder compound locomotives based on his '8B' Atlantic. They were constructed at Gorton and entered service in December, numbered 258 and 259, class '8D'. A further couple, numbered 364 and 365, were built in December 1906 with slight difference in the frame design – the latter two were initially intended as standard simple 2-cylinder Atlantics – and as a result, though differences were small, were classified '8E'. Their dimensions were:

Cylinder diameter:	Inside high pressure 19x26in Outside low pressure (2) 21x26in
Coupled wheel diameter:	6ft 9in
Bogie wheel diameter:	3ft 6in
Trailing wheel diameter:	4ft 3in
Stephenson motion with 10in piston valves for inside HP cylinder	
Stephenson motion with slide valves for the two LP cylinders	
Boiler pressure:	180lb psi
Heating surface:	1,931sqft ('8D'), 1,972sqft ('8E')
Grate area:	26.24sqft
Axleload:	18½ tons
Weight (Engine):	73 tons 6 cwt
(Tender):	48 tons 6 cwt
(Total):	121 tons 12 cwt
Water capacity:	4,000 gallons
Coal capacity:	6 tons
Tractive effort (66 per cent HP, 25 per cent LP): 13, 321lb	

365 *Sir William Pollitt* was named after the previous General Manager in October 1907 and is seen at Neasden shortly afterwards.
(F. Moore/MLS Collection)

The engine crew pose with their locomotive, 364 *Lady Henderson*, at Leicester, 30 June 1910. (W. Bradshaw/MLS Collection)

258 at Neasden just after naming after the Board member Viscount Cross in June 1909. (F. Moore/ML Collection)

259 was named *King Edward VII* in November 1906 and the two 1906 built engines were named in 1907, 364 as *Lady Henderson* and 365 *Sir William Pollitt*. 258 was not named until 1909, when it received the name *The Rt Hon. Viscount Cross G.C.B.G.C.S.I.* 365 was superheated in 1911, and thereafter the compounds showed little advantage in coal consumption over the superheated '8B's and had a more costly maintenance regime, so no more compounds were built. 364 was superheated in 1913, 259 in 1921 and 258 only in 1927. They were fitted with Wakefield mechanical lubricators. 364 was renamed *Lady Faringdon* in 1917.

At the Grouping they were classified 'C5' and renumbered 5258, 5259, 5364 and 5365. Like the C4s, they were repainted in the LNER lined green, only to be downgraded to black with red lining in 1928. Their GC chimneys were replaced by the LNER 'flowerpot' variety in the late 1920s and their boiler fittings were cut down to meet the LNER composite loading gauge, but not until the 1930s. They were renumbered 2895-2898 in the LNER 1946 numbering scheme, but were all withdrawn between December 1946 (2895) and December 1947 (2897).

5365 *Sir William Pollitt*, still in green livery but with 'flowerpot' chimney, at Nottingham Victoria with a stopping train for Leicester, May 1929. (J.A.G. Coltas/MLS Collection)

***Left*: 5365 again**, but now in the LNER black livery, at Leicester, 13 March 1932. (J.A.G. Coltas/MLS Collection)

***Below left*: Black liveried** 5259 *King Edward VII* at Leicester shed, c1931. (Real Photographs/MLS Collection)

***Below right*: A sad** end – 2897 *Lady Faringdon*, with little to confirm its identity after withdrawal and stored at Dukinfield, 1 February 1948. (N. Fields/MLS Collection)

Operation

All four compounds were allocated to Gorton from their construction until 1920. They were used on the shed's prime duties including the two morning Manchester–Marylebone expresses, the 7.45 and 11.25, returning the following afternoon on the 3.25 and 6.20 Marylebone. They worked excursions on bank holidays and other holiday periods and were the company's choice engines for any royal train duties in the first decade of the twentieth century. Rous-Marten corresponded with Robinson, receiving a letter from the great man himself in which he said the compounds were doing 'exceedingly good work' with an economy of 2-2½lb of coal less per mile than the Atlantics working on saturated steam. Being 3-cylinder engines they were better balanced than the 2-cylinder engines and rode more smoothly. He had no regrets about building the compounds and if more express engines were required, he 'would be inclined to continue this type'. Rous-Marten published some outline times of their early performance.

258 *Viscount* *Cross* on the 10.30am Leicester–West of England express near Whetstone. April 1910. (G.M. Shoults/ MLS Collection)

258 *Viscount* *Cross* on a lightweight GC express thought to be near Neasden, c1910. (F. Moore/ MLS Collection)

They were, however, on very lightweight expresses. 258 on the 3.25pm Marylebone slipped a coach of its 150-ton load at Leicester in 108 minutes with sustained minima of 60mph on the long 1 in 176 gradients and a maximum of 82mph. 259, on the 1.45pm from Leicester with just 120 tons, ran to High Wycombe in just 79½ minutes for the 79.8 miles, accelerating to 60mph in the first three miles from Leicester before hitting the 1 in 176 at Whetstone. The time included being brought to a stand by signals at Grendon Underwood Junction, costing nearly six minutes, to which point the 57½ miles had taken just 52 minutes start-to-stop. The maximum speed noted was again 82mph.

364 and 365 were transferred to Leicester in September 1920 when the 'Lord Faringdon' 4-6-0s replaced them at Gorton and 258 and 259 followed in 1921. They were each allocated their regular Leicester crews and worked expresses regularly from Leicester to Marylebone until 1932. The compounds were slightly slower than the C4s in initial acceleration and had no advantage over the

latter for fuel economy since their equipment with superheaters, but they were popular with their regular crews and rode like Pullman carriages. 5259 was timed on the 6.20pm Marylebone in the early 1930s before the slip working was abolished and details of the run are in the table below:

		Marylebone–Leicester, c1930			
		5259 *King Edward VII*			
	Load to Finmere:	**288 tons**			
	to Woodford:	**249 tons**			
	to Leicester:	**210 tons**			
Miles	**Location**	**Times**	**Speed**		**Gradients**
0	Marylebone	00.00		T	
3	Brondesbury	-	32/57½		1/100 R
5.1	Neasden Junction	09.40	40*	¾ L	1/90 F
11.6	Northolt Junction	18.00	50*	1 L	
16.1	Denham	23.00	50		1/264 R
18.7	Gerrards Cross	26.05	52½		1/175 R
23	Beaconsfield	31.10	64		1/225 F
27.8	High Wycombe	36.05	45*	1 L	
32.8	Saunderton	42.30	48½		1/164 R
36	Princes Risborough	46.00		1 L	1/100F, 1/88 F
41.4	Haddenham	50.35	77½		1/176 F
45.4	Ashendon Junction	54.05			L
51.3	Grendon Junction	60.05		T	
53.3	Calvert	62.05	56½ /66		1/176 R, 1/176 F
59	Finmere	67.50		¼ E	
63.8	Brackley	72.55	66		1/176 F, 1/176 R
67	Helmdon	76.35	52½		1/176 R
70.6	Culworth	80.10	68		1/176 F, 1/176 R
73.6	Woodford	82.55		1 L	
76	Charwelton	85.25	56½		1/176 R
78.4	Braunston	91.55	77½		1/176 F
83.1	Rugby	96.00	58½ /68		1/176 R, 1/176 F
86.7	Shawell	-	54		1/176 R
89.9	Lutterworth	102.45	65		1/176 F, 1/176 R
102.9	Whetstone	110.15	77½		1/176 F
107.6	Leicester	114.45		¾ L	

5364 *Lady* *Faringdon* on Charwelton troughs with a Marylebone–Manchester express, c1928. (F. Moore/MLS Collection)

Immingham's 5365 *Sir William Pollitt* near Barnetby with a Cleethorpe–Doncaster train, 1936. (MLS Collection)

2896, formerly 5259, withdrawn from Immingham in April 1947 and in the scrapyard at Gorton Works, 1948. (MLS Collection)

At Leicester, 5259 was exchanged for another compound, 5364, and, with one additional vehicle making the load 245 tons, ran the 23.4 miles to Nottingham in exactly 25 minutes, with 80½mph at Loughborough, a minimum of 64 at Barnston Box at the summit of two miles of 1 in 176 and 79 at Ruddington. 5364 was timed in the late 1920s on a Leicester–Marylebone via Aylesbury train booked to run the 103.1 miles in 110 minutes, but with three severe p-way checks at Quainton Road, Rickmansworth and South Harrow, failed to meet the schedule, completing the run in 113 minutes 45 seconds (108 minutes net). 5364 had a 180-ton load and had minima uphill of 54mph at Whetstone, and 52½ at Amersham, but no higher speed than 72½mph en route. On one of its last runs from Leicester depot in June 1932 5365 had charge of an 8-coach 282 ton semi-fast train, running the 13 miles to the Lutterworth stop including the eight mile climb from Whetstone to a couple of miles short of Lutterworth station in 17 minutes 55 seconds and averaging 48mph over the 4.5 miles on the 1 in 176 from Ashby to Whetstone, clearing the summit at well over 50mph.

5258 and 5365 were placed in store at Nottingham in November 1932 and 5259 was sent to Lincoln, but only stayed a month before all four were transferred to Immingham early in 1933 and remained there until their withdrawal in 1947. They worked between Cleethorpes and Doncaster/Sheffield on through Manchester expresses, semi-fasts and stopping services until 1938 when they were stored, but they were returned to traffic at the beginning of the Second World War when all locomotives were needed. They continued mainly on Cleethorpes–Doncaster services until they were replaced by Thompson B1s, finishing on local New Holland stopping trains, for which – with the compound's slower initial acceleration – they were not really suitable. The last in service was 5364, now 2897, withdrawn days before nationalisation.

Chapter 5

THE NORTH EASTERN ATLANTICS

The class 'V' & 'V/09' (LNER C6)

Wilson Worsdell had designed and built the successful 'R' class of 4-4-0s in 1899 and also a couple of 4-6-0 classes, neither of which were as good as the 4-4-0s. However, train loads were increasing with heavier stock, more restaurant cars and accelerated schedules on the East Coast route. From 1903, the Ivatt Atlantics with larger boilers began to appear at York on the Scottish expresses and the NER was required to provide the locomotive power on to Edinburgh with an engine change at Newcastle. Worsdell was also aware of motive power developments in America and in particular the exploits of the Atlantics of the Pennsylvania Railroad between Philadelphia and Atlantic City. He therefore turned to the Atlantic wheel arrangement with a large boiler, though without the wide firebox of the GNR and Pen RR Atlantics. 532 was constructed at Gateshead as a 2-cylinder Atlantic, class 'V' in November 1903, with 649 and 784 following in December. 295, 742, 1680, 1753, 1776, 1792 and 1794 followed in 1904. Then after a long gap, ten more with slight differences were built at Darlington Works in 1910 just before Worsdell retired. They were his response to the disappointment of the larger 'R1' 4-4-0s designed to enlarge the 'R's to cope with heavier loads which had been built in 1908.

As well as a slight reduction in cylinder diameter, their main frames were strengthened at the front end. They were numbered in sequence 696 – 705 and classified 'V/09' indicating the year their drawing office design was authorised. Their key dimensions were:

Cylinder diameter (2 outside):	20x28in	(19½x28in for V/09)
Coupled wheel diameter:	6ft 10in	
Bogie wheel diameter:	3ft 7½in	
Trailing wheel diameter:	4ft 0in	
Stephenson motion with 10in piston valves		
Boiler pressure:	200lbs psi initially for first three, rest 180lb psi, all later standardised at 175lb psi after superheating	
Heating surface:	2,455sqft (later 1,875.4sqft after superheating)	
Grate area:	27sqft	
Axleload:	20 tons 4 cwt	
Weight (Engine):	72 tons 18 cwt ('V/09' 76 tons 4 cwt)	
(Tender):	45 tons 6 cwt (from 1914 some 46 tons 12 cwt)	
(Total):	118 tons 4 cwt ('V/09' 121 tons 10 cwt)	
Water capacity:	4,125 gallons	
Coal capacity:	5 tons (from 1914, some 5½ tons)	
Tractive effort:	20, 350lb ('V/09' 19,350lb)	

The prototype 'V' Atlantic No.532 as built in 1903 in NER livery. (The Locomotive Publishing Co./ MLS Collection)

Modifications were made to the cab early on as the original design suffered from too low a pitch, restricting forward vision. 532 returned to Gateshead Works for the roof to be raised and deeper windows to be put in the front spectacle plates. All were equipped with Schmidt superheaters between 1914 and 1920, giving 392sqft of heating surface. When superheated, their smokeboxes were extended by 9¼ inches. From 1931 their new boilers had Robinson instead of the Schmidt type. Westinghouse air brakes and pumps provided the braking system until 1932, after which the locomotive had steam brakes and was equipped with vacuum brakes for the train.

Wilson Worsdell 'V' 1794, built at Gateshead in October 1904, classified by the LNER as 'C6', c1925. (B. Roberts/ MLS Collection)

C6 532, the first NER Atlantic, built in November 1903, at Darlington, c1932. (Real Photographs/MLS Collection)

They were painted in the NER Saxony green until the Grouping. LNER lined green was then carried right through to November 1941 when plain black was used. The LNER classified them as 'C6'. The NER engines retained their NER numbers without alteration until the LNER 1946 scheme when the remaining examples were allocated 2931–2948, following on from the GC Atlantics, though only 2931, 2934, 2935, 2937, 2939, 2941 and 2947 ever carried them and none received the BR number with the additional prefix '6'. 532 was withdrawn in 1943 and 649 and 705 later that year, while five more went in 1945. Only 2933 (ex-742) and 2937 (ex-1792) survived beyond nationalisation and both went early in March 1948 making the class extinct.

***Below left*: 705, the** last of the 'V/09's, built at Darlington in September 1910, after overhaul and repainting at Darlington, c1925. (F. Moore/MLS Collection)

***Below right*: 705 again,** at Darlington, 8 August 1935. (MLS Collection)

***Above left*: 700, a** former 'V/09', built at Darlington in July 1910, at Tweedmouth, 5 July 1936. (G. Barlow/MLS Collection)

***Above right*: 2931, formerly** 'V' 784, and two other C6s, in their last days at Gateshead, 27 June 1947. (MLS Collection)

***Below*: 2934, the** former 'V' 1680, in rundown post-war condition, at Gateshead, 29 June 1947. It was withdrawn in November of that year. (MLS Collection)

Operation

The 'Vs' were allocated to York, Gateshead and Tweedmouth (Berwick) for the main line work between York and Edinburgh, and the 'V/09s' similarly although in 1911 they were joined by the Raven 'Z' 3-cylinder Atlantics, to be described later. In fact, both classes of 2-cylinder Atlantics and the 3-cylinder version seemed to be used indiscriminately. The Vs were rougher-riding engines than the 'Zs' and burnt more coal although some drivers were of the view that they were stronger and better for the heaviest expresses. They were also more costly on maintenance, scheduled to run 65,000 miles between Works repairs, 10,000 less than the 'Zs', and in reality by the Grouping were struggling to make 60,000 miles. Amid a flurry of logs published in the 1912 *Railway Magazine,* with interest concentrated on the new 'Z' class, there was one recorded run of a 'V' with a heavy load, which is tabled below.

Edinburgh–Newcastle, c1911

697, 350 tons

2.20pm Edinburgh

Miles	Location	Times	Speed		Gradients
0	Edinburgh	00.00			1/78 F
3	Portobello	05.10		¾ E	
17.25	Drem	22.00	60	2 E	undulating
29.25	Dunbar	33.20	66/60*	2¾ E	
36.5	Cockburnspath	42.05	45		1/200 R, L, 1/96 R
41.25	Grantshouse	53.35	17	1½ L	1/96 R
46.25	Reston Junction	59.05	72½	1 L	1/200 F
52	Burnmouth	64.00	72½		L, 1/190 F
57.5	Berwick	69.50		1¼ E	
0		00.00		T	
1.25	Tweedmouth	03.15			
6.25	Goswick	09.10			1/190 F
15.5	Belford	19.05	56	1 L	1/208 R
24	Christon Bank	28.25	54½		L, 1/150 R
	Longhoughton	-	76½		1/170 F
32.25	Alnmouth Junction	36.50	60*	¾ L	
41.5	Chevington	45.30	64		undulating
50.5	Morpeth	54.10	65/45*	1¾ E	
	Plessey	-	sigs		
67	Newcastle	76.45	(75½ net)	1¼ E	

***Above*: The pioneer,** 532, at Edinburgh Waverley awaiting departure with an express for Newcastle, 7 August 1911. (G.M. Shoults/MLS Collection)

***Below*: V/09 699** at York with an inspection saloon, c1914. (MLS Collection)

Overloaded on the climb to Grantshouse, it recovered time by running faster than the 'Zs' on the favourable gradients.

At the Grouping they retained initially their top-link work, the allocation being:

York:	4
Gateshead:	7
Heaton:	6
Tweedmouth:	3

The LNER was testing the motive power it had inherited in 1924 and the NER Atlantics, then designated as classes C6 and C7, were subjected to comparative tests with the dynamometer car between Newcastle and Edinburgh. Five return trips were made with 360-ton trains and in running there was little to choose between them, but in economy the 'C7' outshone the 2-cylinder 'C6s' substantially with lower water and coal consumption. The C6 averaged over 56lb of coal per mile, some 20 per cent more than the C7. The introduction of both the Raven and Gresley Pacifics seems to have had little impact on the allocation of the Atlantics until 1928 when four were allocated to Darlington, two to act as main line standby engines to cover any failures or other engines struggling. Tweedmouth lost its allocation to C7s in 1930 and increasingly they were used on fast freight work north of Newcastle. They were heavy engines and 532 was involved in the bridge testing committee's work in addition to the C4 mentioned earlier.

By the 1930s, though still occasionally used on express work, they were increasingly involved in lesser turns. In 1938 the

705 at Cross Gates with a Leeds–York stopping train, c1925. (MLS Collection)

A southbound express departs from York double-headed by C6 701 and D17/1 1638, c1925. (MLS Collection)

introduction of the Gresley 'V2s' had removed them from most main line passenger and freight work and they were seen on Leeds–York–Scarborough and Bridlington trains. In September 1939 twelve were based on the east coast resorts of Scarborough and Bridlington and the other eight were at Darlington. This allocation changed because of the changed war demands and by the end of 1940 the allocation was:

York:	3
Darlington:	8
Gateshead:	3
Heaton:	6

The Darlington engines in particular were employed on

532 passing Cowton between Northallerton and Darlington with a train from the Great Western routed via Banbury to Newcastle, c1930. (Photomatic/ MLS Collection)

C6 704 assists an ailing A4, 4489 *Dominion of Canada*, out of Newcastle with the Up *Flying Scotsman*, c1938. (MLS Collection)

parcel trains and all saw military traffic use including troop trains. In 1943 the LNER had a major reallocation of its stock to minimise the holding of spare parts at numerous depots and apart from five which remained at Gateshead, the rest moved to the old Hull & Barnsley Railway territory at Dairycoates (two), Springhead (ten) and Cudworth (two), all working on freight traffic only. Several were withdrawn and the rest finished at Dairycoates, working local freight trains. Just two lasted into the nationalisation era, 2933 (ex-742) at Dairycoates and 2937 (ex-1792) at Gateshead. They were both withdrawn in March 1948.

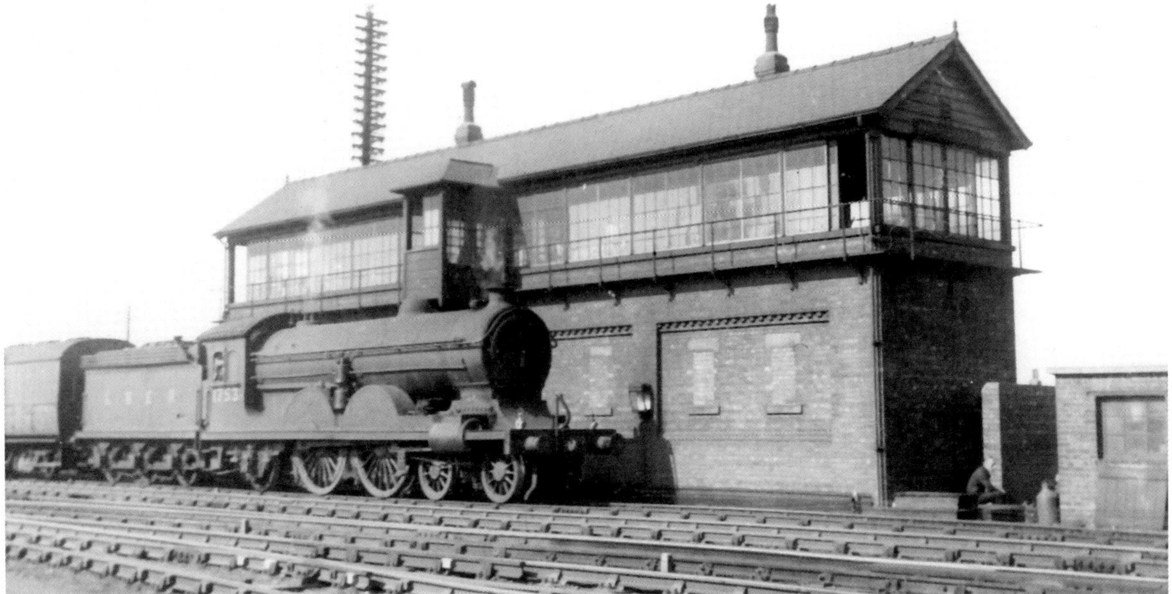

1753, serving as the North End pilot engine at Darlington station, 28 July 1939. (MLS Collection)

696 with a Newcastle–Darlington stopping train at Aycliffe, 25 March 1940. (B. Roberts/ MLS Collection)

The 'Z' class (LNER C7)

The Gateshead Works ceased new construction in 1910 and Wilson Worsdell retired, replaced by Vincent Raven, a long time NER engineer who had been apprenticed under Edward Fletcher. Raven favoured 3-cylinder rather than 2-cylinder engines to give a smoother torque and easier blast on the fire and after successfully using three cylinders on two tank engine designs he got authority to design and build twelve, changed to twenty, 3-cylinder Atlantics to be based on the 'R1' 4-4-0s, though they more closely resembled the 'V' 2-cylinder Atlantics. Because of the change in progress from Gateshead to Darlington for new construction, the twenty were built by the North British Loco Company in 1911, numbered 706, 709, 710, 714, 716-722, 727-729, 732-737. As the advantages of superheating had not yet been proven, the first ten were built using saturated steam and the second ten were equipped with Schmidt superheaters. Their efficacy was soon established and the next ten built at Darlington in 1914, numbered 2163-2172, were given superheaters and the first ten of 1911 were also equipped later. 2193–2211 were added between 1914 and 1917. The first build was classified 'V2', soon changed to 'Z'. Their dimensions were:

Cylinder diameter (3):	15½x26in (first ten), 16½x26in (remainder)	
Coupled wheel diameter:	6ft 10in	
Bogie wheel diameter:	3ft 7½in	
Trailing wheels:	4ft 0in	
Boiler pressure:	175lb psi	(160lb psi – superheated locos, later all 175lb psi)
Stephenson motion with 7½in piston valves		
Heating surface:	2,340sqft, 2,509sqft	(superheated 1911) 1,875.4sqft (incl 392sqft superheating) from 1914.
Grate area:	27sqft	
Axleload:	20 tons 16 cwt	
Weight (Engine):	79 tons 4 cwt	
(Tender):	46 tons 12 cwt	
(Total):	125 tons 16 cwt	
Water capacity:	4,125 gallons	
Coal capacity:	5½ tons	
Tractive effort:	19,300lb	

709, the second 'Z' Atlantic built by the North British Locomotive Company, as delivered in July 1911. (MLS Collection)

***Above left*: 2201 as** built at Darlington in April 1915, outshopped in full NER livery despite the war. (MLS Collection)

***Above right*: 714 moving** down from Haymarket to pick up a southbound express at Edinburgh Waverley, 7 August 1911. (G.M. Shoults/MLS Collection)

***Below*: 2168 built** at Darlington in June 1914. (MLS Collection)

In 1918 Darlington Works built the last authorised Atlantic, 2212, as a Stumpf 'Uniflow' cylinder engine. It was rebuilt as a C7/2 with Lentz poppet valves in 1936. After the Grouping Gresley modified some of the 'Z's, classified by the LNER as 'C7', experimentally, 2163 carrying a Dabeg feedwater system from 1926 until 1937, and 728 and 2206 fitted similarly in 1928 with ACFI water heater equipment, removed in 1942 and 1941 respectively. 727 and 2171 were fitted with boosters in 1931 and reclassified as C9s (see full description later) and 732 was rebuilt in 1933 with Lentz rotary cam poppet valves before using that system on his later orders of the D49 4-4-0. The cylinders were 17in diameter, the same as for the D49/2 'Hunt' class, and the cams gave five cut-off positions, revised to seven positions for the rebuilt 2212. Other revised dimensions were:

Bogie wheel diameter:	3ft 1¼in
Axleload:	21 tons
Weight (Engine):	76 tons 2 cwt
Tractive effort:	20,446lb

The Schmidt superheaters were replaced by Robinson superheaters from 1931 and the total heating surface stabilised at 2,294.5sqft which included 437sqft of superheating. Lubrication had been by an NER type mechanical lubricator until 1924 when they were replaced by Detroit sight feed lubricators in the cab, apart from the Stumpf 'Uniflow' engine until it was rebuilt. The NER used the Westinghouse air brake system, dual braked for the East Coast joint stock which had vacuum brakes only. Between 1932 and 1935 the locomotive brakes were changed from air to steam brake.

Withdrawals commenced in 1943 with 2170 and 2202 and in 1946 the C7s still remaining were renumbered 2963 – 2997. Fourteen were taken into British Railways stock in 1948, but all were withdrawn by the end of that year, the last survivor being 2970, the former 2164. None of the class ever bore their BR allocated number.

720 in LNER livery, c1926. (MLS Collection)

Above left: 719, a rear view, c1925. (MLS Collection)

Above right: 2200 at York, c1925. (MLS Collection)

2206 fitted with ACFI feedwater heater in 1928, at Grantham, c1930. (MLS Collection)

2206 again, at York, c 1929. (Real Photographs/ MLS Collection)

728, the other C7 fitted with ACFI feedwater heater, c1935. The equipment was removed in March 1942. (MLS Collection)

728 again, stored and awaiting removal of the ACFI feedwater equipment in 1942. (Real Photographs/MLS Collection)

729 at Haymarket, 10 April 1939. (MLS Collection)

2163, equipped with the Dabeg system of feedwater heating in 1926, c1930. (Photomatic/ MLS Collection)

Side view of the Dabeg feedwater system C7, 2163, c1934. (Real Photographs/MLS Collection)

***Above left*: 2212, the** Stumpf 'Uniflow' locomotive built in 1918, at York, c1928. (Real Photographs/MLS Collection)

***Above right*: 2212, the** Stumpf 'Uniflow' locomotive at Haymarket, c1930. (Photomatic/MLS Collection)

732 rebuilt in 1933 as a C7/2 with Lentz rotary cam poppet valves, at York, 18 August 1935. (MLS Collection)

732, the C7/2 with poppet valves, December 1938. (Walter Ball/ MLS Collection)

The Stumpf 'Uniflow' engine, 2212, rebuilt as a Lentz poppet valve engine, C7/2, in January 1936, seen here c1939. (MLS Collection)

***Above left*: 2169, which** became one of the last survivors of the C7 class in July 1948, seen here at York in the late 1930s. (Photomatic/MLS Collection)

***Above right*: 2978, the** former 2193, at Darlington a month before its withdrawal, 4 July 1948. (MLS Collection)

***Below*: 2992, ex-2207,** at York shed, 3 July 1948. (H.D. Bowtell/MLS Collection)

2975 stored at Darlington shed, 4 July 1948. (MLS Collection)

732, An unidentified C7 being dismantled for scrap at Darlington North Road Works, 4 July 1948. (MLS Collection)

Operation

Like the earlier 'V's, the 'Z's were based at the key East Coast route depots of York, Gateshead and Tweedmouth/Haymarket. They were fine engines on the level, but their poor adhesion gave them a reputation of being weak on the banks, especially Cockburnspath and on the 1 in 78 approach to Edinburgh Waverley if checked on the arrival there. The *Railway Magazine* of November 1912 published logs of several runs with the 'Z' Atlantics between Newcastle and Edinburgh in both directions and I show in the tables below a few of the best of them, although at this time the schedules for most sections were relatively slack.

		Newcastle–Edinburgh, c1911/12						
		714, 250 tons			**721, 220 tons**			
		11.14am Newcastle			**11.14am Newcastle**			
Miles	**Location**	**Times**	**Speed**		**Times**	**Speed**		**Gradients**
0	Newcastle	00.00			00.00			
10	Cramlington	15.35			14.05			1/200 R, L, 1/224 R
16.5	Morpeth	22.30	57/45*	3½ L	20.30	61/45*	1½ L	1/217 F, 1/251R
25.5	Chevington	31.55	58	3 L	30.05	56	1 L	undulating
34.75	Alnmouth Junction	40.35	72½	3 L	38.20	70½	¾ L	1/220 F
43	Christon Bank	48.50	51		46.50	55		1/170 R
51.5	Belford	56.10	76½	2¼ L	54.55	70	1 L	1/150 F, L
60.75	Goswick	63.50	72½		63.00	69		1/208 F, L
65.75	Tweedmouth	69.05	57/35*		67.50	62½ / 35*		1/190 R
67	Berwick	70.45	25*	¼ E	69.30	25*	1½ E	
72.5	Burnmouth	79.45	36/42½		78.00	43		1/190 R
78.25	Reston Junction	87.05	47	2 L	83.50	59	¼ E	1/200 R
83.25	Grantshouse	93.35	46	2½ L	89.45	51	1¼ E	1/200 R
88	Cockburnspath	98.20	75		94.40	68		1/96 F
95.25	Dunbar	104.50	67	¾ L	101.25	64	2¾ E	L, 1/200 F
106.75	Drem	115.45	63	¼ E	113.20	58	2¾ E	undulating
115	Prestonpans	123.45	62		122.25	55		undulating
	Joppa		sigs			sigs		
121.5	Portobello	131.20	sigs		130.20			1/78 R
124.5	Edinburgh	138.15	(134¾ net)	¼ L	134.45	(133¼ net)	3¼ E	

Three other runs had net times between 133 and 135 minutes and tended to be closer to the even speed run of 721. 714 with the 30 ton heavier load was definitely weaker on the banks but recovered time with higher speeds when the gradients were favourable. The 19 minute schedule to Morpeth was deemed impracticable by the recorders of the day. A couple of runs with superheated 'Zs' were slightly superior on the banks and both recorded net times of 133¼ minutes with 200 ton trains. Southbound, the major obstacle was the five mile climb at 1 in 96 from Cockburnspath to Grantshouse. Three logs have been selected, two with 265 tons and one with a heavy 375 ton load which would often have been double-headed or stopped at Cockburnspath for a banker. All three logs are with superheated 'Z1s'.

Edinburgh–Newcastle, c1911/12

		732, 265 tons			**734, 265 tons**			**735, 375 tons**			
		6.27pm Edinburgh			**6.27pm Edinburgh**			**10am *Flying Scotsman***			
Miles	**Location**	**Times**	**Speed**		**Times**	**Speed**		**Times**	**Speed**		**Gradients**
0	Edinburgh	00.00			00.00			00.00			1/78 F
3	Portobello	05.15		¾ E	04.55		1 E	06.20		¼ L	1/300 F, L
9.5	Prestonpans	13.55	45		12.45	50		15.00	45		1/300 R
17.75	Drem	22.30	59	1½ E	21.30	58	2½ E	24.45	51	¾ L	undulating
29.25	Dunbar	33.25	63	2½ E	32.30	63	3½ E	36.10	60	¼ L	1/300 F
36.5	C'burnspath	41.35	55		40.55	50		44.25	52		1/96 R
41.25	Grantshouse	49.50	28½	2½ E	50.40	23	1¼ E	54.05	29/22	2 L	1/96 R
46.25	Reston Junction	55.40	65	2¼ E	56.20	60	1¾ E	59.20	65	1¼ L	1/200 F
52	Burnmouth	60.50	66½		61.35	66		64.20	72		1/200 F
57.5	Berwick	67.35		3½ E	68.20		2¾ E	71.30		½ L	
0		00.00		T	00.00		T	00.00		T	
1.25	Tweedmouth	03.00			03.15			03.30			
6.25	Goswick	08.45	60		09.00	64		09.15	58		1/190 F
15.5	Belford	18.15	55	¾ E	18.15	57	¾ E	20.00	48	1 L	1/208 R
24	Christon Bank	27.20	56/50		27.05	58		29.40	56		L, 1/150 F
32.25	Alnmouth Jcn	36.45	60/50*	¼ E	35.40	65/55*	1¼ E	38.00	65/60*	1 L	1/170 F
41.5	Chevington	47.10	58		45.15	58		46.45	63		undulating
50.5	Morpeth	57.30	55/35*	½ L	54.50	62/35*	2¼ E	59.00	52/30*	2 L	undulating
59.25	Annitsford	69.00			66.15			66.55	70		1/224 F
	Heaton	-			-	sigs		-	sig stop		
67	Newcastle	78.25		½ E	77.40	(76 net)	1¼ E	81.55	(77 net)	3 L	

728 leaving Newcastle with the 2.20pm Edinburgh–King's Cross, c1912. (MLS Collection)

Unsurprisingly 735 lost time on the banks, but 734 with 265 tons lost time also on the climbs.

At the Grouping the allocation was:

Gateshead:	22
York:	13
Heaton:	8
Haymarket:	4
Neville Hill:	3

Five new Raven Pacifics became available in 1923 and fifteen new Gresley Pacifics were allocated to Gateshead and Heaton in 1924/5, displacing eleven C7s from Gateshead, transferred to York

2208 on a northbound East Coast express between Newcastle and Edinburgh, c1920. (Photomatic/MLS Collection)

and Leeds Neville Hill. Although no longer on the fastest trains, they still often powered heavy secondary expresses and semi-fast trains and frequently needed double-heading. Shortly after the Grouping a York C7 had a working south to Grantham and many NER engines including the 'C7's worked excursion trains to London for the 1924 Wembley Exhibition, Football and Rugby specials. One 'C7' run on a Grantham turn was featured in Cecil J. Allen's 200th article in the *Railway Magazine* of February 1927, which was an extended article covering some of the most meritorious runs over each of the railway companies during the previous five years since his 150th article.

Grantham–York, c1926
721, 8 chs, 264/280 tons
5.30pm King's Cross–Newcastle

Miles	Location	Times	Speed		Gradients
0	Grantham	00.00		T	
4.2	Barkston	06.40	69		1/200 F
6	Hougham	08.14	75		1/300 F
9.9	Claypole	11.20	70½		L, 1/268 R
14.6	Newark	15.15	77½	¾ E	1/300 F
20.9	Carlton	20.20	72½		L
21.9	Crow Park	21.10	71½		L
25.8	Dukeries Junction	24.55	59		1/200 R
26.4	Tuxford	25.30	61½		L
28.2	Markham Box	27.20	59		1/200 R
30	Gamston Box	29.00	67		1/200 F
33.1	Retford	32.00	55*	4 E	L
	Barnby Moor	-	70½		1/198 F, L
38.4	Ranskill	37.00	71½		L
40.3	Scrooby	38.35	75		1/440 F, L
42.2	Bawtry	40.10			1/198 R
44	Pipers Wood Box	41.50	61½		1/198 R
45.8	Rossington	43.30	70½		1/198 F
50.5	Doncaster	47.30		6½ E	
54.7	Shaftholme Junction	51.25		7½ E	L
57.4	Moss	54.10	64		L
61.8	Heck	58.05	68/67		L, 1/270 R
64.3	Templehirst	60.15	71½		L
68.9	Selby	62.05	30*	12 E	
73	Riccall	70.40	57½ /sigs		
80.5	Chaloners Whin Jcn		sig stand		
82.4	York Loco Yard	86.25	(73½ net)	6½ E	

721 had developed a fault and engines were changed there, C7 2172 taking over

***Above left*: 731 near** Lawesley with the Up *Flying Scotsman*, c1907. (MLS Collection)

***Above right*: C8 731** leaving York with a heavy northbound East Coast express in the late 1920s. (Cecil Ord/MLS Collection)

C8 730 near Darlington with a northbound express, June 1930. (Photomatic/MLS Collection)

The 'LNER C9'

After the First World War, express train loads on the East Coast main line remained heavy enough to require frequent double-heading north of Newcastle to avoid difficulties on the climbs in both directions to Cockburnspath. In 1926, Gresley, aware of the use of the booster system in America, had experimentally fitted a booster to Ivatt Atlantic 4419 (see Chapter 2, page 44) and he suggested to his Assistant at Darlington that the fitting of a booster to a C7 Atlantic might overcome the problems and cut the costs of double-heading. The experiment with 4419 had however thrown up a couple of problems that were never really solved with that engine. The extra weight of the booster was not popular with the Civil Engineer and 4419 had a reputation of rough riding caused by inadequate springing with lack of space under the cab filled by the booster.

Gresley suggested a bogie to replace the trailing axle, articulated with the tender, spreading the booster's weight and releasing enough space for improved springing. This would require a new tender and make the locomotive a 4-4-4, or a 4-4-2 with a six wheel tender, the first axle as part of the booster bogie and a further bogie under the rear of the tender. Darlington prepared drawings in 1927, but it was felt that a larger boiler would be necessary to supply the extra steam to the booster and this was incorporated in the proposal during 1928. It was not until 1931, however, that the authority to proceed was obtained for the conversion of two C7s, and the first two to enter Darlington for regular overhaul in January, 727 and 2171, were selected for rebuilding with the booster and redesigned tender. The conversion took nearly a year with 727 re-entering traffic in November 1931 and 2171 in December. The dimensions of the two locomotives were:

Cylinder diameter (3):	16½x26in
Coupled wheel diameter:	6ft 10in
Leading bogie wheel diameter:	3ft 7¼in
Booster & tender wheel diameter:	3ft 8in
Boiler pressure:	200lb psi

Stephenson motion with 7½in piston valves

Heating surface:	2,317.6sqft (incl 417sqft of superheater)
Grate area:	30sqft
Axleload:	20 tons 1 cwt
Weight (Engine & Tender):	135 tons 8 cwt
Water capacity:	4,125 gallons
Coal capacity:	5½ tons
Tractive effort:	22,012lb
Booster tractive effort:	5,000lb

They were designated class C9 but retained their NER/LNER numbers. The cost of the conversion was estimated at £3,894 less £2,444 (the value of materials recovered), leaving a net cost of £1,450 per locomotive. Trials commenced immediately with 727 on the Darlington–Bishop Auckland route where there were sufficient heavy gradients. With dynamometer car

York's C7 2171, before rebuilding with booster equipment, waits to take over a northbound express from Ivatt Atlantic 286, c1922. (E.S. Cox/MLS Collection)

and increasing loads on successive days on a near four mile climb at 1 in 70, 727 with 295 tons covered the four miles from standing start in 9½ minutes, sustaining 26mph on the gradient. In Shildon Yard, 727 succeeded in starting 746 tons on a 1 in 111 gradient. The maximum without the use of the booster was 496 tons. It had taken five years from Gresley's 1926 suggestion to be implemented. The problem was that by 1931 sufficient Gresley Pacifics were available for the main expresses on the Newcastle–Edinburgh route, so in effect the rebuilding was unnecessary.

The booster equipment on 2171 was particularly troublesome with broken springs on the tender putting the engine out of action for six months in the latter half of 1932 and after a general repair

727 after rebuilding with booster and larger boiler in 1931. (Real Photographs/MLS Collection)

727 inside Gateshead roundhouse, 1 April 1934. (H.C. Casserley/MLS Collection)

2171 newly rebuilt with larger boiler and booster, at Darlington Works, December 1931. (Real Photographs/MLS Collection)

2171, booster fitted in December 1931, seen here c1932. (Colling Turner/ MLS Collection)

***Above left*: 2171 at** Gateshead in 1936 before the removal of its booster. (Real Photographs/ MLS Collection)

***Above right*: 2171 at** Darlington after removal of the booster but retaining its articulated engine/tender bogie, 21 August 1938. (J.D. Darby/MLS Collection)

727 in its final form without booster stored and awaiting withdrawal at Darlington in January 1943. (MLS Collection)

in February 1934 it ran without the booster until it was refitted in April 1935. With the introduction of the A4s in 1935 and more A3s available also, there was no need for the booster and 2171's was removed finally in December 1936 and 727's in February 1937. Both engines retained their larger boiler, but the removal of the boosters reduced the total engine and tender weight to 131 tons 13 cwt. Both were withdrawn early compared with the conventional C7s, 2171 in April 1942 and 727 in January 1943. They retained their articulated tenders until withdrawal which were then rebuilt with a normal six-wheel underframe and coupled with new B1s, 1038 and 1039.

Operation

Both locomotives were allocated to Gateshead after rebuilding with the booster equipment and operated mainly on the Newcastle–Edinburgh route. This included the heavy night services and performance on the road seems to have been very satisfactory. Unlike 4419, the riding of the locomotives seems to have been smooth and the boiler coped with the extra demands from the booster used on starting and on the climbs to Cockburnspath though not initially. In the first year, however, the booster could only be used on starting and above 45 per cent cut-off and full regulator, which caused excessively fierce exhaust and a drop in steam pressure. The cam gear was altered to be cut in at 35-40 per cent cut-off which enabled the booster to be utilised more frequently on the banks. Records exist which prior to this modification showed the booster only used on starting when it did give improved acceleration but was rarely used on Cockburnspath bank even when speed dropped to the mid-20s.

The modification on 727 was found to be effective on a run on the Newcastle–York mail in March 1932 when the ability to use the booster at 35 per cent cut-off allowed its operation for four minutes after leaving both Newcastle and Durham. In July 1932, after a successful northbound run to Edinburgh, 727 returned with 321 tons and after a stop at Dunbar, the booster was used on starting at 35 per cent cut-off. Approaching Cockburnspath the cut-off was set at 25 per cent and the booster unused until halfway up the 1 in 96 bank when speed had dropped significantly, and then the cut-off was advanced to 35 per cent and the booster cut in. The engine responded and began accelerating on the bank and the summit before Grantshouse was passed at over 35mph. There seem to be few records of 2171's performance and 727 seems to have been the better of the pair in both performance, reliability and availability.

After the boosters had been removed following the transfer of sufficient Pacifics to cover all express turns north of Newcastle, both C9s were transferred to Tweedmouth where they acted as standby engines for a year before another transfer to Heaton in 1940, from where they worked secondary expresses, semi-fasts and fast freight and fish trains. Occasionally if availability of the Pacifics was poor, they could be called upon to assist a C7 on an express. 2171 is recorded to have occasionally worked between Newcastle and Carlisle. The building of more V2s and their suitability for the increasingly heavy wartime traffic spelt the death knell for the two C9s which were stored and then withdrawn in 1942/3.

Chapter 6

THE LONDON, BRIGHTON & SOUTH COAST ATLANTICS

The 'H1' Atlantics

Douglas Earle Marsh, Assistant to Ivatt at Doncaster, was appointed to the LB&SCR as Locomotive Superintendent on the first of January 1905. He found a large number of locomotives out of action requiring repair, so he gave the Works the priority of maintenance over new construction until the backlog had been addressed. Because of the needs for new construction whilst dealing with the repair situation, he used his GNR contacts to obtain drawings of the Atlantics as a model for the H1 and H2 LB&SCR engines which were his first priorities for new construction. Within four months of arriving at Brighton, he placed a contract with Kitson & Co. to build five Atlantics at a cost of £3,905, sending the contractors the Doncaster drawings of the 'Large Atlantic' suitably amended. The comparative dimensions of the Marsh and GNR Atlantics are shown below. Most significant is the increase in cylinder stroke and even more, the increase in boiler pressure.

	The LB&SCR H1	The GNR C1
Cylinders (2-outside):	18½x26in	18¾x24in
Coupled wheel diameter:	6ft 7½in	6ft 8in
Bogie wheel diameter:	3ft 6in	3ft 8in
Trailing wheel diameter:	3ft 6in	3ft 8in
Stephenson motion with slide valves		Stephenson motion with slide valves
Boiler pressure:	200lb psi	175lb psi
Heating surface:	2,454.5sqft	2,478sqft
Grate area:	31sqft	30.9sqft
Axleweight:	19 tons	20 tons
Weight (Engine):	67 tons	68 tons 6 cwt
(Tender):	39 tons 5 cwt	43 tons 2 cwt
(Total):	106 tons 5 cwt	111 tons 8 cwt
Water capacity:	3,112 gallons	3,500 gallons
Coal capacity:	4 tons	6½ tons
Tractive effort:	19,028lb	15,649lb

There were other more obvious differences. The cab and footplate were lengthened, a distinct improvement on the GNR cab, and the engines had screw-reversing instead of lever operation. They had deeper fireboxes and the running plate was curved over the outside cylinders and coupled wheels. They were delivered by Kitson's between December 1905 and February 1906 and numbered 37-41. Initially described as 'B5' class, then 'H-Atlantic', it was designated as class 'H1' in January 1907. They were delivered in grey primer and after initial tests were painted in a new LB&SCR livery of umber with gold lining, with monograms of the company initials added to the splashers at the first repainting. The new Atlantics had a significantly lower fuel consumption than the 'B4' 4-4-0s though more than

Marsh's later superheated 'I3' 4-4-2 tank engines. They were fitted with Westinghouse air brakes.

The one problem experienced by the new Atlantics was a propensity for the trailing axleboxes to overheat, especially on Nos. 37 and 38, but after the problems were identified and sorted the locomotives performed reliably and each ran up annual mileages between 38,000 and 48,000 in 1907 and 1908 with consistent coal consumption figures of 40-42lb per mile. Hasler speed recorders were acquired in 1908 and fitted to 39-41 in 1909. Marsh's successor, Billinton, proposed to fit Schmidt superheaters to the H1s in 1920, but the Locomotive Committee turned the plan down despite the promised improved efficiency and they were not superheated until Maunsell and the Southern Railway Board approved the expenditure in 1925 and the five engines received the superheaters between December 1925 and December 1927. The heating surface was then reduced to 2,283.5sqft with 337sqft of superheating and the boiler pressure was reduced to 170lb psi to reduce boiler maintenance, the potential reduction in performance being offset by superheating. Maunsell fitted his own design of superheater to the H1s between 1934 and 1939. The revised heating surface was 2,491.5sqft including 460sqft of superheating. In 1935 the cabs and boiler fittings were altered to fit the Southern Railway composite loading gauge as follows – chimney replaced by an Ashford 'U1' pattern, dome cover lowered, safety valves shortened, cab roof lowered and buffer beam ends cut to reduced width. After electrification of the Brighton line in 1933, the Atlantics were found new work including the heavy Newhaven boat trains which often required piloting. As a result the 'H1' boilers were upgraded back to 200lb psi

In 1925 as part of a new Southern Railway locomotive naming policy, the H1s were named and painted in the SR green livery: 37 *Selsey Bill,* 38 *Portland Bill,* 39 *Hartland Point,* 40 *St Catherine's Point,* and 41 *Peveril Point.* For a short time in 1913 39 had been named *La France,* when it hauled the train for the visiting French President, but this was only temporary. At the Grouping ex-LB&SCR locomotives had 2000 added to their former numbers.

LB&SCR No.40 as built in February 1906 and with the Company's initials entwined as a monogram on the splashers placed there at the first repainting in 1907, seen at Brighton in 1907 or 1908. (Locomotive Publishing Co./MLS Collection)

No.38 at Brighton, the monogram on the splashers replaced by the Company's coat of arms, c1912. (MLS Collection)

***Above left*: The fifth** LB&SCR Atlantic No.41, also at Brighton shed, c1912. (MLS Collection)

Above right*: 2040 *St Catherine's *Point* at New Cross shed, 16 April 1939. It is seen after the boiler mountings and cab had been reduced in size to fit the Southern Railway's composite loading gauge and as repainted in February 1939 in the Bulleid dark green livery. (W. Potter/MLS Collection)

Below*: 2038 *Portland *Bill* at Eastleigh, 11 June 1949. 2038 was the only H1 that was painted in malachite green after the war and is seen here two years before its withdrawal. (J.D. Darby/MLS Collection)

2039 *Hartland* *Point* as rebuilt experimentally in 1947 with sleeve valves and multiple jet blastpipe and wide chimney, seen here at Brighton, 1947. (Real Photographs/ MLS Collection)

The new Bulleid green livery was applied from 1939 initially to 2040 (dark green), then to 2037 (olive green) and 2041 (light green), but after February 1941 wartime plain black was applied to all of them. The first withdrawals took place in the war years, 2040 and 2041 being condemned at the beginning of 1944, both having been in traffic for around a million miles. After the war 2038 was repainted in malachite green and the three remaining 'H1s' became BR property in 1948 and were renumbered 32037-32039. 2039 became the subject of a Bulleid experiment, being fitted in 1947 with sleeve valve gear which Bulleid was intending to fit to his new 'Leader' class. Out-shopped from Brighton Works in November 1947, it had new cylinders, and multiple jet blastpipe and wide chimney. After various trials, it was stored and scrapped in February 1951. Both 32037 and 32038 were also withdrawn in 1951.

Operation

The five Atlantics were all based at Brighton and after running in, were rostered to the main London–Brighton expresses including Pullman services. The basic schedule for the non-stop run over the 50.9 miles was sixty minutes and in June 1907 the run was completed in just 51 minutes 48 seconds, No.38 hauling seven Pullmans and two vans with a tare weight of 228 tons, 240 gross. This was clearly a test run being scrutinised by management as full details were taken by an inspector on the footplate. Cut-off was kept in the 40-50 per cent range and, after the start, the regulator was left half open until Three Bridges was passed when it was fully opened. Speed remained in the mid-50s to that point on the steady climb at 1 in 264, steepening to 1 in 169 in the last mile and a half to Stoats Nest, passed at 53mph, with 66mph then attained down similar grades to Horley. Now working hard, 38 held 59mph on

The sleeve valve engine renumbered in the BR era as 32039, and still retaining its name, *Hartland Point,* seen at Brighton with the prototype 'Leader' in the background, for which the H1 was undergoing the valve gear experiment, 1949. (MLS Collection)

the 1 in 264 through Three Bridges to Balcombe Tunnel and kept steam on, passing Haywards Heath at 78mph and reaching a maximum of 86½mph at Wivelsfield. Speed fell away to 65mph on the last climb to Clayton Tunnel and then it was easy into Brighton. The boiler pressure dropped after Haywards Heath, but that did not matter as the terminus was near. A maximum of 1,400 indicated horse power was calculated over the last two miles on the 1 in 169 to Stoats Nest.

A more normal routine run was described in a 1908 *Railway Magazine* article when 38 had the 11am Victoria–Brighton *Sunday Pullman* as its task. The gross load was 250 tons and the run with two severe p-way slowings at Stoats Nest and Clayton Tunnel made the train's arrival three minutes late in 63 minutes 8 seconds (net 56 minutes). Clapham Junction was passed in 6 minutes 8 seconds and the 1 in 166 to Wandsworth was climbed at 47mph and the 1 in 94 through Balham brought the speed down to 40mph. 53-54mph was maintained up the 1 in 264 to Thornton Heath, the 1 in 100/165 to the Quarry Tunnel causing a drop to 45mph minimum before the first 10mph p-way restriction, which lost the chance of high speed down to Horley. 38 accelerated the train from 45mph through Earlswood to 53mph on the climb to Balcombe Tunnel and 72½mph was the maximum down through Haywards Heath. No.40 was on the return *Sunday Pullman* that day and ran the 50.9 miles in 54½ minutes, passing Haywards Heath (13 miles) in 15 minutes 5 seconds despite a moderate p-way slowing at Wivelsfield. After that it was

***Above*: No.37 with** a London–Brighton express including two Pullman cars, at Balham, c1908. (F. Moore/MLS Collection)

***Below*: No.38 leaving** Brighton with a London train, c1912. (MLS Collection)

unchecked and ran at a remarkably even speed with nothing over 65mph and the long climbs of 1 in 264 taken at an exceptional 60-62mph.

Pullman cars were included in the weekday expresses, usually a couple amid the standard stock. One exceptionally popular and heavy train was the 8.45am Brighton – London Bridge which had eleven coaches including two Pullmans through to London Bridge, slipping two coaches and another Pullman at East Croydon for Victoria. This schedule and load (392 tons) was regular for the 1909/10 period when rostered for an H1 Atlantic. No.39 was the 'star' engine in the early years before the superheated H2 Atlantics were built, and was used for George V's Coronation Naval Review at Portsmouth in June 1911.

No.37 was involved in a number of potentially dangerous incidents, two on Brighton shed in 1906 and 1908 and in 1914 a heavy collision with the stock of the 6.5pm London train when it backed on at Brighton station. Most serious was the fracture of the tyre of one of the coupled wheels at speed on the *Southern Pullman* in 1919 but luck and prompt actions by the crew avoided complete derailment of the train. No.40 was the train engine when the last six vehicles of the 3.40pm Brighton–Victoria Pullman became derailed at Stoats Nest killing seven people, five of whom were passengers in a coach that swung broadside and slammed into the platform ramp. No. 40, however, had remained on the track and was undamaged.

When six new superheated Atlantics (class H2) were built in the autumn of 1911, they shared the Brighton line work with the H1s, and the latter began more frequent working to Newhaven, Eastbourne, Bognor and Portsmouth. The *Railway Magazine* published an account of a run to Portsmouth in one of C.J. Allen's articles in 1913.

Victoria–Fratton, c1913

39, 145 tons

11.35am Victoria–Portsmouth

Miles	Location	Times	Speed		Gradients
0	Victoria	00.00		T	
	Grosvenor Bridge	-	36		1/64 R
2.6	Clapham Junction	05.45	40*		
8.6	Mitcham	16.10	25*		
15.6	Epsom	26.45	39.6 ave		1/86 R, undulating, 1/100 R
	Leatherhead	-	60		1/112, 1/128 F
23.9	Dorking	37.15	25*		
28.8	Holmwood summit	-	36		1/100 R
	Warnham	-	64½		1/90 F
37.4	Horsham	54.55	20*		
	Arundel Junction	-	15*		L
	Barnham	-	30*		L
69.1	Chichester	91.50	51.5 ave from Horsham		L
77.9	Havant	103.00	47.3 ave/15*	2 E	L
81.7	Fratton	107.25	sigs	¼ L	

No speeds were quoted for the long level stretch from Arundel Junction through Chichester but taking the permanent speed restrictions at the junction and Barnham into account, the maximum is likely to have been between 65 and 70mph.

The same locomotive, 39, was recorded in the article with a run on the *Southern Belle* Pullman train:

Victoria–Brighton, c1913

39, 165 tons

The Southern Belle

Miles	Location	Times	Speed		Gradients
0	Victoria	00.00		T	1/64 R, L
2.6	Clapham Junction	05.50	pws 10*		
6.9	Streatham Common	-	56½		1/186 R, L, 1/264 R
8.8	Thornton Heath	-	sigs		
10.6	East Croydon	17.05		1 L	
13.6	Purley	20.35			
15.1	Coulsdon North	-	pws		1/264 R
18.8	Quarry	-	40*		1/264 R
21.9	Earlswood	31.55	65		1/200 F
29.6	Three Bridges	39.45	60		1/264 R
31.9	Balcombe Tunnel Box	-	58½		1/264 R
34.1	Balcombe	44.40	pws 5*		
38	Haywards Heath	48.00			1/264 F
41	Wivelsfield	-	75		1/264 F
41.2	Keymer Junction	50.40			
45	Clayton Tunnel	-	60		1/264 R
49.5	Preston Park	58.48	68½		1/264 F
50.9	Brighton	61.00	(54 net)	1 L	

Despite three severe p-way slacks and a signal check at Thornton Heath, the engine and driver did well in the second half of the run to arrive only a minute late.

The *Railway Magazine* ran another article about performance on the Brighton line in November 1922 when loads were considerably more than pre-war, although the one hour schedule to Brighton was unchanged. 41 found itself with a heavy load of 330 tons gross on the *Southern Belle* earlier that year and would have just made the hour had it not been for signal checks at Balham and Battersea Park.

		Brighton – Victoria, c1922 **41, 315/330 tons** ***The Southern Belle***			
Miles	**Location**	**Times**	**Speed**		**Gradients**
0	Brighton	00.00		T	
1.3	Preston Park	04.05			1/264 R
4.7	Clayton Tunnel	09.05	48½		1/264 R
7	Hassocks	11.25			1/264 F
9.7	Keymer Junction	13.45		¾ E	L
	Wivelsfield	-	75		1/264 F
12.9	Haywards Heath	16.20			1/330 R
16.8	Balcombe	20.20			1/264 R
19	Balcombe Tunnel	22.40	56½		1/264 R
21.3	Three Bridges	24.30	sigs 20*	½ E	1/264 F
24.9	Horley	28.05	70½		1/264 F
29	Earlswood	34.50	sigs 44*		1/264 R
32.1	Quarry	39.10	44	3 L	1/200 R
35.9	Coulsdon North	43.35		3½ L	1/165 F
37.3	Purley	44.50	69		1/264 F
40.5	East Croydon	47.35	60*		1/264 F
46	Balham	55.25	sigs		L, 1/94 F
48.2	Clapham Junction	59.25		4½ L	
49.6	Battersea Park	62.05	sigs		
50.9	Victoria	65.00	(58 net)	5 L	

2040 ***St Catherine's*** *Point* at Victoria at the head of the *Sunday Pullman* to Brighton, c1930. (MLS Collection)

The Brighton line was busy with military traffic during the First World War, but both sets of Atlantics remained on top express work until the mid-1920s when the six-wheeled tender 'King Arthurs' and the 'River' 2-6-4 tanks took over much of the Brighton line top link work. Some of the Atlantics were then moved from Brighton to Eastbourne and Bognor sheds. Their most important work remained the Newhaven boat trains, which could load heavily – indeed one

Atlantic coped with a 484 ton boat train in the summer of 1939. After the electrification to Brighton in 1933, the H1s were all transferred to Eastbourne. This did not last long and 2038 and 2039 were transferred to Newhaven and 2037, 2040 and 2041 moved to New Cross.

The 'H2' Atlantics

Marsh resigned in 1911 with ill health and L. Billinton was Acting Locomotive Superintendent for a few months before it was clear Marsh could not return and so he was appointed permanently to the post. Marsh had built a couple of 4-6-2 express tanks in 1910 which he might have standardised as the company's express engines, but they were still undergoing trials and the correction of teething problems, so Billinton and the Locomotive Committee decided that the extra express locomotives needed should be a superheated version of the H1. Six locomotives, 421-426, were constructed at Brighton Works between June 1911 and January 1912 at a cost of £3,265 each. Their dimensions that were different to the H1 Atlantics were:

Cylinders (2-outside):	21x 26in
Boiler pressure:	170lb psi (200lb psi later)

Stephenson motion with 10in piston valves

Heating surface:	2,528.5sqft (incl 479sqft of superheating)
Axleload:	19¾ tons
Weight (Engine):	69 tons 15 cwt
Water capacity:	3,500 gallons
Tractive effort:	20,840lb (24,518lb later)

423 as built in the autumn of 1911 and before painting in LB&SCR Livery. (MLS Collection)

421 entered service in a grey livery lined black and white and 422, 424-426 in unlined grey while 423 ran the initial 1,000 miles in only red oxide undercoat.

The superheated locomotives gave excellent service immediately, based as they were on the successful H1s. They were estimated to have a fuel economy of around 10-12 per cent compared with the H1s though Billinton was expecting more, complaining that they were being driven at high fixed cut-off with regulator adjusted, whereas the H1 driving method was to use full regulator and adjust the cut-off. Like the H1s, they accumulated respectable annual mileages between 32,000 and 42,000 in 1912, 426 accumulating over 47,000 in 1913. Annual coal consumption in 1912 was between 35.9 and 37.1lb per mile. By the time of the Grouping in 1923, the H2 Atlantics had run between 292,000 miles (424) and 363,580 (426). Like all former LB&SCR engines, they had 2000 added to their numbers. Their umber livery

421 as built in June 1911 and after its repainting in LB&SCR livery with the company's initials as monograms on the splashers. The short cab roof was quickly extended as seen here. (F. Moore/MLS Collection)

424 at Brighton with the company's coat of arms as the splasher monograms, c1913. (MLS Collection)

was replaced by Southern Railway dark green, but not until 1926/7 for 2425 and 2423 respectively. In 1925, like the H1s, they were selected for naming with the theme being continued:

2421	*South Foreland*
2422	*North Foreland*
2423	*The Needles*
2424	*Beachy Head*
2425	*Trevose Head*
2426	*St Alban's Head*

B424 repainted in Southern green livery in September 1924 and before naming in 1926. (MLS Collection)

The H2s, like the H1s, exchanged their Schmidt superheaters for ones designed by Maunsell between 1935 and 1938 and had their boiler fixtures and cab modified to fit the SR composite loading gauge between 1935 and 1937. The H2s had their boiler pressure increased to 200lb psi, 2426 as early as 1936, 2424 and 2425 in 1938, 2423 in 1939 and 2421 and 2422 in 1940. Bulleid introduced new liveries in 1939, 2423 appearing in olive green, 2421, 2422 and 2425 in dark green, but all became wartime black from February 1941 onwards. After the war, 2423 was painted in malachite green in June 1945, whilst 2422, 2424 and 2426 retained unlined black after their first post-war Works overhaul. All the H2s had, however, received the malachite green livery by October 1947. After nationalisation in 1948 all except

2423, which was withdrawn with badly cracked frames in 1949, received the new BR numbers, at first retaining the malachite green livery and later the BR mixed traffic lined black livery between 1949 (32421) and September 1951 (32424).

In 1955 the Eastern Region 'W1' 60700 derailed because of flaws in the bogie frame and the surviving H2s were taken out of traffic for they had similar bogie frame designs. 32421 and 32426 were withdrawn without re-entering service and 32422 and 32425 both returned to traffic on restricted duties but were soon withdrawn also, leaving just 32424 in traffic. It survived a visit to Eastleigh Works in August 1956 and it was finally withdrawn in April 1958, although it is being replicated with a new build '32424' by the preservation movement.

***Above left*: 2422 *North* ***
Foreland at Stewarts Lane, 22 September 1947. (J.D. Darby/MLS Collection)

***Above right*:**
2424 *Beachy* *Head* and B4X 2056 at New Cross Gate shed, 21 May 1948. (MLS Collection)

32425 *Trevose* *Head* at Newhaven depot with H1 2038 *Portland Bill*, 28 August 1949. (A.C. Gilbert/MLS Collection)

Operation

The initial allocation of the H2 Atlantics was:

Brighton:	421, 425
Battersea:	422, 426
Eastbourne:	423, 424

They were of course allocated to the best expresses and their performance was excellent. They still shared duties with the H1s, the two Pacific and the Baltic tanks, but there were now enough express engines ably assisted by the I3 4-4-2 tank engines to relegate the B4 4-4-0s to secondary services. The Cecil J. Allen article of December 1913 quoted a run by one of the new H2 Atlantics on the *Southern Belle,* a diagram it shared with the Brighton allocated H1 Atlantics.

This was a typical rather than an exceptional performance and with the same energy over the last dozen or so miles displayed by 39 and its driver in the log quoted earlier, an on time arrival could easily have been achieved with a net time of 56 minutes or less. 425 and its driver were more energetic on the 8.35pm from Victoria with a heavier load of 205 tons. East Croydon was passed in 14 minutes 21 seconds and 425 actually accelerated from 55mph through Purley to 60mph at Quarry Tunnel, passed in 23 minutes 53 seconds (18.8 miles) at the summit of the ten miles of 1 in 264 gradient from Streatham Common. With time well in hand, 425 was eased and arrived at its Haywards Heath stop 2½ minutes early. 422 on the 12.20pm *Southern Belle* up from Brighton had 175 tons and maintained 47mph on the initial 1 in 264 to Clayton Tunnel, 69 in the dip through Burgess Hill, 51½ at Balcombe Tunnel and 74 through Horley. The 32 miles to Quarry Tunnel, passed at 53mph, took exactly 36 minutes but there was then a two mile p-way slack and despite 66mph through East Croydon, another p-way check and signal slowings from Clapham Junction, arrival was 1¼ minutes late, net 56 minutes.

424 was timed on the 2.25pm from Eastbourne to Victoria with 305 tons and after 66mph though Glynde, slowed for Lewes (11.5 miles) in 13 minutes 40 seconds and averaged 46mph over the following 9½ uphill miles (mostly 1 in 143/145) to Keymer Junction. The climb to Balcombe tunnel was maintained at 50mph for most of the way, a slip near the summit reducing the final speed to 47½mph. 64mph through Horley was average and speed fell away to only 36mph at Quarry Tunnel suggesting that steam pressure may have been dropping from its earlier efforts. There was then another long p-way slack and arrival at East Croydon was 3¼ minutes late. The load was reduced to 210 tons there after a portion for London Bridge had been detached and with another stop at Clapham Junction, a minute was recovered to Victoria.

The logs of two up runs were published in a *Railway Magazine* article of 1915, one with the 12.20pm Brighton *Southern Belle Pullman* and one with the 5pm Brighton, the second run unusually free of p-way and signal checks.

Victoria–Brighton, c1913

425, 160 tons

The Southern Belle

Miles	Location	Times	Speed		Gradients
0	Victoria	00.00		T	1/64 R, L
2.6	Clapham Junction	-	40*		
4.7	Balham	07.50			1/168 R
10.6	East Croydon	14.55	sigs	1 E	L
15.1	Coulsdon North	-	sigs		1/264 R
18.8	Quarry Tunnel	26.45			
26	Horley	-	69		1/264 F
29.6	Three Bridges	37.30	60		1/264 R
31.9	Balcombe Tunnel Box	-	51		1/264 R
41	Wivelsfield	48.55	69		
45	Clayton Tunnel	-	50		1/264 R
49.5	Preston Park	-	v. slow in		1/264 F
50.9	Brighton	61.00	(58 net)	1 L	

		Brighton–Victoria, c1914						
		422			425			
		175 tons			290 tons			
		12.20pm *Southern Belle*			5pm Brighton			
Miles	Location	Times	Speed		Times	Speed		Gradients
0	Brighton	00.00		T	00.00		T	
0.7	Preston Park	03.00			03.35			1/264 R
	Clayton	-	45		-	47		1/264 R
7.1	Hassocks	10.30			10.47			1/264 R
9.7	Keymer Junction	12.55		T	13.13		¼ L	
	Wivelsfield	-	65		-	73		1/264 F
12.9	Haywards Heath	15.55			15.50			
16.8	Balcombe	20.20	51½		19.51	54		1/264 R
21.3	Three Bridges	25.10		¼ L	24.31		½ E	1/264 F
25	Horley	28.15	74		27.31	72		1/264 F
29	Earlswood	32.20			31.32			1/264 R
32.1	Quarry Tunnel	36.00	53/pws	T	35.10	46	¾ E	1/200 R
37.3	Purley	45.10	67		40.52	66		1/264 F
40.4	East Croydon	48.00		3 L	43.45		1¼ E	
48.2	Clapham Junction	57.00		2 L	52.21		2½ E	
50.9	Victoria	61.15	(58½ net)	1¼ L	56.30		3½ E	

The second run is clearly the superior, making better time with a significantly heavier load. One can feel that the driver of 422 might have made a little more effort earlier in the run to have time in hand to compensate for the planned engineering work at Quarry, and then made a punctual arrival.

Towards the end of the First World War, the two London based engines joined their sisters at Brighton. This allocation remained static until the Grouping, by which time the H1s had run over half a million miles in traffic

426 on a Victoria–Brighton express, c1912. (F. Moore/MLS Collection)

and most of the H2s well in excess of 300,000. Regular loads had increased but the Atlantics were still expected to keep the 60 minute Brighton schedules. A couple of logs were published in a *Railway Magazine* article in 1922, one of which was by an H2 which maintained the quality of the 1914 run of 425:

Brighton–Victoria, c1922

422

290/305 tons

Miles	Location	Times	Speed		Gradients
0	Brighton	00.00		T	
1.3	Preston Park	03.40			1/264 R
4.7	Clayton	-	45		1/264 R
7.1	Hassocks	11.15			1/264 R
9.7	Keymer Junction	13.45		¾ L	
	Wivelsfield	-	71½		1/264 F
12.9	Haywards Heath	16.25			
16.8	Balcombe	20.20	57		1/264 R
19	Balcombe Tunnel	22.40	56½		1/264 R
21.3	Three Bridges	24.55		T	1/264 F
25	Horley	27.50	75		1/264 F
29	Earlswood	31.55			1/264 R
32.1	Quarry Tunnel	34.55	53/45	1 E	1/200 R
37.3	Purley	40.30	69/sigs		1/264 F
40.4	East Croydon	44.05		1 E	
46	Balham	51.20	sigs		
48.2	Clapham Junction	56.00		1 L	
49.3	Battersea Park	59.30	sigs		
50.9	Victoria	64.00	(56½ net)	4 L	

The Central Section of the Southern received an allocation of six-wheeled tender 'King Arthurs' (793-806) in 1926 and the Brighton based engines joined their sisters at Eastbourne or were allocated to Bognor. New train loads for different motive power groups were calculated when new Maunsell corridor stock was introduced in 1930 with the H2s being restricted to six coaches on the West Sussex route to Bognor and ten coaches on the Newhaven boat trains. This caused a flurry of piloting in the first month, followed by a reduction in the formations, but the H2s soon found these precautions unnecessary and the Atlantics were soon trusted to take the former heavier loads unassisted.

The Brighton line was electrified in 1933 and the H2 allocation at Eastbourne was 2421 and 2422 with the other four at Bognor, where they monopolised the main London expresses until 1938. 2421 and 2422 with the remaining H1s at Eastbourne were replaced by 'Schools' 910-916, the two H2s then moving to New Cross with the two H1s going to Newhaven for the boat trains. Further electrification of the Portsmouth and Bognor routes in the late 1930s displaced the Atlantics once more with 'Schools' and 'King Arthurs' being found regularly on the Newhaven boat trains and tests were made with firstly 2041, then 2423, on the former South Eastern Chatham route. 2423 successfully worked the 12.35pm Victoria–Ramsgate 'returning on the 8.13pm Ramsgate' and as a result 2421, 2423, 2425 and 2426 were all allocated at Battersea in the summer of 1938 for the Victoria–Kent Coast expresses. 2039 and 2424 had then returned to the Newhaven boat trains and gave satisfaction with ever increasing train loads, though when the formation grew to thirteen coaches plus luggage vans, an ex-SE&CR 4-4-0 would be called upon to assist. Performance was assisted by the upgrading of the H2 boilers to 200lb psi in line with that of the H1s.

B422 on a Brighton–Victoria express, between Clayton Tunnel and Burgess Hill, with the South Downs in the background, c1924. (Real Photographs/ MLS Collection)

***Below left*: B423 at** speed with the *Southern Belle* Pullman train, c1925. (Railway Photographs/ MLS Collection)

***Below right*:** B426 departing from Brighton with the *Southern Belle* Pullman train, c1924. (MLS Collection)

2421 *South* *Foreland* with a Bognor–Victoria train, c1928. (Real Photographs/MLS Collection)

2422 *North* *Foreland* and B4 2053 on arrival at Victoria with a heavy boat train from Newhaven, c1930. (MLS Collection)

At the outbreak of war, boat train traffic ceased and some were stored while in November 1940 all the H2s were sent to Basingstoke to replace the rebuilt Baltic tanks (the N15X) which had gone on loan to the GWR and LNER for freight working. The heavy wartime loads on the Bournemouth route were proving overtaxing for the Bournemouth based Schools, so Lord Nelsons 850-855, no longer needed for Dover and Folkestone boat trains, displaced a number of Schools, which then in turn cascaded to Basingstoke in place of the H2 Atlantics. The six H2s were then transferred to Ashford, taking over work from former SE&CR 4-4-0s, five 'Ls' at Ashford moving on in turn to Faversham and Ramsgate. The Atlantics were not ideal locomotives for the variety of duties on the heavily graded Chatham route and in 1944 they went back to their original home at Brighton.

2425 *Trevose Head* on wartime freight traffic duty on the South Western main line between Woking and Basingstoke during the period when the H2s were all based at Basingstoke, 28 December 1940. (J.B. Latham/MLS Collection)

2422, 2423 and 2426 joined 2038 for Newhaven boat train work again in 1947 and Brighton's 2421 started on what became a well known Atlantic turn, the 6.10pm Victoria–Oxted–Uckfield having worked up in the morning on

2424 ***Beachy*** *Head* at Bromley in the summer of 1938. (Real Photographs/ MLS Collection)

2425 *Trevose* *Head* departing from Lewes with a Newhaven train, 25 June 1948. (MLS Collection)

the 8.18am Uckfield. The author remembers seeing 2422 and later, 2421, passing through Clapham Junction on the 6.10pm during his first train-spotting trips to London in 1950 and being very impressed as the malachite green Atlantics swept round the curve past the platforms.

2423 and 2425 were at this time regularly working the Newhaven boat trains until May 1949 when the Southern electric locomotives 20001–20003 took over. The Atlantics then appeared regularly on the Brighton–Southampton–Bournemouth route, including on the Brighton–Plymouth daily service. P. Ransome-Wallis described a footplate run he had on 32421 *South Foreland* in 1955 on the 9.40am Brighton–Bournemouth West and 1.50pm return, when the normal power was a Bulleid Light Pacific. The train was eight coaches, very full and nearly 300 tons gross. Along the gently undulating stretch to Fareham, despite full regulator and cut-off varying from 30-40 per cent, 32421 was hard pressed to get the speed higher than 53mph between stops at Worthing and Chichester,

32421 *South* *Foreland* departing from Southampton Central with a Brighton–Bournemouth train, 3 August 1953. (MLS Collection)

the train arriving at Fareham, 47.4 miles, in five minutes over the 70 allowed, just about accounted for by a 20mph restriction at Arundel Junction and a p-way slack to 15mph at Bedhampton. Time was held to Southampton and improved on through the New Forest with 61mph before the Brockenhurst stop and 63½ down the gradient after Hinton Admiral. However, falling boiler pressure and difficulty in restarting from the final stops at New Milton, Christchurch, Pokesdown and Boscombe made the train over nine minutes late at Bournemouth Central. The return train had seventeen stops instead of ten on the outward journey and 32421 managed well to Southampton Central despite seven scheduled stops, with a top speed of 66mph at Lyndhurst Road. A signal stand at Northam Junction cost over three minutes and arrival at Fareham was nearly five minutes late, after falling to 29mph on the 1 in 81 to Swanwick. Station overtime at Fareham shunting a horsebox to the rear and signal checks before Barnham made the train eight minutes late into Brighton despite 64mph before the Worthing stop. With steam pressure dropping to 150lb psi and half regulator and 30 per cent cut-off, 32421 responded better than when pushed harder and actually regained four minutes on the last leg, having left Worthing twelve minutes late.

In the 1950s the remaining Atlantics were popular choices for enthusiast railtours, both 32424 and 32425 being so employed in 1952. Both included runs from London to Brighton on the old 60 minutes non-stop schedule, 32424 going down in 58 minutes 40 seconds (54¾ net) and returning in 60 minutes 14 seconds (54½ net). 32425 in wet windy weather got to Brighton in 61 minutes 24 seconds (59¼ net) and returned in exactly the hour (58 minutes net). Then in 1955 32421 worked the *Hampshireman* from Waterloo to Woking via Staines and back from Redhill to Victoria. In August 1955 32426 worked the

32425 *Trevose* Head at Kensington Olympia with a return South Coast–Leicester & Nottingham holiday express, August 1956. It was withdrawn at the end of that month. (MLS Collection)

32424 climbing Grosvenor Bank out of Victoria with an RCTS special Pullman train, 5 October 1952. (C.C. Herbert/Rail Archive Stephenson/MLS Collection)

Wealden Limited from Lewes to New Cross Gate via Horsted Keynes.

The final runs of the last surviving Atlantic in Great Britain were made by 32424 on the *Sussex Coast Limited* in April 1958, when it ran the 56.8 miles to Newhaven with 255 tons in 81 minutes 11 seconds (70 net) against the 90 minute schedule. From its overhaul in August 1956 until the end of 1957 it frequently worked the Brighton–Bournemouth service, plus Christmas parcel van specials in November/December 1957. On 24 April 1958 it hauled the 7.28am Lancing–Micheldever empty stock train and then ran light to Eastleigh for withdrawal and scrapping.

***Above and right*: Two views** of 32424 *Beachy Head* at Victoria before the departure of its last run on the RCTS special railtour, the *Sussex Coast Ltd*, to Newhaven, 13 April 1958. (MLS & G. Shuttleworth/MLS Collection)

32424 *Beachy Head* on arrival at Newhaven Town, completing the last run of a British Atlantic in active service, 13 April 1958. (MLS Collection)

32424 *Beachy* *Head* back at Brighton shed after its last run. It was withdrawn the following day. Unfortunately efforts to preserve it failed and now some 65 years later progress is being made in building a replica for use on heritage lines and special railtours. (MLS Collection)

Chapter 7

THE NORTH BRITISH ATLANTICS

The North British Railway was in the doldrums at the beginning of the twentieth century. The Midland and the Caledonian railways had introduced heavier rolling stock with new modern facilities and powerful locomotives to pull them. The North British was losing business to the Caledonian's competition on the Glasgow–Edinburgh–Aberdeen routes and was struggling to maintain schedules when taking over Midland trains at Carlisle for the run over the Waverley route. The North British Board, influenced by Dr John Inglis, wanted a new powerful locomotive rather than any rebuilding of earlier 4-4-0s and Reid was instructed to provide one. He submitted two designs – a 3-cylinder compound and a 2-cylinder simple, both 4-4-2 Atlantics as it was thought that the curvature of the NB routes to both Aberdeen and Carlisle would put undue stress on the frames of a 4-6-0.

The 2-cylinder simple version was chosen and the North British Loco Company was contracted to build fourteen powerful Atlantics in 1905, which were delivered in July and August 1906 and were numbered 868–881. Their names were:

868	*Aberdonian*
869	*Dundonian (Bonnie Dundee* after 1912)
870	*Bon-Accord*
871	*Thane of Fife*
872	*Auld Reekie*
873	*Saint Mungo*
874	*Dunedin*
875	*Midlothian*
876	*Waverley*
877	*Liddesdale*
878	*Hazeldean*
879	*Abbotsford*
880	*Tweeddale*
881	*Borderer*

They were given the class identification 'H'. Their main dimensions were:

Cylinder diameter (2-outside):	20x28in (21x28in later)
Coupled wheel diameter:	6ft 9in
Bogie wheel diameter:	3ft 6in
Trailing wheel diameter:	4ft 3in
Boiler pressure:	200lbs psi
Stephenson motion with 10in piston valves	
Heating surface:	2,256.2sqft
Grate area:	28.5sqft
Axleload:	20 tons
Weight (Engine):	74 tons 8 cwt
(Tender):	45 tons 8 cwt
(Total):	119 tons 16 cwt
Water capacity:	4,240 gallons
Coal capacity:	7 tons
Tractive effort:	23,324lb

The design's large outside cylinders and Belpaire firebox were innovations for the NBR and there appears to have been contact between the NB Board, the North British Loco Company and the drawings of the Great Central Robinson Atlantics, as well as tests with Highland Railway and LNWR 4-6-0s. The new Atlantics did not have the immediate success expected. They were late for the newly introduced faster schedules with improved heavier rolling stock and there were immediate complaints about their rolling and oscillation causing concern about safety and also their impact upon track maintenance, a subject about which the Civil Engineer was very vociferous. The Directors called upon Ivatt to investigate

Class 'H' Reid Atlantic 878 *Hazeldean* as constructed by the North British Loco. Co. in August 1906, as seen shortly afterwards at Carlisle Canal dept. (MLS Collection)

881 *Borderer*, also class 'H' built in August 1906, seen around 1908. (F. Moore/MLS Collection)

and after riding on them in the autumn of 1906, he submitted a report suggesting limiting them to a maximum of 55mph in descent of gradients on the severely curved Waverley route and a number of other proposals to reduce their reciprocating weight and stresses. However, the report was mostly favourable. The Board did not accept his recommendations and called on Vincent Raven of the NER to make a similar investigation. Raven travelled on the engines on both NB main routes and also conducted dynamometer tests on the Edinburgh–Newcastle route normally worked by NER engines. He found no fault with them, although he made one or two minor suggestions about blastpipe and piston valve dimensions.

Six further locomotives to the same basic design with a few minor modifications and boiler pressure of 190lbs psi were built by Robert Stephenson & Co. in 1911,

1911 built 'I' class 906 *Teribus*. (MLS Collection)

numbered 901–906, also class 'H'. In 1915 868 and 873 were superheated, 880 and 881 in 1917, 870 and 878 in 1919 and the rest of the first batch in 1920 and 1921. New cylinders, diameter increased to 21in x 28in, were provided. The engines with the larger diameter cylinders were easily recognisable by the flattened cladding of the cylinders to maintain clearances. Two more, 509 and 510, were built by the North British Loco. Co. in 1921 and were equipped with Robinson superheaters from new. Inflation had escalated during the war years and the pair cost £15,450 each, three to four times the pre-war price. The superheated locomotives retained the classification 'H', but those still unsuperheated became class 'I' until so equipped. The heating surface of the superheated engines was 2,188.8sqft (incl 385sqft of superheating). Boiler pressure of all the superheated engines was further reduced to 180lbs psi. The six constructed in 1911 were named:

901	*St.Johnstoun*
902	*Highland Chief*
903	*Cock 'o the North* (renamed *Aberdonian* in 1934 after the naming of P2 2-8-2 2001 and the withdrawal of 9868 in 1933)
904	*Holyrood*
905	*Buccleugh*
906	*Teribus*

The last two built in 1921 were:

509	*Duke of Rothesay*
510	*The Lord Provost*

904 ***Holyrood*** of the 1911 series at Aberdour, c1912. (MLS Collection)

At the Grouping the superheated locomotives were given the class identification of C11, the unsuperheated 901-906 becoming class C10. All had 9 added to their numbers to become LNER 9868-9881, 9509-9510 and 9901-9906. The C10s were all then superheated between November 1923 and June 1925, also becoming class C11. The heating surface of the LNER superheated engines became 2,066sqft with 263sqft of superheating, boilers from 1929 being further modified to give 2,020.65sqft including 241.1sqft of superheating. 9903 was equipped in 1926 with a Worthington feed water heater and pump which was reliable and efficient and was retained by this engine until its withdrawal although no other locomotives were fitted in a similar way.

The locomotives were dual-fitted with vacuum and Westinghouse brakes, though the Westinghouse system was removed between 1930 and 1932. They were liveried in NB bronze green with yellow, red and black lining initially and the LNER apple green with black and white lining from 1923. Initially a couple (874 and 876) had 'L N & E R' on the tender. The new numbers and standard LNER livery were applied to the rest of the class from March 1924, and numbers moved from tender to cabside in 1929, though the C11s retained green livery at a time when the pre-grouping 4-4-0s became lined black.

The 1911 boilers were due for replacement in the early 1930s and a decision was made to withdraw them rather than re-boiler as there were sufficient Pacifics for the main line work and D49s for secondary traffic needs. The first to go was 9874 in May 1933, with 9868 following in September. Just 9873 went at the end of 1934 and another three of the earliest batch in 1935. The rest were withdrawn in 1936 and 1937, 9875 and 9901 the last in December 1937. A late decision was made to preserve 9875, but by the time the order was received most of the engine had been dismantled. It was then rebuilt pending preservation, but the war needs for steel sealed its fate and it was withdrawn a second time in November 1939. Five of the C11 boilers were retained as stationary boilers, four at Cowlairs Works and one (believed to be off 9875) at Stratford. The latter was not taken out of service until 1960.

9509 *Duke of Rothesay*, one of two superheated Reid Atlantics built in 1921, at Aberdeen, Ferryhill shed, September 1930. (J.A.G. Coltas/ MLS Collection)

9510 ***The*** *Lord Provost*, the second 1921 built 'H', at Haymarket, c1928. The flattened cylinder cladding and mechanical lubricator are easily seen in this photograph. (Real Photographs/ MLS Collection)

9903 *Cock o'* *the North,* superheated in 1924 and fitted with the Worthington feed water heater in 1926, at Perth station, c1927. (MLS Collection)

9880 *Tweeddale* in LNER livery, c1925. (MLS Collection)

***Above left*: 1911 built** 9902 *Highland Chief* at Dundee shed, superheated in November 1923 with new 21in cylinders (note the flattened cladding), seen in June 1929. (Photomatic/MLS Collection)

Above right*: 9901 *St. Johnstoun at Aberdeen Ferryhill shed, 9 June 1936. (MLS Collection)

9902 *Highland* *Chief* at Dundee shed, 5 June 1936. (MLS Collection)

Above*: 9876 *Waverley at Aberdeen Ferryhill shed, 28 March 1937. (MLS Collection)

Below left*: 9905 *Buccleugh at Glasgow Eastfield, 16 August 1937. (MLS Collection)

Below right*: 9875 *Midlothian, one of the last three Reid Atlantics remaining in service in July 1937 (the other two were 9901 and 9905), seen here taking water at Perth. 9875 was withdrawn in December 1937, and after part dismantling, was reconstructed in August 1938 pending preservation, only to be scrapped in November 1939 as steel was needed for the war effort. (B. Roberts/MLS Collection)

Operation

The initial allocation of the first fourteen Atlantics was:

Glasgow Eastfield:	868–873
St.Margaret's Edinburgh:	874–879
Carlisle:	880, 881

The Eastfield engines worked expresses to Edinburgh and the Glasgow portions of Aberdeen expresses as far as Dalmeny where they were attached to Edinburgh–Aberdeen trains. In 1907, however, the North British and Caledonian came to an agreement to cut their intense competition between Glasgow and Aberdeen and the number of North British turns to Dalmeny was reduced. The Eastfield allocation was then transferred to Aberdeen. In 1908 the St.Margaret's engines moved to Haymarket with their regular crews (and cleaners!) as the shed facilities were better, apart from 879 which joined 880 and 881 at Carlisle. The Atlantic work was then mainly restricted to the Edinburgh–Aberdeen main line and Edinburgh–Carlisle via the Waverley route. The Edinburgh–Aberdeen diagrams involved a daily return trip, three starting from the Edinburgh end and three with Aberdeen engines.

The first experiences of the new engines were not good. F.E. Charlewood reported a poor run on the 6.30am Aberdeen to Edinburgh in 1907 with 872 and 330 tons which, with a combination of poor operating and sluggish running by the engine, managed to lose 40 minutes. Reports of performance on the Waverley route mentioned very restrained running downhill, unaware of the fact that the civil engineer's concerns had resulted in a speed limit of 55mph being applied to the Atlantics on that route. Complaints were made about loss of time by the Atlantic drivers frequently stopping to take assistant engines or bankers rather than risk losing a couple of minutes when load was near (but under) the limit. It would appear that the caution of some drivers with the new substantially bigger engines, a shortage of experienced firemen and the doubts raised by the vociferously critical civil engineer caused an initial lack of confidence in the new engines.

Between 1908 and 1910 the Reid Atlantics were involved in a number of exchange trials, partly as a result of the initial problems and the involvement of Henry Ivatt and Vincent Raven – the other engines involved in the comparative trials were the NER 4CC Atlantics (one of which failed at Hawick after uncontrolled slipping), Midland compound 1032, a Highland Railway 'Castle' 4-6-0, and in 1910 a test between Carlisle and Preston, with Carlisle's 881 in comparison with an LNWR 'Experiment' 4-6-0, 1483 *Redgauntlet*. Whilst apparently none of the other railways' engines impressed, the coal consumption figures of the NB engines were high (as much as 71lb per mile on the LNWR route) and tests with different types of coal at the same time revealed coal consumption varying between 47lb and 61lb per mile.

880 *Tweeddale* was recorded on a 195 ton Edinburgh–Carlisle train in 1908 which struggled on the 11½ mile 1 in 70 climb to Falahill, falling to 27mph and taking over half an hour to pass the summit (18 miles from Edinburgh). However, the performance improved and the 11 miles from Hawick to Whitrope Tunnel, the last three at 1 in 75, were cleared in 20½ minutes, speed 33mph minimum. Speed was 60mph maximum on the descent from Whitrope, constrained by the temporary limit imposed on the Atlantics and unknown to Charlewood. His successor in the *Railway Magazine's* articles, J.F. Gairns, reported a much better run on the 12.45pm Carlisle with the same locomotive in 1909 when the driver, given the incentive of a 3½ minute late start from Carlisle, gained time steadily on both major climbs and would have arrived early in Edinburgh but for signal checks outside Waverley station. 879 *Abbotsford* with 120 tons on the 9.30am Edinburgh got to Galashiels (33½ miles) in 48 minutes 35 seconds with a minimum of 28½mph on the 1 in 70 to Corbridge, accelerating to 34mph on the 1 in 111 easing through Fushiebridge and topping the 1 in 100 at Falahill Box at 36mph. 875 *Midlothian* with 190 tons on the 6.11pm from Carlisle ran the 25 miles to Newcastleton in 31½ minutes with 34½mph maintained on the 1 in 100 to Penton. The 21.2 miles on to Hawick took 35½ minutes, with 32mph sustained on the 1 in 75 ten mile climb to Whitrope Box. After stops at Melrose and Galashiels, 875 passed Falahill Box, 18 uphill miles from Galashiels culminating in 1 in 100, in 24 minutes 50 seconds at 36mph. C.J. Allen, in his articles a couple of years later after describing runs with 878 and 879 on the Waverley route, wrote 'These records serve to show the excellent work that Mr Reid's engines can be depended upon to perform'.

Despite the initial doubts, a further six class 'H' Atlantics were built in 1911 and these were all allocated at first to St.Margaret's for services to Carlisle and Perth. However, 905 and 906 were transferred to Carlisle, making a fleet of five there. They took over nearly all of the through working of the Midland Railway trains to Edinburgh and in the First World War, the Naval leave train (Euston–Thurso and return) between Carlisle and Edinburgh with the assistance of a superheated 'Scott' (D30) cut inside. At Edinburgh the Atlantic was replaced by a second Perth based 'Scott' for the run to that city before the Highland Railway assumed command there.

The April 1917 *Railway Magazine* published some interesting accounts of Reid Atlantic performance over the Waverley route during the war. Firstly, a couple of logs of Edinburgh–Carlisle day trains, with both superheated and unsuperheated 1906 built Atlantics.

Edinburgh Waverley – Carlisle, 1916

		868 *Aberdonian* (superheated 5/15) **170 tons** **9.30am Edinburgh**			**869 *Bonnie Dundee*** (unsuperheated) **275 tons** **10.30am Edinburgh**			
Miles	**Location**	**Times**	**Speed**		**Times**	**Speed**		**Gradients**
0	Edinburgh	00.00		T	00.00		T	1/78 F
3	Portobello	05.35	53	½ L	07.00	sigs	2 L	L
8	Eskbank	13.25	sigs/pws		15.00	att banker		1/70 R
12	Gorebridge	19.40	38		25.30	30		1/70 R
18	Falahill	32.50	27/23½		37.30	30 det banker		1/70/100 R
					38.15			
22.6	Fountainhall	38.10	52		44.15	46/55		1/100/150 F
29.8	Bowland	45.50	57		51.30	60		1/175 F
33.5	Galashiels	50.00	**	1 E	55.45		4½ L	
		51.30		½ L	00.00		4½ L	
37.2	Melrose	56.40			06.00		4½ L	
40.6	St Boswell's	60.20		3¼ L	06.45		4¼ L	
45.2	Belses	65.40	53/65		07.30			1/120 R/1/120 F
52.9	Hawick	73.10	**	1¾ E	17.00		4¼ L	
		76.00		1 L	00.00	banker	5 L	
56.7	Stobs	85.30	32½		08.00	35		1/80 R
59.9	Shankend	91.00	40½		13.30	38½		1/117/121 R
63.7	Whitrope	98.00	32/30	2 E	20.30	30 (banker off)	½ L	1/75 R
65.9	Riccarton Jcn	100.40	50	3¼ E	23.00	55	1 E	1/80 F
74	Newcastleton	109.45	55	3¼ E	32.30	60	½ E	1/75 F
81.6	Penton	117.15	65	3¾ E	40.30	60	1½ E	undulating
84.2	Riddings	120.00	pws		43.15	58		1/100 F
88.6	Longtown	125.35		3½ E	47.45		1¼ E	L
93.8	Harker	130.45	60		53.00	58		
98.2	Carlisle	137.05		3 E	59.15		¾ E	

** Conditional stops.

902 *Highland Chief* and 906 *Teribus* were noted on the night sleeper to St Pancras towards the end of 1916. 902 got its 225 tons to Galashiels in exactly 50 minutes, a minute early (49 net), with a minimum of 27mph on the climb to Falahill. *Teribus* had a 265 ton load and took assistance in the form of NBR 4-4-0 321 to Falahill reached in 29½ minutes, minimum speed 30mph. After a 1¾ minute stop to detach the pilot, 906 easily made Galashiels in 49¼ minutes, 1¾ minutes early. In all the runs described, the Atlantics were still descending the steep winding gradients exceedingly cautiously, dropping the odd minute from the gains they made on the climbs.

In the other direction. I show in the table below two runs around the similar date, 878 *Hazeldean* with 240 tons on a day train and 902 *Highland Chief* leaving Carlisle at 4.28am on the 9.30pm sleeper train from St Pancras.

		Carlisle–Edinburgh Waverley, 1916						
		878 *Hazeldean*			**902 *Highland Chief***			
		240 tons			**220 tons**			
Miles	**Location**	**Times**	**Speed**		**Times**	**Speed**		**Gradients**
0	Carlisle	00.00		T	00.00		T	
4.4	Harker	07.30			07.13			
9.6	Longtown	12.30		½ E	12.16		¾ E	L
14	Riddings	17.30			17.30			1/100 R
16.6	Penton	21.45	36½	¼ E	21.31	39	½ E	1/100 R
24.2	Newcastleton	32.00	50	T	30.55	54	1 E	
28.8	Steele Road	40.30	36		39.09	33½		1/70 R
32.3	Riccarton Jcn	47.30	31½	2½ E	48.10	23	1¾ E	1/70 R
34.5	Whitrope	51.30	33	2½ E	53.40	24	¼ E	1/96 R
38.3	Shankend	56.30	50		58.05	55		1/75 F
45.3	Hawick	65.15	30*	1¾ E	66.45		¼ E	
53	Belses	75.30			11.37			1/175R, 1/120F
57.6	St Boswell's	80.15	60	¾ E	16.25		1½ E	
61	Melrose	83.45	58		07.41			L
64.7	Galashiels	88.00	30*	1 E	10.40		¼ E	
68.4	Bowland	94.15			07.41			1/155/99 R
71.5	Stow	98.15	46		11.52	44		1/175 R
75.6	Fountainhall	103.15	49		17.02	47½		1/150 R
80.2	Falahill	109.45	42½	3¼ E	24.02	39½	2 E	1/100 R
86.2	Gorebridge	116.15	60		30.39	55		1/70 F
90.2	Eskbank	121.00	50		35.02	55	2 E	1/70 /228 F
95.2	Portobello	127.45		2¼ E	41.05		2 E	1/80 F
98.2	Edinburgh W	133.45		1¼ E	45.50		2¼ E	

876 *Waverley* on an Aberdeen–Edinburgh express near Aberdour c1911. (G.M. Shoults/ MLS Collection)

901 *St Johnstoun* had the Edinburgh portion of the 8.02pm from St Pancras, a lightweight 110 tons, and skipped up the ten miles of 1 in 75 to Whitrope Tunnel in 16¼ minutes (ave 37mph), entering the tunnel at 38mph. With nothing more than 55mph on the descent, it arrived in Hawick nearly five minutes early. It then stopped at St Boswell's and Melrose and arrived punctually at Galashiels, where the load was made up to 240 tons. It passed Falahill in 24¾ minutes, just under schedule at 36mph and arrived at Edinburgh Waverley a couple of minutes early.

In 1919, the working hours of the crews were reduced to an eight hour day, necessitating a change of engines at Dundee if the engines were to retain their regular crews and three of Aberdeen's allocation – 868, 869 and 902 – were

St.Margaret's 901 *St Johnstoun* near Carlisle with an Edinburgh–Carlisle train made up of Midland Railway heavy bogie coaches, c1912. (MLS Collection)

transferred to Dundee to pick up the morning starters from Edinburgh. There was just one through working from Edinburgh to Aberdeen daily on a stopping service worked on alternate days by Haymarket's 874 and 876, their crews lodging in Aberdeen overnight. The two new Atlantics built in 1921 were allocated respectively to Dundee and St Margaret's, 509 sharing the Dundee–Aberdeen and Dundee–Edinburgh turns, whilst 510 ran two return trips to Perth every day for a prolonged period.

Changes took place at the Grouping. Former railway demarcation lines disappeared and St Margaret's men learned the road to Tweedmouth and Newcastle. After a test run with 510 between Edinburgh and Newcastle in October 1922, 510 joined the

1911 built 'H' Atlantic 904 *Holyrood* runs into Aberdour with the Edinburgh–Aberdeen stopping service, C1912. (G.M. Shoults/MLS Collection)

874 *Dunedin* runs into Edinburgh Waverley station with an express from Aberdeen, 6 August 1911. (G.M. Shoults/MLS Collection)

Haymarket stud and 877, 878 and 510 began regular working south of Edinburgh on East Coast expresses from May 1923. In 1923 trials of GN, NE and NB Atlantics between Newcastle and Edinburgh took place, on both booked and special test trains, the NB representative being 878 which compared well in the running with the C1 and C7, although the coal consumption was heavier. 9902 *Highland Chief* attended the 1925 Centenary Cavalcade at Darlington as no.25 in the exhibition list. However, allocation of Gresley Pacifics to Haymarket in 1924 reduced the working of the now designated C11s on both the Waverley and Edinburgh–Newcastle routes. The allocation of the Atlantics at the Grouping and in the early 1920s was:

St Margaret's:	9510, 9873, 9901, 9904
Haymarket:	9874-9878
Dundee:	9509, 9868, 9869, 9902
Aberdeen:	9870-9872
Carlisle:	9879-9881, 9905, 9906

The practice of changing engines at Dundee continued throughout the 1920s and the tonnages allowed the superheated C11 Atlantics were as follows:

Edinburgh–Aberdeen	370
Aberdeen–Dundee	340
Dundee–Edinburgh	370
Edinburgh–Perth	325
Perth–Edinburgh	320
Edinburgh–Glasgow	410
Glasgow–Edinburgh	435 (banked from Queen St–Cowlairs)
Edinburgh–Carlisle	290
Carlisle–Edinburgh	290
Edinburgh–Berwick	380
Berwick–Edinburgh	380

Most of the Haymarket, Dundee and Aberdeen engines had their regular crews, double-shifted and were working two return trips between Edinburgh and Dundee or Aberdeen and Dundee daily, and the Carlisle engines (which gained 9876 during the 1920s) also were double-shifted with regular crews. The St Margaret's engines worked mainly to Carlisle and Perth, although as more Gresley Pacifics came to Haymarket, the C11s became more frequent sights on the Edinburgh–Glasgow expresses, including the *Queen of Scots* Pullman. Loads on the Edinburgh–Aberdeen services in particular often exceeded the tonnages allowed for the C11s and therefore double-heading with a 4-4-0 cut inside the Atlantic was common. As well as haulage of the express passenger trains, the fast fish trains from Aberdeen were often allocated to C11s.

O.S. Nock recorded a number of journeys in Scotland during the years after the Grouping when most of the Atlantics were superheated. His attention was on the main Aberdeen–Edinburgh route where very heavy summer loads were prevalent, and piloting the Atlantics was necessary, especially on the night sleeper services. The first run below is with a superheated C11 with a maximum load unassisted and the other two on the 7.35pm Aberdeen sleeper. 9902 was one of the first C10s to be superheated by the LNER and had been so modified by the time of the run below. It was assisted by an unnamed D31 cut inside in the usual fashion. 9869 on the second run had the help of a superheated 'Scott'.

872 *Auld* *Reekie* leaving Aberdour with the 10.20am Aberdeen – Edinburgh train, 5 August 1910. (G.M. Shoults/ MLS Collection)

		Aberdeen–Dundee, post-Grouping						
		9869 *Bonnie Dundee*		9902 *Highland Chief*		9869 *Bonnie Dundee*		
	Pilot	-		9769		9413 *Caleb Balderstone*		
		333/355 tons		434/470 tons		523/565 tons		
		12.45pm Aberdeen		7.35pm Aberdeen		7.35pm Aberdeen		
		c1935		c1928		4.1934		
Miles	**Location**	**Times**	**Speeds**	**Times**	**Speeds**	**Times**	**Speeds**	**Gradients**
0	Aberdeen	00.00		00.00		00.00		1/96 R
4.8	Cove Bay	10.43	36/30½	09.30	39/35	09.33	41/35	1/118/154/116 R
7.1	MP234	14.52	36	13.15		13.11	41	1/153 R
11.6	Muchalls	19.47	64	18.20	64½	18.05	64½	1/170/310 F
16.2	Stonehaven	25.00		24.00		23.42		
		00.00		00.00		00.00		
2.6	Dunnottar Box	07.17	30/36½	05.40	30/42	06.39	38½	1/92 R
5.5	Carmont	12.17	33	10.00	37	11.13	34½	1/102 R
11.2	Fordoun	18.17	65	16.10	68/sigs 45*	17.20	62½	1/141/170 F
14.5	Laurencekirk	23.15		20.15	49	20.41	52	1/285 R
19.8	Craigo	07.33	69½	-	69	26.23	62½	1/104 F
21.9	Kinnaber Jcn	09.53	25*	28.15	37*	29.10		
24.5	Montrose	13.40		32.00		33.40		
		00.00		00.00		00.00		1/88 R
2.1	Usan Box	05.32	30	05.20	30	04.53	32½	1/111 R
4.9	Lunan Bay	10.14	35/51	10.05	34½	09.28	38½	1/121 R, 1/93 F
7.5	Inverkeilor	12.49	68/pws 25*	12.40	68/56	12.11	pws 45*	1/100 F, 1/103 R
10.7	Letham Grange	16.49		16.15	63½	16.54	62½	L, 1/103 F
13.7	Arbroath	21.35		20.40		21.15		
		00.00		00.00		00.00		
1.8	Elliott Junction	03.51		03.25		03.27		L
6.1	Carnoustie	09.20	58	09.00	56	08.25	60	L
13	Broughty Ferry	16.15	60	16.35	60	14.59	64½	L
17	Dundee	22.05		22.30		21.05		

Nock was on the footplate of 9869 on the 12.45pm Aberdeen and recorded the cut-off and regulator opening throughout. Driver Campbell of Dundee left the cut-off at 53 per cent for most of the journey, adjusting the regulator for the gradient. He did not drop below 44 per cent and raised it to 60 per cent on the climb out of Stonehaven to Carmont. Regulator opening varied from 2/5s to 3/5s, and only once, on the climb out of Aberdeen to Cove Bay, was it as much as three quarters open. On the return journey on the 3.55pm Dundee with 9509 *Duke of Rothesay* and a maximum load

380 ton train, Driver Moodie of Dundee used 44 per cent cut-off on the adverse gradients and 34 per cent on the level with a fuller regulator opening. The first level leg to Arbroath(17 miles) took 22 minutes 20 seconds (21½ net) with 67mph maximum. Arbroath to Montrose (13.7 miles) was run in 19min 43sec, gaining a minute and a quarter on schedule with 72mph at Inverkeilor and nothing below 40 on the 1 in 91 to Lunan Bay. Montrose to Stonehaven (24½ miles) took 33½ minutes with 37½mph on the 1 in 104 through Marykirk, 66 on the slight descent to Fordoun, 39½ on the 1 in 141 to Dunnottar Box and 71 down the 1 in 102 descent, arriving at Stonehaven 1½ minutes early. The last stretch to Aberdeen was run comfortably inside the schedule with 34mph on the initial 1 in 100/108 climb and a maximum of 64 after Cove Bay. Steam was maintained between 170 and 180lb psi on both journeys. The difference in driving methods was marked and the sluggishness of the Atlantic on the level and downhill experienced on 9869's run disappeared and Nock assessed the coal consumption in this direction as hardly more than 40lb per mile – much less than observed on the southbound run

Nock continued to Edinburgh on the two sleeper trains but a different run timed by C.J. Allen is included to show what could be done with a maximum unassisted load south of Dundee. Nock comments that both the runs above and below Dundee were punctuated by thunderous exhaust with the Atlantic working extremely hard on the banks.

		Dundee–Edinburgh Waverley, post-Grouping						
		9875 ***Midlothian***		**9877** ***Liddesdale***		**9510** ***The Lord Provost***		
	Pilot	**-**		**9427** ***Lord Glenvarloch***		**9427** ***Lord Glenvarloch***		
		364/390 tons		**434/475 tons**		**511/550 tons**		
		12.45pm Aberdeen		**7.35pm Aberdeen**		**7.35pm Aberdeen**		
				1928		**4.1934**		
Miles	**Location**	**Times**	**Speeds**	**Times**	**Speeds**	**Times**	**Speeds**	**Gradients**
0	Dundee	00.00		00.00		00.00		1/66/74 R
2.7	Tay Bridge Box	07.55	37½	07.05		07.05		1/114 R
4.6	St. Fort	10.35	62/52	09.40	65	09.45	57	1/100 F
8.3	Leuchars Jcn	14.35	60½	13.40	62	13.38	63	L
11.6	Dairsie	18.25	44½	17.40	45	17.22	50½	1/160 R
14.6	Cupar	22.05	55½	21.00	57½	20.27	61	1/400 F
16.9	Springfield	25.10	39	23.40	48	23.12	47½	1/161 R
20.1	Ladybank Jcn	29.35	50½	27.35	60	26.52	58½	L
24.3	Lochmuir Box	37.05	28½	34.05	33	32.30	35	1/95, 105 R
25.9	Markinch	39.25	63/pws	35.35	60	34.40	60/pws	1/102 F
28.5	Thornton	41.55	35*	38.50	slack*	38.32	20*	
	Dysart		34		35½		32	1/131/158 R
33.3	Kirkcaldy	48.15	66	45.45	64½	46.19	63½	1/100/143 F
39	Burntisland	54.20	45*	52.20	35*	53.20	20*	
41.8	Aberdour	58.15		56.25	48/37½	57.48	45½ /39	1/100 R
43.2	Dalgetty Box	61.10	28½	58.35	39	59.50	39	1/100 R

		Dundee–Edinburgh Waverley, post-Grouping						
		9875 *Midlothian*		9877 *Liddesdale*		9510 *The Lord Provost*		
	Pilot	-		9427 *Lord Glenvarloch*		9427 *Lord Glenvarloch*		
		364/390 tons		434/475 tons		511/550 tons		
		12.45pm Aberdeen		7.35pm Aberdeen		7.35pm Aberdeen		
				1928		4.1934		
Miles	**Location**	**Times**	**Speeds**	**Times**	**Speeds**	**Times**	**Speeds**	**Gradients**
46	Inverkeithing	64.45	60/35*	62.05	60/45*	63.27	54/40*	1/94 F
48	Forth Bridge N.	68.35	23	65.45	28	67.50	23½	1/70 R
52.7	Turnhouse	75.30	61½	72.10	65	74.42	63½	L
58	Haymarket	81.10		78.20	sigs stand	80.35		
59.2	Edinburgh	84.00	1 L	82.40	(80½ net) ¼ E	83.55	1 E	

Haymarket's 874 departing from Edinburgh through the Princes Street Gardens with an express for Dundee and Aberdeen just before the Grouping, c1922.
(F. Moore/MLS Collection)

The Edinburgh–Perth trains were worked by St Margaret's engines and the *Railway Magazines* of January 1927 and January 1928 published southbound runs from Perth which included the seven mile climb at 1 in 75 from Bridge of Earn to Glenfarg. Both the Reid C10 Atlantics had been superheated shortly after the Grouping and were then classified as C11s.

		Perth–Edinburgh Waverley c1926/7						
		9901 *St Johnstoun*			**9906 *Teribus***			
		281/290 tons			**224/240 tons**			
		12.25pm Perth			**12.25pm Perth**			
Miles	**Location**	**Times**	**Speed**		**Times**	**Speed**		**Gradients**
0	Perth	00.00		T	00.00		T	L, 1/168 R
2	Hilton Junction	04.50		¾ L	-	sigs 15*		1/315 F
3.5	Bridge of Earn	06.40		¾ L	08.55	53	3 L	L
4.8	MP 43	08.10	47½		-			1/75 R
9.8	MP 38	18.14	26		-	27		1/75 R
10.1	Glenfarg	18.55	26½	T	20.53	31	1¾ L	1/75 R
13.6	Mawcarse Jcn	23.10	64½		24.41	65½		1/94 F
17.2	Kinross Jcn	27.25		1½ E	29.07	(26½ net)	T	
0		00.00		T	00.00		T	
3.7	Blairadam	05.20	57		05.32	62		undulating/1/78 F
5.9	Kelty	08.00	30*	2 E	07.57	45*	2 E	
8.1	Cowdenbeath	12.10	26½	1¾ E	11.37	31	2¼ E	1/80 R
11.5	Halbeath	16.10	61½		14.05	53/pws 40*		1/100 F
11.9	Townhill Jcn	16.40	35*	1¼ E	-			1/72 F
13.7	Dunfermline	19.50		1¼ E	19.21		1¾ E	
0		00.00		T	00.00		T	
2.2	Rosyth	03.30	62½		03.37	64		1/89 F
3.7	Inverkeithing	05.15	40*	¼ L	05.17	35*	¼ L	
5.7	Forth Bridge N	08.50	36	¼ E	08.59	32½	T	1/70 R
7.4	Dalmeny	12.25		½ L	12.07	41*	T	L
10.4	Turnhouse	15.55	64½/56		15.37	60/57		L, 1/110 R
13.4	Saughton Jcn	18.55			18.49			
16.9	Edinburgh W	23.40		1¼ E	24.42		¼ E	

As the Haymarket allocation of A3s increased and some were also stationed at Carlisle Canal depot, the C11s were demoted to stopping and semi-fast services, appeared on Carlisle–Newcastle trains and increasingly on the Edinburgh–Glasgow services. A couple of runs on the latter service were documented in 1935, with comparatively heavy loads. 9878 *Hazeldean* with 320 tons ran the 46 miles comfortably within the 56 minute non-stop schedule with steady running in the low 60s, top speed 64mph at Manuel. 9901 *St Johnstoun* started from Haymarket station with 355 tons and arrived at Glasgow Queen St just over a minutes early in 54½ minutes, with 64mph at Manuel and a late sprint to 68½ between Croy and Lenzie, though C.J.Allen commented that these engines were more suited to slogging uphill than running on the level higher speed routes as they seemed to need hard driving to overcome an apparent sluggishness on the flat.

Because of the condition of the track and bridges, the A3s were not allowed north of Dundee until around 1930, so the C11s kept their work between Dundee and Aberdeen on all the main expresses including the heavy overnight sleepers until then. The A3s replaced some of the Carlisle based C11s between 1928 and 1930, although the St Margaret's engines continued to work to Carlisle from that end. Most of the Carlisle C11s were dispersed as follows:

St Margaret's:	9906
Haymarket:	9876, 9880
Aberdeen:	9879
Carlisle (remaining):	9881, 9905

As stated earlier, by the mid-1930s they were running out of suitable work with not only the A3s but the powerful P2 2-8-2s taking over much of the Edinburgh – Aberdeen traffic, and withdrawals began. One of the last accounts of their work

Aberdeen's 9870 *Bon-Accord* assisted by D29 9420 *The Abbot* on a typical heavy formation Aberdeen–Dundee/Edinburgh express passing Ferryhill and an ex-Caledonian 'Dunalastair' 4-4-0, c1925. (Real Photographs/MLS Collection)

was a run with 9906 *Teribus* on a semi-fast Perth–Edinburgh train of 340 tons gross which was checked by signals at Hilton Junction, losing momentum for the climb to Glenfarg. 9906 did well to accelerate hard to 56mph by Bridge of Earn, but struggled to maintain 23mph near the end of the seven mile climb which was, however, passed just a quarter of a minute early, and despite 66mph after Milnathort was a bit over a minute late into Kinross Junction (29mins 22 seconds for 17.2 miles, net time 28½ minutes). Most still looked externally in good condition and were light on maintenance and rode well despite their initial reputation (the early problems were as much about

St Margaret's 9904 *Holyrood* passing Haymarket with an Edinburgh–Perth stopping train, c1928. (MLS Collection)

St Margaret's 9906 *Teribus,* still in superb external condition, runs into Carlisle Citadel station with the 12.10pm Edinburgh luncheon express, including a Pullman car, c1934. (MLS Collection)

track condition as the fault of the engines), but they did have a high coal consumption working with heavy loads over steeply graded routes. The very last turns worked by a C11 were undertaken by the resurrected 9875 allocated after its semi-restoration to St Margaret's from whence it worked on three different diagrams – the 4.10pm Edinburgh–Perth and 8.10pm return, the 4.55pm Edinburgh–Glasgow and 8.25pm return or the 12noon Edinburgh–Carlisle and 6.29pm return. It ran light from St Margaret's to Cowlairs on 5 November 1939 and that unfortunately was the end of the NB Atlantic era. 9875 had accumulated the highest mileage in traffic – 1,408,823 miles, whereas 9509 and 9510, with only 15-16 years' service, had barely run around 700,000 miles.

St Margaret's 9904 *Holyrood* leaving Edinburgh Waverley station with a northbound express, probably for Perth, c1930. (Colling Turner/ MLS Collection)

9906 ***Teribus*** passing through Princes Street Gardens with an Edinburgh–Perth stopping train that unusually contains a Pullman coach, 18 June 1936. (MLS Collection)

Chapter 8

THE MOST SIGNIFICANT ATLANTICS IN THE WORLD

Between 1895 and the start of the First World War the number of Atlantic locomotives increased significantly, especially over flatter routes where high speeds were possible. By 1914 the number had reached over 3,500 of which more than 2,000 were in the USA. In mainland Europe, the German Railways led the way, especially the Prussian Railway on the northern plains, with over 400, followed by the British with 310, the vast majority on the East Coast route from London to Aberdeen. There were a couple of late unique designs, streamlined and designed for high speed lightweight trains in the USA on the Chicago, Milwaukee, St Paul & Pacific Railroad, and in Belgium for fast boat trains between Ostend and Brussels. However, train loads became significantly heavier after the First World War and the 4-4-2 was replaced by Pacific locomotives in most countries, though in Britain the 4-6-0 was as significant as the 4-6-2. Many of the earlier Atlantics were withdrawn in the 1920s and most by the Second World War. The American classes disappeared under the onslaught of the diesels in the 1940s and early 1950s and the last British Atlantic in active service was the former LB&SCR's H2 *Beachy Head* which was withdrawn in 1958. The last Atlantics in Europe in service were the four Class 12 streamlined Belgian Atlantics, their final withdrawal being in 1962. In the rest of the world the final examples seem to have been the Indian 'EM' class, the last of which were not withdrawn until the 1970s, one of those now preserved in the Indian Railway Museum in Delhi, and four Henschel built Atlantics for the Mozambique railway which lasted into the twenty-first century.

The very first 4-4-2 locomotives were built in the USA in 1888, evolved from a 2-4-2 wheel arrangement to give a more stable ride. Competition between railroads was growing and there was pressure to increase train speeds and cut scheduled times. More were built in 1894 by Baldwin for the Atlantic Coast Line of the Philadelphia & Reading Railroad. They were a development of the common 4-4-0 type, the additional space behind the coupled wheels allowing a large, wide and deep firebox. It was from their use on this route that the name of 'Atlantic' for locomotives of the wheel arrangement were named. The majority of American Atlantics were built in the early and mid first decade of the twentieth century, with the Santa Fe Railroad building a 4-cylinder compound in 1904, the class '510', which is alleged to have achieved 106mph with a three-car special over a 2.8 mile stretch, although this was unauthenticated. The Atlantic City Railroad built 48 'Camelbacks' with the cab moved forward astride the boiler which although looking clumsy, were fast, regularly running the 55½ miles from Camden to Philadelphia in 50 minutes, the record being 46½ minutes at an average speed of 71.6mph after a maximum speed of 90mph. They had 7ft coupled wheels, a huge 76sqft grate, a 200lb psi boiler and had a tractive effort of 22,906lb.

The best known of the American Atlantics were the 'E' series of the Pennsylvania Railroad, the first emerging in 1902. They had two cylinders with the large diameter of 20½in by 26in and 6ft 8in coupled wheels. The E3 of 1906 had cylinders of 22 by 26in, Walschaerts valve gear and piston valves, a grate area of 55.5sqft, boiler pressure of 205lb psi and a huge tender with a capacity of 5,660 gallons and 15½ tons of coal. Engine and tender weighed a massive 165 tons. Tractive effort was 27,400lb. The E3sd was a superheated version. The Penn RR track could accept high axleloads and the company continued to develop the design culminating in the E6s of 1913/14 which had 23½in by 26in cylinders. Eventually the company had 576 Atlantics of which at least two were preserved – No. 460 of class E6 and an earlier superheated E2sd, 8063, which was renumbered 7002 of the same class which was credited with achieving 120mph although the evidence from the times of the record run does not back this up with the high 80s or 90 being the probable maximum speed. They certainly regularly ran the 189 miles from Jersey City to Harrisburg at an average speed of 57.8mph with 360 ton loads. The E6s were capable of hauling 800-900 tons on the New York–Philadelphia–Washington route and in 1933 were running the *Detroit Arrow* from Fort Wayne to Chicago at a scheduled 75.5mph, the world's fastest train, and the 64 miles from Plymouth to Fort Wayne at 75.3mph, thus beating the previous world's fastest, the Great Western's *Cheltenham Flyer,* although that train held the record of the fastest actual time of 81.7mph held by a 4-6-0, (5006 *Tregenna Castle*). The later preserved E6, 460, ran a special in 1927 to carry the newsreels of the record-breaking transatlantic flyer Charles Lindbergh from Washington to Manhattan in 175 minutes for the 216 miles, averaging over 72mph over that huge distance.

The most powerful of all the American Atlantics was the Philadelphia and Reading Railroad's 1915 built locomotive which had no less than a 108sqft grate area, 23½ by 26in cylinders, 6ft 8in coupled wheels and 215lb psi boiler pressure, giving a tractive effort of 32,800lb. Then in 1935 the Chicago, Milwaukee, St Paul and Pacific Railroad built four streamlined 4-4-2 'Hiawathas' to work at planned 100mph scheduled speeds with lightweight trains of 5-6 cars, with a 431 mile route scheduled in 400 minutes including several stops. They were oil-fired with 7ft coupled wheels, 300lb psi boiler pressure and 69sqft grate area. Their tractive effort was 30,685lb. They were supplanted of course by diesels and were withdrawn between 1949 and 1951. Five of the earlier E2s survived to 1947 and the E6s lasted into the 1950s.

The first European Atlantics were the Austro-Hungarian class IId of the Kaiser Ferdinand Nordbahn of 1895 which became class '308' of the ŐBB and the class XVIb of the Austrian North West Railway (ŐBB '208' class). There were over a hundred of these locomotives. The Pfalz (Palatinate) Railway ordered twelve inside cylinder P3/1 Atlantics from Krauss in 1898 which were rebuilt as 4-cylinder compounds in 1913 and a further eleven locomotives classified P4 in 1905 which were

The Pennsylvania RR's record-breaking superheated E2 Atlantic 7002 (in reality 8063, another member of the class) at Northumberland USA, 9 August 1964 and now housed in the Penn RR's museum at Strasburg. (D.A. Somerville/ MLS Collection)

The Pennsylvania RR's E6, 1067. (Wikipedia)

The Chicago, Milwaukee, St Paul & Pacific Railroad's 1935 streamlined No.1 built for the *Hiawatha* train, seen on a passenger train shortly before its withdrawal in 1951. (MLS Collection)

similar to the Maffei built S2/5 of the Bavarian Royal State Railway, with a longer gap between the rear coupled wheel and the trailing axle which allowed a deeper firebox. The Bavarian railway had purchased two Baldwin USA 4-4-2s in 1900 before deciding to build ten of their own 4-cylinder compound version, but these were superseded by the highly successful Maffei Pacifics of 1908 (class S3/6). The Saxon State Railway ordered fifteen de Glehn Atlantics of class XV from Hartmann in 1900, one of which was exhibited at the Paris Exhibition that year.

The Saxon railway had Hartmann build a further eighteen 3-cylinder Atlantics of class XH1 in 1913 of which seventeen entered DR service in 1920, the last being withdrawn by 1930. The most numerous Atlantics of German design and operation were the Prussian Railway's S9 of

1907 of which 90 were built by Hanomag as 4-cylinder compounds, but unsuperheated. Although initially successful, because of increasing loads only one survived to enter DR stock although many went as war reparations to the French railways.

The most famous and influential European Atlantics were the French de Glehn compounds of the Nord Railway of France. The first de Glehn compound was a 2-2-2-0 (No.701) of 1891 but the design was developed and between 1900 and 1902 twenty 4-4-2 de Glehn 4-cylinder compounds were delivered by the SACM company of Belfort. They were followed by a further 15 engines built by SFCM of Fives-Lille in 1903 and 1904. The high pressure cylinders measured 13 3/8 in by 25 3/16 in and the low power 22 1/8 in by 25 3/16 in. Grate area was 29.5sqft and the total heating surface 2,455.77sqft. Boiler pressure was 227lb psi, the engine weighed 64 tons 13 cwt without tender and the tractive effort was 23,716lb. The first twenty of the class were causing attention by sustaining 75mph (120 km/hr) on the level between Paris and Calais with 300 tons, and 64-70 with 360 tons, surmounting the 1 in 125 of Caffiers bank at 62mph with the former tonnage. The Paris & Orleans Railway 3001 class was also a 4-cylinder compound engine with larger diameter high pressure cylinders at 14 5/16 in by 25 3/8 in and the low pressure of 23 5/8 in and similar stroke. The boiler pressure was similar to the Nord Atlantics but the grate area was larger at 33.35sqft and total heating surface was 2,757sqft. The engine weighed 71 tons 14 cwt and tractive effort was 27,174lb.

The Austro-Hungarian Atlantic of 1895, ŐBB 308.44, later DR 14.002. (Carl Bellingrodt/MLS Collection)

***Left*: The Saxon** railway's XV Atlantic of 1902, renumbered by the Deutsches Reichbahn in the 1920s as 14.315. (Carl Bellingrodt/MLS Collection)

***Below*: One of** the few S9s that survived the First World War without being sent as a war reparation to France, 915 of the Prussian State Railway, with wide and deep firebox, c1919. (Carl Bellingrodt/MLS Collection)

2.663, a de Glehn 4-cylinder compound of the Northern Railway of France, c1925. (Photomatic/ MLS Collection)

Danish class P Atlantic 917, built by Hanomag in 1909 and preserved and seen at Naestved shed, 24 September 1970. (MLS Collection)

Other significant European Atlantics included the Danish class P, designed by the company's Chief Mechanical Engineer, O.F.A. Busse, nineteen constructed by Hanomag in 1907 and fourteen by Schwartzkopf, the last delivered in 1910. They were numbered 901-933. They had coupled wheels of 6ft 6in diameter, weighed 117 tons including tender with an axleweight of 19 tons and boiler pressure of 213lb psi. They were used mainly on the relatively level routes from Copenhagen to Korsor and Fredericia to Esbjerg. Seven were rebuilt as Pacifics in 1943 to lower their axleweight and two have been preserved, one in the Danish Railway Museum at Odense.

The last Atlantics built in Europe were six streamlined locomotives of the Belgian Railways, class 12, based on the 1936 streamlined 'Jubilee' 4-4-4 locomotives of Canada. They were designed by Chief Engineer Raoul Notesse and built by Cockerill in 1938/9. They had two inside cylinders of 19in by 28½in, had 6ft 10½ in diameter coupled wheels and boiler pressure of 256lb psi. They weighed 116 tons, had a tractive effort of 26,644lb and were numbered 12.001-006. They were built to deliver a fast service between Brussels and Ostend and in June 1939 one completed the 65 miles in 57 minutes with a maximum speed of 103mph, although they were normally restricted to 87mph in passenger service. After the war and electrification of the main Ostend–Liège route, the locomotives were used on the Brussels–Mons and Tournai lines. They were withdrawn in 1962 and 12.004 was preserved and is currently in the Train World Museum in the former Schaerbeek shed.

The British engineering practice influenced the railways of the British Commonwealth and the results were seen particularly in the Atlantic designs for the Indian and Egyptian railways. 117 broad gauge (5ft 6in) 4-4-2s were built for five different Indian railway companies. Nineteen were de Glehn 4-cylinder compounds, most of which were withdrawn in the 1920s, but the others were outside 2-cylinder simple engines, forty of which were built by the North British Locomotive Company for the Great India Peninsular Railway in 1907 and forty-six for the East Indian Railway in 1908/9.

***Above left*: An SNCB** class 12 streamlined Atlantic arriving at Lille with a train from Brussels in the 1950s. (P. Laurent/ MLS Collection)

***Above right*: Indian 'EM'** Atlantic 922 (named *Queen Empress* in 1911 after the visit of King George V and Queen Mary) of the North Western Railway, preserved and restored for display at the India Railway Museum in New Delhi. (MLS Collection)

Oil burning Atlantic No.56 of the Egyptian State Railway at Cairo in 1947. (R.K. Blencowe/ MLS Collection)

No.8, a Chinese Tao Ching Railway Kerr-Stuart Atlantic. (A.C. Gilbert/MLS Collection)

They were superheated in the late 1920s and the GIPR engines were further rebuilt with new frames and enlarged cylinders in 1940/1, becoming class EM and survived to the 1970s. The EIR engines were class AP and were numbered 113-158 with 6ft 7in coupled wheels and 19in by 26in cylinders. The GIPR engines, numbered 900-939 and mostly named after British Imperial aristocrats (which were removed after independence), had 6ft 6in coupled wheels, 19½in by 26in outside cylinders (20½ by 26 after 1941), boiler pressure of 180lb psi, heating surface of 1,990sqft, grate area of 32sqft, axleload of 17½ tons and a total weight of 113½ tons. After electrification of the railway through the Ghats, the forty GIPR Atlantics were transferred to join the few already owned by the North Western Railway. They were particularly imposing and handsome and an example can be viewed in the Indian Railway Museum in New Delhi. A similar Atlantic was the Class '35' of the Egyptian Railways, five oil-burner locomotives built in 1913, designed by R.G.Peckitt. They were built by Berliner Maschinenbau, were superheated, had Belpaire fireboxes, 6ft 6in diameter coupled wheels, grate area of 30.9sqft, 20in by 26in cylinders and a tractive

A 3ft 6in gauge Baldwin 4-4-2 of the 6600 class, built for the Japanese railway in 1897, and subsequently for the South African railway system. (Wikipedia)

Mozambique's Henschel built Atlantic 812 on a Nampula–Nacala passenger train, September 1974. (P.A.G. Michie/Ted Talbot Collection)

effort of 20,860lb. They worked the Cairo–Alexandria service before dieselisation and were capable of conveying 450 ton trains on the level at 60mph. Another locomotive designed with British engineering influence was the Kerr-Stuart Atlantic for the Chinese Tao Ching Railway. They weighed 120 tons, had 19in by 24in cylinders, a grate area of 35sqft and total heating surface of 1,876sqft with a tractive effort of 23,132lb.

A number of 3ft 6in gauge railways also used Atlantics. As early as 1897 the Japanese railway acquired twenty-four of the 6600 class built in the USA by the Baldwin Locomotive Company, and Baldwin followed delivering a further six of the same design to the South African railway. Last of all, however were some Atlantics owned by the Mozambique railway which surprisingly outlived some newer classes and didn't disappear until the beginning of the twenty-first century, the last working examples of Atlantics in the world. They were four Henschel built 4-4-2s constructed in 1923, numbered 811-814 and based at Nampula and worked passenger trains over the 6-hour journey to Nacala on the Indian Ocean.

It is of interest that the best and most powerful of the British designs, the Great Western 4-4-2s, that were of course later converted to 4-6-0s, were influenced by Churchward's study of the best American Atlantics and those of the Nord and Paris-Orleans in France. And that these Churchward engines went on to influence the design of passenger and mixed traffic 4-6-0s in Great Britain for decades. And on the other hand, British Atlantics of the twentieth century's first decade influenced the design of 4-4-2s, many built by British companies, for the British Empire railways in Africa and Asia.

APPENDIX

Theoretical power comparison of the British Atlantics

Class	Tractive Effort (85%) lbs
GW P&O, 103 & 104	27,174
GW 'Star' 40	25,090
LB&SCR H2	24,520
GW '171' (29XX)	24,395
GW De Glehn 102	23,710
NB/LNER C10	23,375
NB/LNER C11	23,325
GC/LNER C4	21,660
NE/LNER C6	20,350
NE/LNER C7	20,317
GC/LNER C8	19,387
LNER C9	19,260
LB&SCR H1	19,028
GN/LNER C1 (20" cyls)	17,450
L&Y 'Highflyer'	16,505
GN/LNER C1 (18¾" cyls)	15,400
GN/LNER C2	15,400
GC/LNER C5	13,231
(in compound mode)	

British Atlantics in date order

GN/LNER C2	1898
L&Y 'Highflyer'	1899
GN/LNER C1	1902
GW de Glehn 102	1903
GC/LNER C4	1903
NE/LNER C6	1903
GW P&O 103 & 104	1904
GW '171' (29XX)	1904
GC/LNER C5	1905
LB&SCR H1	1905
GW 'Star' 40	1906
NB/LNER C11	1906
NE/LNER C8	1906
LB&SCR H2	1911
NE/LNER C7	1911
NB/LNER C10	1911
LNER C9	1931

The Lancashire & Yorkshire 'L1' 'Highflyers'

Dimensions: See page 15

Statistics

All were built at the L&Y Horwich Works.

No.	Built	Rebuilt	LMS No.	Withdrawn
1400	2/1899	5/1910	10300	1933
1392	3/1899	5/1912	10301	1927
1393	3/1899	7/1914	10302	1927
1394	4/1899	5/1915	10303	1927
1395	4/1899	10/1912	10304	1926
1396	5/1899	-	10305	1928
1397	5/1899	-	10306	1927
1398	5/1899	11/1918	10307	1933
1399	6/1899	6/1913	10308	1927
1401	6/1899	6/1913	10309	1933
1402	6/1899	4/1914	10310	1933
1403	7/1899	4/1913	10311	1932
1404	7/1899	6/1912	10312	1930
700	7/1899	8/1913	10313	1927
702	8/1899	11/1918	10314	1926
708	9/1899	7/1916	10315	1930
711	9/1899	2/1911	10316	1934
718	10/1899	7/1915	10317	1931
735	10/1899	12/1912	10318	1927
737	10/1899	6/1916	10319	1930
1405	1/1902	11/1911	10320	1933
1406	2/1902	7/1911	10321	1931
1407	2/1902	12/1909	10322	1933
1408	2/1902	6/1915	10323	1929
1409	3/1902	1/1912	10324	1932
1410	3/1902	5/1912	10325	1930
1411	3/1902	4/1914	10326	1927
1412	3/1902	2/1913	10327	1929
1413	4/1902	6/1914	10328	1929
1414	4/1902	5/1913	10329	1928
1415	4/1902	1/1912	10330	1928
1416	4/1902	12/1909	10331	1930
1417	5/1902	11/1910	10332	1927
1418	5/1902	-	10333	1927
1419	5/1902	3/1910	10334	1927

No.	Built	Rebuilt	LMS No.	Withdrawn
1420	5/1902	-	10335	1933
1421	6/1902	11/1909	10336	1929
1422	6/1902	9/1912	10337	1930
1423	6/1902	3/1915	10338	1927
1424	7/1902	2/1913	10339	1932

The Great Northern Atlantics, 'C2' 'Klondykes'

Dimensions: See page 26

Statistics

All were built at Doncaster.

No.	Built	Rebuilt PVs	Superheated	LNER No.	1946 No.	Withdrawn	Mileage
990*	5/1898	12/1922	12/1922	3990	-	10/1937	1,231,700 (approx)
949	3/1900	4/1923	4/1923	3949	-	8/1938	
950	4/1900	-	1/1916	3950	-	12/1937	
982	5/1900	-	2/1914	3982	-	11/1935	
983	5/1900	-	9/1923	3983	-	4/1936	
984	6/1900	-	5/1924	3984	-	10/1937	
985	6/1900	11/1925	12/1923	3985	-	5/1936	
986	5/1900	11/1918	2/1914	3986	-	10/1937	
987	6/1900	2/1918	2/1918	3987	-	8/1936	
988	6/1900	5/1909	5/1909	3988	-	12/1935	
989	6/1900	-	2/1919	3989	-	4/1938	
271	7/1902	7/1911**	7/1911	3271	-	6/1936	
250	6/1903	12/1921	10/1920	3250	(2893)	6/1944	
252	5/1903	-	5/1924	3252	(2892)	7/1945	
253	5/1903	4/1929	1/1918	3253	-	5/1937	
254	6/1903	-	2/1922	3254	-	4/1943	
255	5/1903	8/1924	6/1919	3255	-	8/1938	
256	5/1903	-	7/1920	3256	-	3/1943	
257	6/1903	4/1918	4/1918	3257	-	3/1936	
258	6/1903	10/1929	11/1923	3258	-	4/1937	
259	6/1903	-	4/1921	3259	-	10/1943	
260	6/1903	-	8/1919	3260	-	9/1936	

* named *Henry Oakley*

** built as a 4-cylinder engine, rebuilt to 2-inside cylinders

The Great Northern Atlantics, 'C1' 'Large Atlantics'

Dimensions: See page 41

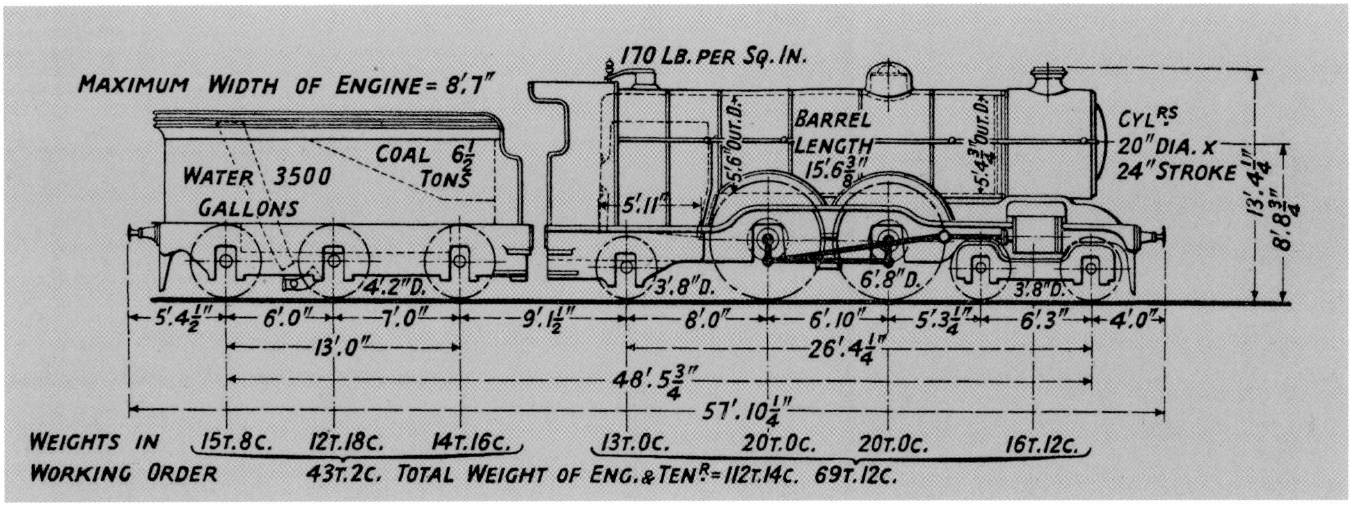

Weight diagram of a GN 'Large Atlantic' LNER C1.

Statistics

No.	Built	Rebuilt PVs	Superheated	LNER No.	1946 No.	BR No.	Withdrawn
251	12/1902	12/1923	8/1918	3251	2800	-	7/1947*
272	5/1904	2/1916	2/1916	3272	2801	-	8/1947
273	6/1904	3/1916	3/1916	3273	2802	-	1/1947
274	6/1904	6/1920	6/1920	3274	(2803)	-	5/1946
275	6/1904	-	8/1921	3275	(2804)	-	5/1945
276	6/1904	-	10/1918	3276	(2805)	-	1/1946
277	6/1904	-	4/1919	3277	(2806)	-	1/1945
278	6/1904	9/1920	9/1920	3278	(2807)	-	7/1945
279	6/1904	5/1915**	5/1915	3279	2808	(62808)	2/1948
280	6/1904	1/1931	7/1922	3280	(2809)	-	10/1946
281	6/1904	10/1935	7/1920	3281	2810	(62810)	5/1949
282	6/1904	-	8/1917	3282	2811	-	1/1947
283	6/1904	12/1924	8/1923	3283	2812	-	8/1947
284	6/1904	9/1917	9/1917	3284	(2813)	-	1/1946
285	6/1904	12/1919	3/1918	3285	(2814)	-	5/1946
286	6/1904	-	5/1924	3286	2815	-	10/1947
287	6/1904	-	6/1922	3287	(2816)	-	10/1945
288	6/1904	12/1919	3/1918	3288	2817	(62817)	5/1950
289	6/1904	2/1919	2/1919	3289	(2818)	-	12/1945
290	6/1904	6/1922	4/1920	3290	(2819)	-	11/1945
291	6/1904	-	7/1922	3291	(2820)	-	4/1945

No.	Built	Rebuilt PVs	Superheated	LNER No.	1946 No.	BR No.	Withdrawn
292***	3/1905	-	-	3292	-	-	1/1927
1300+	7/1905	11/1917+	-	(4300)	-	-	10/1924
293	4/1905	7/1926	10/1919	3293	2821	-	7/1948
294	5/1905	9/1917	9/1917	3294	2822	62822	11/1950
295	5/1905	10/1915	10/1915	3295	2823	-	8/1947
296	4/1905	-	8/1917	3296	(2824)	-	12/1945
297	4/1905	8/1932	9/1923	3297	2825	-	2/1947
298	5/1905	2/1917	2/1917	3298	(2826)	-	4/1945
299	5/1905	-	6/1919	3299	(2827)	-	5/1945
300	6/1905	1/1920	1/1918	3300	2828	(62828)	9/1949
301	5/1905	3/1917	3/1917	3301	2829	(62829)	7/1948
1400	6/1905	-	6/1921	4400	2830	-	12/1947
1401	6/1905	9/1915	9/1915	4401	2831	-	11/1946
1402	6/1905	2/1934	8/1917	4402	2832	-	8/1947
1403	6/1905	8/1916	8/1916	4403	2833	-	7/1947
1404	6/1905	3/1914	3/1914	4404	2834	-	8/1947
1405	6/1905	4/1914	4/1914	4405	2835	-	8/1947
1406	6/1905	4/1914	4/1914	4406	(2836)	-	2/1946
1407	7/1905	9/1915	9/1915	4407	(2837)	-	6/1944
1408	7/1905	-	11/1921	4408	(2838)	-	7/1945
1409	7/1905	4/1917	4/1917	4409	2839	(62839)	1/1950
1410	8/1905	8/1919	7/1917	4410	2840	-	4/1947
1411	3/1906	11/1926	5/1924	4411	2841	-	8/1947
1412	3/1906	7/1916	7/1916	4412	2842	-	5/1947
1413	3/1906	9/1923	9/1923	4413	(2843)	-	1/1946
1414	3/1906	-	6/1918	4414	(2844)	-	10/1944
1415	4/1906	4/1927	6/1920	4415	2845	-	4/1947
1416	4/1906	1/1915	1/1915	4416	(2846)	-	10/1945
1417	4/1906	5/1917	5/1917	4417	(2847)	-	4/1945
1418	5/1906	8/1920	6/1917	4418	(2848)	-	2/1945
1419	5/1906	7/1923++	7/1923	4419	2849	(62849)	7/1948
1420	5/1906	8/1928	5/1919	4420	2850	-	8/1947
1421	8/1907	7/1920#	12/1914	4421	2851	-	8/1947
1422	3/1907	10/1924	6/1919	4422	(2852)	-	9/1946
1423	4/1907	8/1919	8/1919	4423	2853	-	5/1947
1424	4/1907	9/1935	4/1924	4424	2854	(62854)	4/1950
1425	4/1907	10/1916	10/1916	4425	2855	-	1/1947
1426	5/1907	7/1926	4/1924	4426	(2856)	-	2/1944
1427	5/1907	-	11/1919	4427	(2857)	-	2/1945

No.	Built	Rebuilt PVs	Superheated	LNER No.	1946 No.	BR No.	Withdrawn
1428	5/1907	5/1942	7/1913	4428	(2858)	-	6/1946
1429	6/1907	11/1930	5/1919	4429	2859	-	8/1947
1430	6/1907	12/1935	7/1913	4430	(2860)	-	2/1944
1431	6/1907	-	7/1913	4431	(2861)	-	10/1944
1432	11/1907	11/1916	11/1916	4432	(2862)	-	7/1945
1433	11/1907	4/1932	1/1927	4433	(2863)	-	5/1946
1434	11/1907	-	11/1912	4434	(2864)	-	4/1945
1435	11/1907	5/1922	10/1913	4435	(2865)	-	12/1945
1436	11/1907	10/1915	10/1915	4436	2866	-	8/1947
1437	3/1908	-	2/1923	4437	(2867)	-	3/1944
1438	3/1908	-	6/1923	4438	2868	-	8/1947
1439	3/1908	7/1927	9/1916	4439	2869	-	1/1947
1440	4/1908	-	7/1920	4440	2870	(62870)	2/1948
1441	4/1908	-	6/1918	4441	2871	(62871)	5/1948
1442	6/1908	11/1918	4/1914	4442	2872	-	1/1947
1443	5/1908	11/1934	3/1920	4443	2873	-	5/1946
1444	5/1908	7/1929	5/1917	4444	(2874)	-	10/1945
1445	6/1908	-	4/1918	4445	2875	(62875)	1/1949
1446	6/1908	-	3/1922	4446	2876	(62876)	1/1948
1447	6/1908	5/1914	5/1914	4447	2877	(62877)	11/1949
1448	7/1908	3/1926	3/1919	4448	(2878)	-	6/1946
1449	8/1908	6/1940	5/1922	4449	2879	-	7/1947
1450	8/1908	1/1920	1/1920	4450	(2880)	-	6/1946
1451	8/1908	2/1937	3/1922	4451	2881	(62881)	4/1949
1452	8/1910	as new	as new	4452	(2882)	-	2/1946
1453	9/1910	as new	as new	4453	2883	-	7/1946
1454	9/1910	as new	as new	4454	2884	-	9/1946
1455	9/1910	as new	as new	4455	2885	62885	1/1950
1456	10/1910	as new	as new	4456	2886	-	8/1947
1457	10/1910	as new	as new	4457	(2887)	-	3/1946
1458	11/1910	as new	as new	4458	2888	-	4/1947
1459	11/1910	as new	as new	4459	-	-	7/1943
1460	11/1910	as new	as new	4460	(2890)	-	10/1945
1461	11/1910	as new	as new	4461	(2891)	-	8/1945

* Preserved
** Rebuilt again in 6/1938 as 2-cylinder standard Atlantic
*** 4-cylinder compound
\+ Vulcan Foundry 4-cylinder compound, rebuilt 11/1917 as a 2-cylinder 'simple'
++ Fitted with booster from 7/1923 – 11/1935
\# Built as a 4-cylinder compound and rebuilt as standard 2-cylinder simple in 7/1920

The Great Western Atlantics

The French du Bousquet/de Glehn Compounds

Dimensions: See pages 78, 80

Statistics

No.	Name	Built	Rebuilt with GW boiler	Superheated	First depot	Last depot	Withdrawn	Mileage
102	*La France*	1903	1916	1916	Westbourne Pk	Oxford	1926	728,031
103	*President*	1905	1910	1914	Westbourne Pk	Oxford	1928	
104	*Alliance*	1905	1907*	*	Westbourne Park	Oxford	1928	

* received P&O boiler back in 1909, but later a superheated GW boiler

The Churchward Atlantics

173-178 were built as 4-6-0s and never ran as Atlantics

Dimensions: See page 79

Statistics

No.	Name	Built	Rebuilt as 4-6-0	1912 No.	First depot	Last depot	Withdrawn	Mileage
171	*Albion***	12/03	7/07	2971	Westbourne Pk	Swindon	1/1946	1,789,333
172	*The Abbot**	2/05	4/12	2972	Laira	Canton	3/1935	1,268,611
179	*Quentin Durward**	4/05	1912	2979	Bath Road	Ebbw Jcn	1/1951	1,802,144
180	*Coeur de Lion*	5/05	1912	2980	Westbourne Pk	Gloucester	5/1948	1,901,031
181	*Ivanhoe*	6/05	7/12	2981	Newton Abbot	Banbury	3/1951	1,838,884
182	*Lalla Rookh*	6/05	11/12	2982	Laira	Ebbw Jcn	6/1934	1,251,744
183	*Redgauntlet**	7/05	4/12	2983	Westbourne Pk	Tyseley	3/1946	1,860,269
184	*Guy Mannering*	7/05	8/12	2984	Westbourne Pk	Bath Road	5/1933	1,238,079
185	*Peveril of the Peak*	7/05	1912	2985	Westbourne Pk	Landore	8/1931	1,175,432
186	*Robin Hood*	7/05	5/12	2986	Westbourne Pk	Swindon	11/1932	1,272,865
187	*Bride of Lammermoor*	8/05	6/12	2987	Exeter	Hereford	10/1949	1,764,046
188	*Rob Roy*	8/05	5/12	2988	Newton Abbot	Tyseley	5/1948	1,795,453
189	*Talisman*	9/05	5/12	2989	Bath Road	Chester	9/1948	1,776,101
190	*Waverley*	9/05	11/12	2990	Laira	Canton	1/1939	1,328,335

* 172 named *Quicksilver* until 3/07
179 named *Magnet* until 3/07
183 named *Red Gauntlet* until 6/15
184 named *Viscount Churchill* until 4/07
185 named *Winterstoke* until 4/07
187 named *Robertson* until 4/07
** 171 was built as a 4-6-0, rebuilt as a 4-4-2 in 10/04, and back as a 4-6-0 in 7/1907

The Churchward 4-cylinder Atlantic

Dimensions: See page 84

Statistics

No.	Name	Built	Rebuilt as 4-6-0	1912 No.	Reb. as Castle	First depot	Last depot	Withdrawn	Mileage
40	*North Star*	1906	1909	4000	11/1929	W'bourne Pk	Landore	5/1957	2,110,396

The Great Central Atlantics

8B (LNER C4)

Dimensions: See page 97

Weight diagram

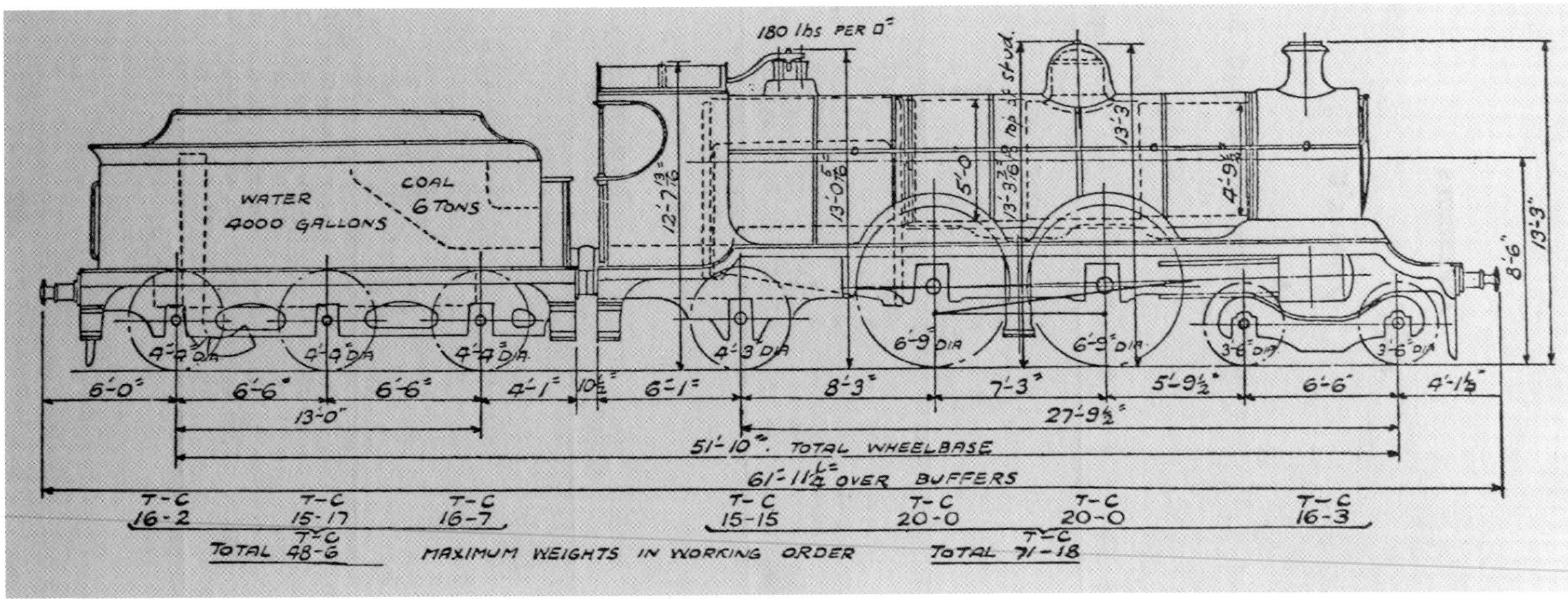

Statistics

No.	Built	Builder	Superheated	PVs	LNER No.	1946 No.	BR No.	Withdrawn
192	12/1903	Beyer Peacock	9/1920	11/1927	5192	2900	(62900)	11/1950
194	12/1903	Beyer Peacock	10/1925	10/1932	5194	2901	(62901)	11/1950
263	7/1904	Beyer Peacock	6/1926	-	5263	2902	(62902)	4/1949
264	7/1904	Beyer Peacock	7/1921	11/1931	5264	2903	(62903)	6/1949
265	7/1904	Beyer Peacock	9/1920	4/1927	5265	2904	-	12/1947
266	7/1904	Beyer Peacock	5/1921	-	5266	(2905)	-	10/1943

No.	Built	Builder	Superheated	PVs	LNER No.	1946 No.	BR No.	Withdrawn
267	7/1904	Beyer Peacock	9/1920	4/1927	5267	2906	-	11/1947
1083	10/1905	N.B. Loco Co	1/1921	10/1932	6083	2907	-	12/1947
1084	10/1905	N.B. Loco Co	8/1929	-	6084	2908	(62908)	11/1950
1085	10/1905	N.B. Loco Co	1/1925	1/1925	6085	2909	(62909)	11/1950
1086	10/1905	N.B. Loco Co	8/1914	12/1925	6086	2910	(62910)	2/1949
1087	10/1905	N.B. Loco Co	9/1920	11/1930	6087	(2911)	-	11/1944
1088	10/1905	N.B. Loco Co	12/1926	-	6088	2912	(62912)	8/1949
1089	11/1905	N.B. Loco Co	6/1920	-	6089	2913	-	4/1947
1090	11/1905	N.B. Loco Co	3/1914	9/1922*	6090	-	-	11/1939
1091	11/1905	N.B. Loco Co	4/1925	4/1925	6091	2914	(62914)	3/1948
1092	11/1905	N.B. Loco Co	3/1921	7/1925	6092	2915	(62915)	6/1949
1093	11/1905	N.B. Loco Co	11/1927	6/1937	6093	2916	(62916)	11/1948
1094	11/1905	N.B. Loco Co	1/1936	-	6094	2917	(62917)	5/1949
260	2/1906	Gorton	2/1935	-	5260	2918	(62918)	12/1950
261	3/1906	Gorton	1/1927	2/1937	5261	2919	(62919)	11/1950
262	4/1906	Gorton	4/1925	4/1925	5262	2920	(62920)	2/1948
358	5/1906	Gorton	5/1920	2/1932	5358	2921	(62921)	4/1948
360	6/1906	Gorton	10/1920	2/1931	5360	2922	(62922)	6/1948
361	7/1906	Gorton	3/1912	3/1912	5361	2923	(62923)	2/1949
362	6/1906	Gorton	3/1928	1/1942	5362	2924	(62924)	1/1948
363	8/1906	Gorton	2/1921	9/1933	5363	2925	(62925)	4/1949

* rebuilt with 3 cylinders, 12/1908, reverted to 2 cylinders 9/1922.

8D & E (LNER C5)

Dimensions: See page 117

Statistics

No.	Name	Built	Superheated	LNER No.	1946 No.	Withdrawn
258	*The Rt.Hon. Viscount Cross GCB GCSI*	12/1905	12/1927	5258	2895	12/1946
259	*King Edward VII*	2/1906	10/1921	5259	2896	4/1947
364	*Lady Faringdon*	12/1906	3/1913	5364	2897	12/1947
365	*Sir William Pollitt*	12/1906	5/1911	5365	2898	8/1947

V & V/09 (LNER C6)

Dimensions: See page 123

Statistics

No.	Built	Built at	LNER 1946 No.	Withdrawn
532	11/1903	Gateshead	-	1/1943
649	12/1903	Gateshead	-	8/1943
784	12/1903	Gateshead	2931	11/1947
295	6/1904	Gateshead	(2932)	3/1944
742	6/1904	Gateshead	2933	3/1948
1680	6/1904	Gateshead	2934	11/1947
1753	8/1904	Gateshead	(2935)	7/1946
1776	10/1904	Gateshead	(2936)	4/1944
1792	10/1904	Gateshead	2937	3/1948
1794	10/1904	Gateshead	(2938)	5/1944
696	5/1910	Darlington	2939	12/1947
697	5/1910	Darlington	(2940)	10/1945
698	6/1910	Darlington	2941	12/1947
699	6/1910	Darlington	(2942)	7/1944
700	7/1910	Darlington	(2943)	5/1946
701	7/1910	Darlington	(2944)	8/1944
702	8/1910	Darlington	(2945)	7/1946
703	8/1910	Darlington	(2946)	1/1945
704	9/1910	Darlington	2947	11/1947
705	9/1910	Darlington	(2948)	12/1943

'Z' (LNER C7)

Dimensions: See page 133

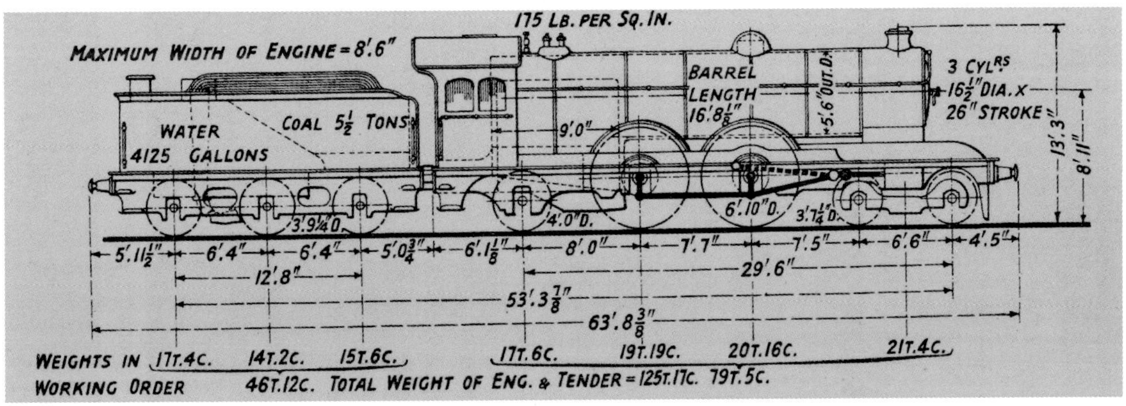

Weight diagram of an NER Z Atlantic,' LNER C7.

Statistics

No.	Built	Built at	LNER 1946 No.	BR No.	Withdrawn	
706	7/1911	N.B.Loco. Co.	(2950)	-	12/1946	
709	7/1911	"	(2951)	-	3/1946	
710	7/1911	"	(2952)	-	2/1944	
714	7/1911	"	(2953)	-	1/1944	
716	7/1911	"	2954	(62954)	6/1948	
717	8/1911	"	(2955)	-	4/1944	
718	8/1911	"	2956	-	6/1946	
719	8/1911	"	(2957)	-	4/1944	
720	8/1911	"	2958	-	11/1947	
721	9/1911	"	(2959)	-	2/1944	
722	8/1911	"	2960	-	3/1946	
727	9/1911	"	-	-	11/1931	rebuilt as C9
728	9/1911	"	(2961)	-	11/1945	
729	9/1911	"	(2962)	-	11/1945	
732	10/1911	"	2963	-	12/1946	rebuilt 12/33 as C7/2
733	10/1911	"	(2964)	-	8/1945	
734	10/1911	"	(2965)	-	9/1944	
735	10/1911	"	(2966)	-	6/1945	
736	11/1911	"	(2967)	-	4/1946	
737	12/1911	"	(2968)	-	12/1945	
2163	5/1914	Darlington	(2969)	-	1/1946	
2164	5/1914	"	2970	(62970)	12/1948	
2165	6/1914	"	2971	-	2/1947	
2166	6/1914	"	2972	(62972)	8/1948	
2167	6/1914	"	2973	(62973)	6/1948	
2168	6/1914	"	2974	-	5/1947	
2169	6/1914	"	2975	(62975)	7/1948	
2170	6/1914	"	(2976)	-	8/1943	
2171	7/1914	"	-	-	12/1931	rebuilt as C9
2172	8/1914	"	(2977)	-	12/1944	
2193	12/1914	"	2978	(62978)	8/1948	
2194	12/1914	"	(2979)	-	9/1944	
2195	12/1914	"	2980	-	6/1947	
2196	2/1915	"	2981	(62981)	7/1948	

No.	Built	Built at	LNER 1946 No.	BR No.	Withdrawn	
2197	2/1915	"	2982	(62982)	7/1948	
2198	3/1915	"	2983	(62983)	7/1948	
2199	3/1915	"	(2984)	-	6/1944	
2200	3/1915	"	(2985)	-	4/1946	
2201	4/1915	"	2986	-	9/1947	
2202	5/1915	"	(2987)	-	10/1943	
2203	6/1915	"	2988	(62988)	7/1948	
2204	6/1915	"	2989	(62989)	8/1948	
2205	11/1916	"	(2990)	-	2/1945	
2206	11/1916	"	2991	-	11/1947	
2207	1/1917	"	2992	(62992)	11/1948	
2208	2/1917	"	2993	(62993)	3/1948	
2209	4/1917	"	(2994)	-	2/1944	
2210	5/1917	"	2995	(62995)	7/1948	
2211	6/1917	"	2996	-	11/1947	
2212*	6/1918	"	(2997)	-	10/1945	rebuilt 1/36 C7/2

* Stumpf Uniflow engine

'4CC' (LNER C8)

Dimensions: See page 153

Statistics

No.	Built	Built at	Superheated	Withdrawn
730	4/1906	Gateshead	3/1915	1/1935
731	5/1906	Gateshead	3/1915	12/1933

LNER C9 (C7 Booster fitted)

Dimensions: See page 156

Statistics

No.	Built	Rebuilt with booster	booster removed	Withdrawn
727	9/1911	11/1931	2/1937	1/1943
2171	6/1914	12/1931	12/1936	4/1942

The LBSCR 'H1' & 'H2' Atlantics

Dimensions: See pages 161, 169

Weight diagrams

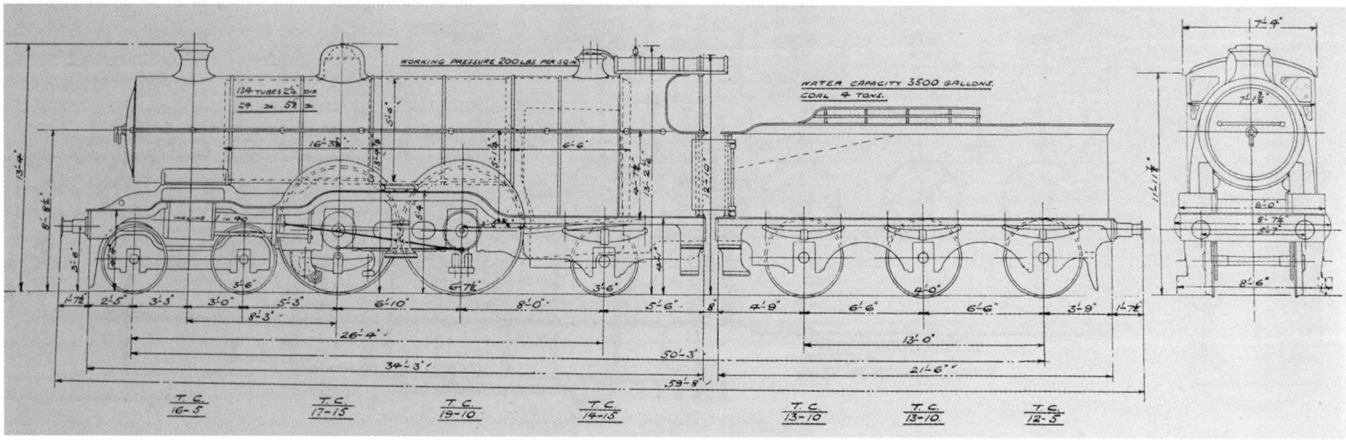

Weight diagram of an H1 Atlantic, LB&SCR.

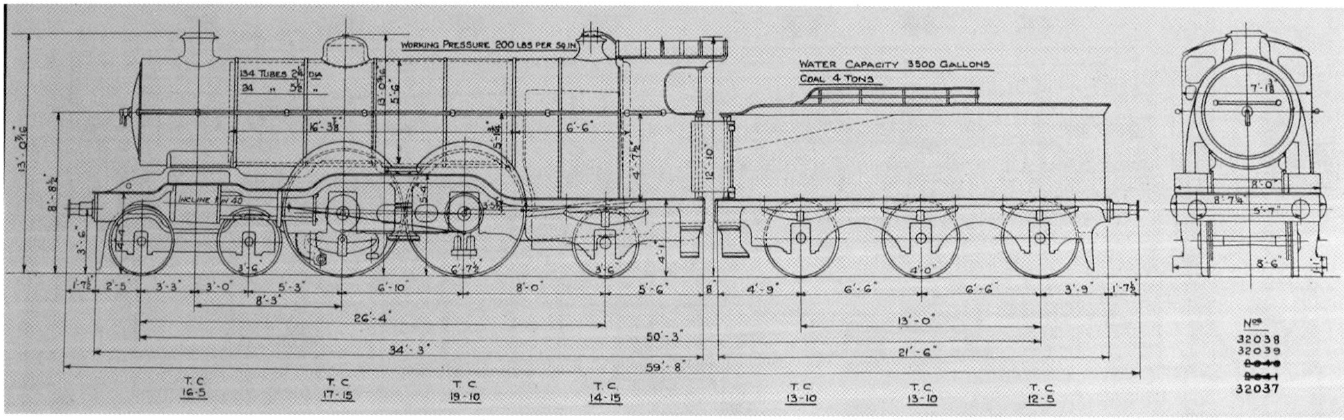

Weight diagram of an H1 Atlantic, SR.

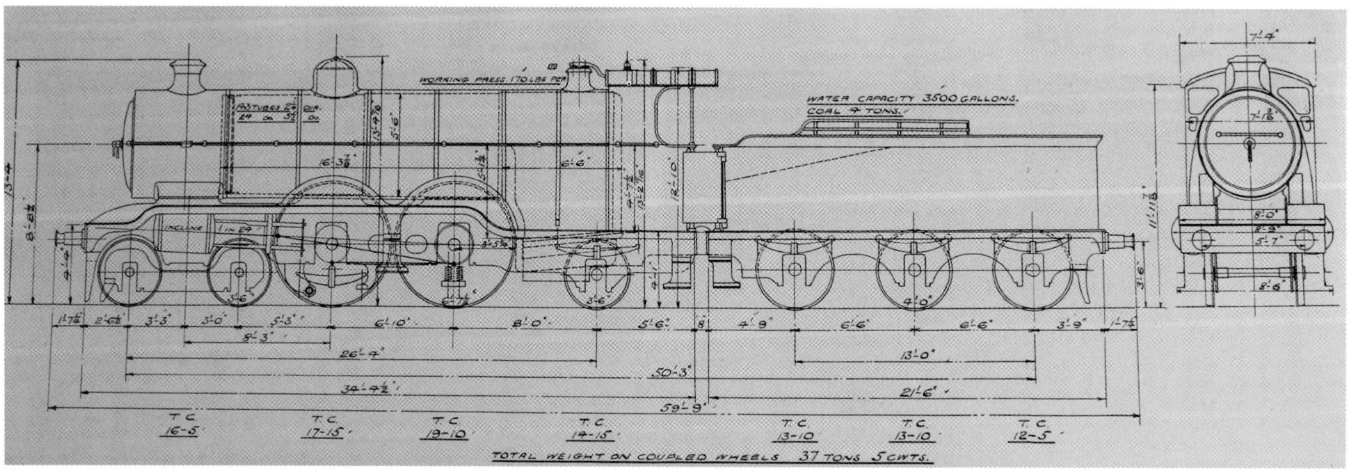

Weight diagram of an H2 Atlantic, LB&SCR.

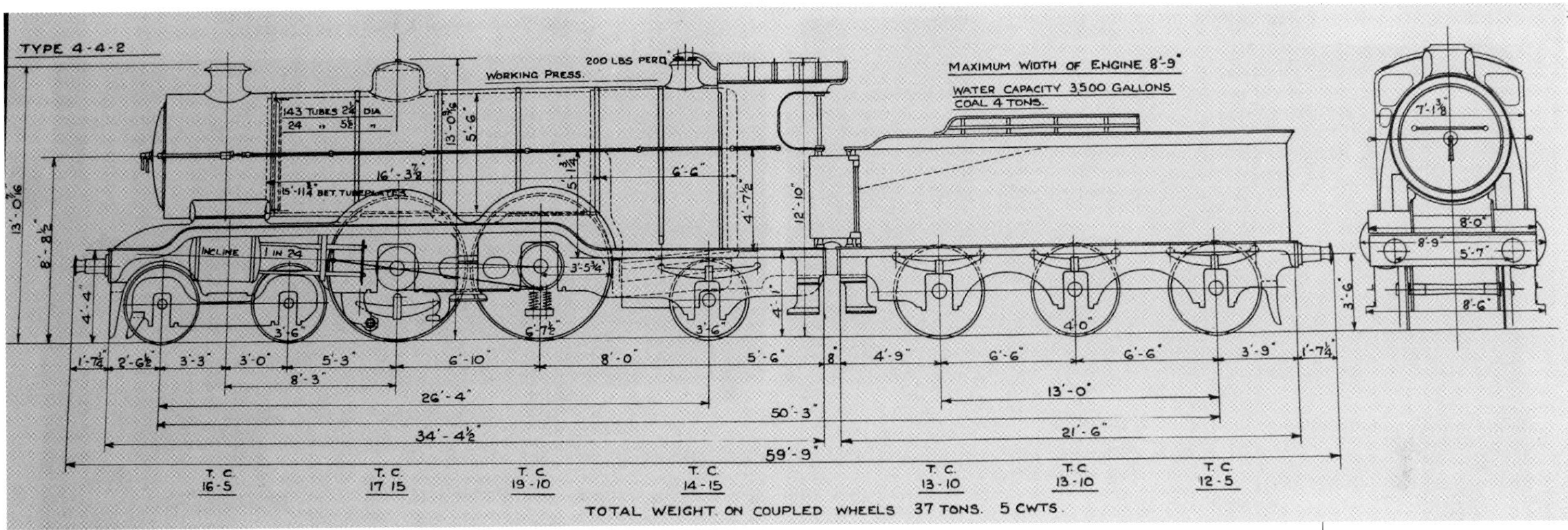

Weight diagram of an H2 Atlantic, SR.

Statistics

No.	Built	Built at	Superheated	SR No.	BR No.	Withdrawn	Mileage
37	12/1905	Kitson & Co	3/1926	2037	32037	7/1951	1,080,697
38	12/1905	Kitson & Co	12/1925	2038	32038	7/1951	1,095,117
39	1/1906	Kitson & Co	1/1926	2039	32039	2/1951	1,116,454
40	2/1906	Kitson & Co	12/1927	2040		1/1944	
41	2/1906	Kitson & Co	6/1927	2041		3/1944	999,994
421	6/1911	Brighton	as new	2421	32421	8/1956	1,112,849
422	7/1911	Brighton	as new	2422	32422	9/1956	
423	9/1911	Brighton	as new	2423	(32423)	5/1949	905,146
424	9/1911	Brighton	as new	2424	32424	4/1958	1,090,661
425	12/1911	Brighton	as new	2425	32425	9/1956	
426	1/1912	Brighton	as new	2426	32426	8/1956	

Names applied by the Southern Railway

No.	Name	Date applied
2037	Selsey Bill	5/1926
2038	Portland Bill	5/1925
2039	Hartland Point	1/1926
2040	St Catherine's Point	7/1925
2041	Peveril Point	3/1925

No.	Name	Date applied
2421	South Foreland	2/1926
2422	North Foreland	6/1925
2423	The Needles	4/1927
2424	Beachy Head	6/1926
2425	Trevose Head	8/1926
2426	St Alban's Head	6/1925

The NBR 'H' & 'H1' Atlantics (LNER C10 & C11)

Dimensions: See page 184

Weight diagram

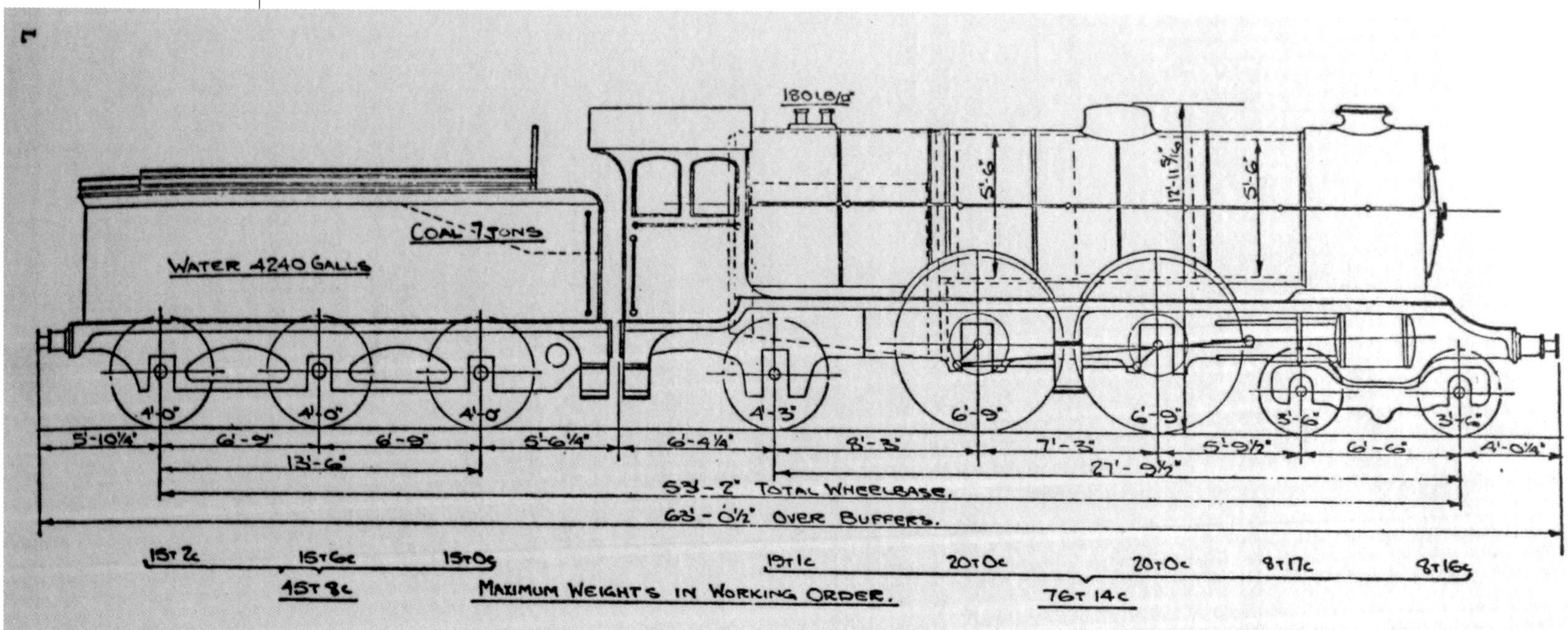

Statistics

No.	Name	Built	Builder	Superheated	LNER No.	Withdrawn
868	***Aberdonian***	7/1906	NB Loco Co.	5/1915	9868	9/1933
869	*Bonnie Dundee*	7/1906	NB Loco Co.	5/1920	9869	10/1935
870	*Bon-Accord*	7/1906	NB Loco Co.	6/1919	9870	5/1937
871	*Thane of Fife*	7/1906	NB Loco Co.	10/1921	9871	1/1935
872	*Auld Reekie*	7/1906	NB Loco Co.	6/1921	9872	8/1935

No.	Name	Built	Builder	Superheated	LNER No.	Withdrawn
873	*Saint Mungo*	7/1906	NB Loco Co.	9/1915	9873	11/1934
874	*Dunedin*	8/1906	NB Loco Co.	5/1921	9874	5/1933
875	*Midlothian*	8/1906	NB Loco Co.	12/1920	9875	11/1939*
876	*Waverley*	8/1906	NB Loco Co.	2/1921	9876	5/1937
877	*Liddesdale*	8/1906	NB Loco Co.	4/1921	9877	4/1936
878	*Hazeldean*	8/1906	NB Loco Co.	9/1919	9878	11/1936
879	*Abbotsford*	8/1906	NB Loco Co.	9/1920	9879	11/1936
880	*Tweeddale*	8/1906	NB Loco Co.	1/1917	9880	10/1936
881	*Borderer*	8/1906	NB Loco Co.	6/1917	9881	11/1936
901	*St Johnstoun*	7/1911	R. Stephenson & Co.	6/1925	9901	12/1937
902	*Highland Chief*	7/1911	R. Stephenson & Co.	11/1923	9902	10/1936
903	*Cock o' the North***	8/1911	R. Stephenson & Co.	9/1924	9903	5/1937
904	*Holyrood*	8/1911	R. Stephenson & Co.	11/1924	9904	8/1936
905	*Buccleugh*	8/1911	R. Stephenson & Co.	5/1924	9905	9/1937
906	*Teribus*	8/1911	R. Stephenson & Co.	7/1924	9906	2/1937
509	*Duke of Rothesay*	6/1921	NB Loco Co.	6/1921	9509	2/1937
510	*The Lord Provost*	6/1921	NB Loco Co.	6/1921	9510	9/1936

* withdrawn 12/1937 and reinstated
** renamed *Aberdonian* in 5/1934

BIBLIOGRAPHY

Bradley, D.L., *Locomotives of the LB&SCR Part 2*, RCTS, 1972

Hennesey, R.A.S., *Atlantic, The Well Beloved Engine,* Tempus Publishing Ltd., 2002

Hughes, Hugh, *Indian Locomotives Part 1 (Broad Gauge 1851-1940),* The Continental Railway Circle, 1990

Knowles, Adrian, *Three French Fancies,* Great Western Echo No.241 article, Spring 2023

Nock, O.S., *LNER Steam*, David & Charles, 1969

Nock, O.S., *The Lancashire & Yorkshire Railway, A Concise History,* Ian Allan, 1969

Obermayer, Horst J., *Taschenbuch Deutsche Dampflokomotiven (Regelspur),* Franckh'ische Verlagshandlung, Stuttgart, 1969

The Railway Magazine, *Gradients of the British Main-Line Railways,* The Railway Publishing Co., 1947

RCTS, *Locomotives of the LNER, Part 3A, Tender Engines – Classes C1 to C11,* RCTS, 1979

Rush, R.W., *The Lancashire & Yorkshire Railway and its Locomotives, 1846-1923,* Railway World Ltd., 1949

Talbot, E., *Steam from Kenya to the Cape,* The Continental Railway Circle & Halcyon Books, 1975

Waters, Laurence, *Great Western Saint Class Locomotives,* Pen & Sword, 2017

Waters, Laurence, *Great Western Star Class Locomotives,* Pen & Sword, 2017

INDEX